D1094332

PLAYING THE NUMBERS

PLAYING THE NUMBERS

GAMBLING IN HARLEM BETWEEN THE WARS

Shane White · Stephen Garton
Stephen Robertson · Graham White

HARVARD UNIVERSITY PRESS

Cambridge, Massachusetts, and London, England

2010

Library of Congress Cataloging-in-Publication Data
Playing the numbers : gambling in Harlem between the wars /
Shane White . . . [et al.].
p. cm.
Includes bibliographical references and index.
ISBN 978-0-674-05107-2 (alk. paper)
1. Gambling—New York (State)—New York—History—20th century.
2. Lotteries—New York (State)—New York—History—20th century.
3. City and town life—New York (State)—New York—History—20th century.
4. African Americans—New York (State)—New York—Social conditions—
20th century. 5. Harlem (New York, N.Y.)—Social conditions—20th
century. 6. New York (N.Y.)—Social conditions—20th century. 7. Informal
sector (Economics)—New York (State)—New York—History—20th century.
8. Harlem (New York, N.Y.)—Economic conditions—20th century.
9. New York (N.Y.)—Economic conditions—20th century. I. White, Shane.
HV6721.N5P54 2010
306.4′82097471—dc22   2009052262

Larry Levine
(1933–2006)

Roy Rosenzweig
(1950–2007)

Greg Dening
(1931–2008)

CONTENTS

Playing the Numbers

PROLOGUE

I'd rather be a lamppost in Harlem than governor of Georgia.

—Folk saying

Henry Moon sat on the edge of his chair in Madame Queen's tastefully modern apartment at 409 Edgecombe Avenue. In 1933, this fourteen-storey building was the tallest on Sugar Hill, Harlem's ritziest area, which sloped north from 145th Street to 155th Street and was bounded by Amsterdam Avenue to the west and Edgecombe Avenue to the east. It was a few blocks of stately apartment buildings and uniformed doormen overlooking the Valley, as Central Harlem, densely populated with mostly poor blacks, was known. Quite simply, then, 409 Edgecombe was the best address in Harlem. At various times, W. E. B. Du Bois, the preeminent black intellectual and for decades editor of the *Crisis*, Walter White and Roy Wilkins, both officials of the National Association for the Advancement of Colored People, and the painter Aaron Douglas all lived there. So too did Madame Queen, who had amassed a fortune from "numbers," the gambling game that, in the early 1920s, had taken Harlem by storm. She was a numbers "banker"—the most successful bankers were known as Kings and Queens—and it was scores of thousands of Valley residents wagering, and losing, their pennies and nickels that had enabled Madame Queen to reach the heights of Harlem. Some on Sugar Hill looked askance at the way this middle-aged woman had made her money, viewing her as little better than a racketeer, but Madame Queen never had any doubts about her position and shrugged off any such aspersions. Her regal presence and sense of entitlement made it abundantly clear that she belonged on Edgecombe Avenue.

Madame Queen stalked the generously proportioned room. She was "a slim figure, dark and sinister, clad as always in a pale gray dress." Her hair was not straightened and "her eyes were flashing like orbs of polished anthracite." As she strode up and down, Madame Queen spoke animatedly. Later on, Moon would remember "the words cascading from her lips in a furious stream." Her audience was transfixed. There were two bodyguards, both of whom obviously carried guns and one of whom had just been released from prison. A young woman, trying to convince Madame Queen to hire her as a secretary, "sat speechless with terror, her lips quivering like jelly atop a throbbing motor." Moon lit a cigarette and inhaled deeply, letting the nicotine course through his veins and relax his body. After all, as he later wryly noted, this "was a time to appear nonchalant."

"WHAM!" Madame Queen thumped her fist on the heavy plate glass covering the table. The young woman started, her timid face a shaking "muddy colored mass." One gunman "blinked," the other stared ahead impassively. Moon "flattened the cigaret held tightly in his fingers." Madame Queen let loose a torrent of words: "To think that dey should put it in ze paper that goddam Dutchman keel one of my men. And put me on de spot? Me? Me? Don't everybody know I ain't scared nothing! Run me out of beezness? Me?" She laughed, and "her laughter was no less sinister than her boastings."

A mesmerized Moon thought, *"Christ, what a woman! What a story!"* In all of his thirty-two years, the currently unemployed reporter had never seen anything quite like it, and he had hardly led a sheltered existence. It was only a few months since Moon had returned from the Soviet Union, where he had been part of the entourage accompanying the newly radicalized Harlem Renaissance writer Langston Hughes, who had been invited to view the progress made since the Russian Revolution and to make a film about the "American Negro at work and play." Moon, who knew Hughes from their teenage years in Cleveland, was particularly embittered when the Soviets abruptly canceled the film. Although Moon may have fancied himself a hard-bitten newspaperman familiar with the ways of the world, he was unprepared for the scene now playing out before his eyes.

Madame Queen not only behaved idiosyncratically—she also sounded unlike other residents of the Black Metropolis. Though everyone in Harlem believed she came from the Caribbean island of Martinique, she always claimed this wasn't true. "Moi? Je suis française," she would gesticulate to the inquisitive. She had arrived in Harlem in 1912, just over two decades before, but had burnished every skerrick of her French accent. Moon drolly noted that "even in her fury, she never forgot it." And Madame Queen's rage was now incandescent. She resumed her tirade: "I'll show dese niggers how to hold on to ze game. I'll show them how to fight back. I'll show that Dutch Schultz he can't muscle in and take ze numbers away from us like that. Yes, dey keel Harris. But me, I ain't scared and dey know it. I ain't like dese niggers." As Moon unnecessarily explained to his readers, "Madame never considered herself a *nigger*." After all, she was French.

"Take this. I'm going to write to that newspaper!" she snapped. The would-be secretary simply crumbled—"the words she tried to force through her lips were formless, meaningless sounds." For the first time, the young woman's terror penetrated Madame Queen's consciousness. She laughed again. "What's matter?" At this point, unable to bear the tension any longer, the newspaperman stepped in: "Let me write the letter." "All right," said Madame. "Take this." But Moon wasn't interested in taking dictation from anyone. "Never mind. I know what you want to say and how it should be said. I'll write it. You sign it." At last in his element, Moon ambled into the next room, lit a cigarette, and began to type.

> To the Editor of the Amsterdam News:
>
> In your issue of last week you wrote: "It is believed that the slain banker was one of a group of Negro operators which the 'policy Queen' has been trying to draw into a union to support her in her active crusade against the usurpers" and further that "the finger has been placed on" me.
>
> This letter is to let you know that Martin L. Harris was in no way connected with any activity in which I may have been engaged. I assure you that had he been affiliated with me in any way, he would never have come to such an untimely and ill-fated end. The gangsters who killed Harris know better than to molest me or my associates.

Madame Queen read and reread the letter, nodded her head, and said, "I guess that'll do." Calmer now, she picked up her pen and in a characteristically confident hand signed, "STEPHANIE ST. CLAIR."[1]

Henry Moon's awe was understandable. Madame Queen was one of the most extraordinary people ever to set foot in the Black Metropolis. She is mostly forgotten now, mentioned only in passing, if that, in histories of Harlem. But in her heyday in the 1920s and 1930s, Stephanie St. Clair, or Madame Queen, or occasionally Queenie, was a household name. No one who met her ever forgot the encounter.

Almost by happenstance, Henry Lee Moon had landed right in the middle of a life-and-death struggle for the heart and soul of the new black culture being forged in northern cities. Numbers came straight out of Harlem: it was invented there in 1920, or maybe 1921, and rapidly insinuated itself into the very fabric of everyday life. The rhythms of the game, with the morning rush of getting bets on before the books were closed at 10:00 A.M., followed by the less frenetic afternoons and early evenings, when winners were paid off and black men and women "doped out" what "gig" they would back the next day, fitted so well into the pulse of the streets that it seemed numbers had been around forever. Most of all, though, numbers took on a central role in the economic life of the African American areas of New York City. Indeed, those who controlled the numbers game possessed a license to print money. And there, of course, was the rub.

Dutch Schultz, perhaps the second best-known gangster in America (admittedly, he was a distant second to Chicago's Al Capone), was the "Beer Baron of the Bronx"—but with Prohibition's days numbered, he needed to diversify his criminal empire. Cashed up and lethal, the Dutchman made his move soon after Thanksgiving 1931. He was like a hawk among the pigeons. Over the ensuing months almost all of the Black Kings and Queens became, voluntarily or otherwise, "partners" with Dutch Schultz, and consequently most of the numbers profits flowed out of Harlem to the Bronx. The holdout was Stephanie St. Clair, who would never bend her knee to the Dutchman, a white interloper in her Harlem. In the early weeks of March 1933, things were coming rapidly to a head.

There was something magnificent about the way Madame Queen fought the good fight. Desperately outnumbered and outgunned, she used every conceivable stratagem at her disposal. She leaked details of Schultz's operations in Harlem to anyone who would listen, including the police, the newspapers, the district attorney, and the federal authorities, who, as a result, would make the Dutchman's life a misery as they pursued him for unpaid income taxes. On several occasions, a black Carrie Nation, she had stormed into one of the countless white-owned and white-run stores on Seventh Avenue that wrote numbers and, as the *Amsterdam News* recorded, "smashed plate glass cases, snatched and destroyed innumerable policy slips, and warned the operators to 'get out of Harlem.' Admittedly, Madame Queen's motives were slightly less exalted than those of the nineteenth-century temperance crusader, notorious for attempting to demolish bars with a hatchet. Rather than promoting the prohibition of numbers, Stephanie St. Clair was trying to ensure that Harlem residents placed their bets with her, or, failing that, at least with one of the other Black Kings or Queens. Probably, the result was inevitable—numbers was far too lucrative an invention to be left in the hands of African Americans. But Stephanie St. Clair was neither the first nor the last self-made millionaire to believe that willpower was enough to hold back the tide.

Of course, this was more than a struggle between two willful people squabbling over who could play in the sandbox. There were larger forces at work. The invention and phenomenal success of numbers was ultimately a product of the Great Migration that took place from 1915 to 1930. In those years well over a million black Southerners moved to the North, creating large concentrations of African Americans in northern cities, most famously in New York's Harlem and on the South Side of Chicago, but in a host of other urban areas as well. The Great Migration transformed black life and race relations in America. If the black experience of the nineteenth century was principally southern, rural, and for much of the time enslaved, that of the twentieth century would be increasingly northern, urban, and free.

And of course the whole drama of who would control numbers was played out against the backdrop of the Great Depression, which was particularly devastating in Harlem. Indeed, Martin Harris was shot and Moon witnessed Madame Queen's stellar performance in her apartment in the first few days of Franklin Delano Roosevelt's first term in office. Newspapers across the United States ran blaring headlines about the banking crisis, bank closures, and enforced bank holidays, while the *New York Age* and the *Amsterdam News* almost eerily featured stories about Harlem's own homegrown banking crisis. As it happened, FDR, with his first fireside chat and decisive legislation restored confidence in the nation's banking system in very short order. But the struggle for control of Harlem's numbers banks would take considerably longer to sort out. This book is our attempt to put numbers into such larger contexts, to explain why this gambling game was so important, and to use it as a prism through which to examine African American culture in the most important city in the world.

That is all right and proper, and in due course we will get to it, but for the moment let us return to the two hellions lunging at each other's throats and to a time and place where individuals knew that they could make a difference. Stephanie St. Clair was one of those people who seized history by the scruff of the neck and gave it a good shake, and even Dutch Schultz in his more introspective moments sensed that he too was shaping history. Central casting could hardly have come up with a more unlikely pair: a West Indian who wanted to be French, a spitfire of a woman who loved nothing better than dressing to the nines and attending the opera or a concert at Carnegie Hall; and a diminutive white gangster, always garbed in cheap, ill-fitting suits and known as the Dutchman, a man who, with more than a modicum of self-identification, enjoyed reading about Napoleon. This odd couple feuded for control of the most lucrative franchise that had ever come out of Harlem, in a deadly struggle that ultimately would break both of them.

And what of the letter that Henry Moon wrote for St. Clair? The *Amsterdam News,* one of Harlem's weekly African American newspapers, published it the following week, on March 22, 1933. It was a time far different from our own. Newspapers still counted for a lot in the early 1930s. In New York City alone, there were close to a dozen dailies vying for a share of the market. Many Harlem residents did in fact read the *Sun* or the *Mirror,* but those interested in a black perspective and some sort of coverage of Harlem could read the two long-running and established weeklies, the *Amsterdam News* and *New York Age,* or others such as the *Negro World* or the *Interstate Tattler.* Madame Queen, an inveterate writer of letters to the editor, knew the power of the press. Indeed, it was her belief in the importance of newspapers that had brought Henry Moon to her apartment in the first place. There were rumors that she was going to start her own newspaper, as a means of persuading ordinary black gamblers to support her struggle to oust the white intruders. The out-of-work Moon had paid her a visit to try "to get her to be an angel for a proposed newspaper venture."

Henry Moon wrote a brief unpublished piece about his meeting with St. Clair and entitled it "Policy Queen." Near the top of the first page, he typed in a subhead—"Personal Participation"—as if acknowledging that this was the stuff of history and that he had not only been a witness but also contributed to the way things had unfolded. And if that was his intention, he was right. Who said that you had to go to the Soviet Union or some such place to be at the center of things? This was Harlem, the Negro Mecca, the Black Metropolis, the black capital of the world. And who could argue with the recently coined old Negro adage, "I'd rather be a lamppost in Harlem than governor of Georgia"? Stephanie St. Clair was a Policy Queen, a Numbers Queen—and back in the day, on the Harlem streets that Henry Moon knew and loved, these were titles that meant something.

INTRODUCTION

> You might almost say the numbers is the salvation of Harlem, its
> Medicare, and its Black Draught, its 666, its little liver pills, its vi-
> tamins, its aspirins and its analgesic balm combined.
>> —Langston Hughes, *New York Times,* March 1, 1971[1]

It was hardly news, more of a filler item making page
seventeen of a Sunday edition of the *New York World* in late March
1928, wedged among advertisements for Phillips' Milk of Magnesia,
Freezone, a guaranteed cure for painful corns, and S. Baumann &
Bro., who apparently had been supplying New Yorkers with home
furnishings since 1854.

"Spring is here!" began Lester A. Walton, a special writer for the
World and one of the few black reporters working for the white
press, and "the soap-box orator has made his reappearance on the
street corners." Walton then proceeded to give a potted history of
public speaking in Harlem, from its beginnings ten years previously, with party political speeches, often greeted with hurled eggs
and howls of derision, through the flowering of the genre in the
1920s, with Hubert Harrison and William Bridges discoursing in an

"intelligent and forceful" fashion on all manner of subjects, even if they usually ended up ruminating on some facet of the "race question." Large crowds of blacks gathered on Seventh Avenue to listen to these and numerous other orators, many lingering to buy the pamphlets and books that were usually offered for sale when the speaker stepped down from his box. The speeches were a mixed bag—"Some are worth listening to," Walton conceded, "others are not."

Walton's piece was pervaded by an air of decline. Harrison had died a few months earlier, and, more important, early in the summer of the previous year, in the side streets off Lenox, "a new type of street entertainer [had] gained a foothold in the district—the vender of quack medicine." According to the black reporter, most of these newcomers had been East Indians or native Africans, who had been dressed "in gaudy costumes of supposedly foreign make," and whose platforms had been festooned with "multi-colored ribbons, bunting and the like." Now, however, in the spring of 1928, the first of the soapbox orators "was not one to discourse on economics, local politics, international affairs, Marcus Garvey, the race problem in the South or Communism." Indeed, Walton told his mostly white readers, it was not until after the man had talked "incoherently for nearly fifteen minutes [that] his real mission became apparent." The year's first black public speaker was trying "to sell the Black Cat Dream Book to those who daily play the Clearing House numbers, sometimes known as policy."[2]

Lester Walton, a resident of Harlem, was baffled by the harangue of the huckster on the soapbox for only a few minutes; anyone today relying on the historiography of Harlem in the 1920s and 1930s for knowledge would likely remain puzzled for a while longer. The Clearing House numbers and dream books have hardly been the standard coin of writing about Harlem. Readers will thumb through the authoritative *Encyclopedia of New York City* without finding much in the way of illumination.[3] Perhaps understandably, historians and literary critics writing about Harlem in these years have concentrated on the Harlem Renaissance, the efflorescence of black creativity, particularly writing, that took place in the 1920s; but this approach renders the social and cultural history of ordinary residents peripheral, at best a colorful backdrop for the likes of Langston Hughes, Jessie Fauset, and Countee Cullen.[4] Yet if one broadens the focus to include the lives of ordinary African American men and women as part of the object of inquiry, the picture necessarily changes. Indeed, the numbers were about as peripheral to the way life was lived in Harlem as was the cockfight to Balinese village society. In 1929, the African American writer and essayist Wallace Thurman noted that "there are some phenomena peculiar to Harlem alone, phenomena which are inherently expressions of the Negro character before it was conditioned by the white world that now surrounds [it]." The prime example that Thurman had in mind was "the game of Numbers."[5] In fact, the numbers slip, millions of which were written in the 1920s and 1930s, was Harlem's "authentic" text; dream books were its bestsellers; and those who ran the numbers game, the so-called Black Kings and Queens of Harlem, were larger-than-life figures who bestrode its streets with style and flamboyance.

The game of "Clearing House numbers" was a brilliant scheme—simple, transparent, and elegant. It was a form of gambling in which individuals wagered on the single numeral between 0 and 999 that would turn up as the day's number. Particularly ingenious was the way in which the daily numbers were randomly generated, and in a fashion that was, so far as ordinary gamblers were concerned, impossible to "fix."

Founded in 1853, the New York Clearing House was a financial institution that facilitated the daily exchanges and settlements of money between the city's banks. In the years following World War I, at precisely 10:00 every workday morning, an employee descended to the lobby of the Clearing House building at 77 Cedar Street, in Lower Manhattan, and chalked up on a blackboard three freshly calculated figures, each of which acted as a basic economic indicator, and two of which, to the embarrassment of this august financial institution, were used in the game of numbers. One of these figures was the total of the daily clearances among member banks; the other was the Federal Reserve Bank credit balance. The daily number, avidly awaited by tens of thousands of Harlem residents, was worked out by combining the second and third digits from the bank clearings with the third digit from the Federal Reserve Bank balance. For example, on the last Monday before Christmas 1930, the clearings were $5**89**,000,000 and the balance was $11**6**,000,000; hence, the winning number was **896.** Within seconds of 10:00 A.M., the daily Clearing House figures were phoned through to Harlem numbers bankers and to the afternoon newspapers. On placards at Harlem newsstands, the *Sun* shamelessly boasted that it was "FIRST with the BANK Clearing NUMBER."[6]

The standard transaction in numbers was to bet anything from one cent to a few dollars on a three-digit number. If, for example, five cents was wagered on 896, the runner would write it down as 896-5. There were other possible ways of betting. The box play, more common in the 1930s, was a way of gambling on all possible combinations of the three digits in a number—not just 896, but also 869, 689, 698, 968, and 986—and the bet was written as ⌐896⌐-6. In the argot of Harlem, this was also known as "combinating" a number, or a "combo."[7] In addition, there was the one-number play, where the gambler bet on just one digit which could be either the first, middle, or last of the three. This bet was written 8xx, or x9x, or xx6. Similarly, a "bolita" was a bet on the last two of the three digits.

The chance of any number "hitting" was one in a thousand, but anyone who managed to overcome these odds and win was paid off on his or her bet at the rate of 600:1. Numbers runners spread out all over Harlem and San Juan Hill (a neighborhood on the West Side, approximately where Lincoln Center is today), collecting bets from individual gamblers. The game was often derisively called "nigger pool," and these two areas were where most of New York City's black population was concentrated in the 1920s and 1930s.

Nowadays, West 125th Street is usually seen as the heart of Harlem, but in the 1920s there were more whites than blacks on that thoroughfare. It was necessary to travel ten blocks, or one subway stop, further north in order to find the mass of black faces that signified Harlem. The first building given over to black tenants, in 1903, stood on West 134th Street, and it was from that hub that subsequent waves of migrants from the South and immigrants from the West Indies pushed out the boundaries of black settlement. In 1920, the area occupied almost entirely by blacks stretched from 130th Street to 144th Street and from Fifth Avenue to Eighth Avenue, an area of forty-eight blocks that was home to 73,000 people. Five years later, black Harlem reached south to 128th Street, and, below 135th Street, east as far as Park Avenue. By 1930, blacks, now numbering over 200,000, almost one-fifth of whom hailed from the West Indies—had spilled beyond Eighth Avenue to Amsterdam Avenue and the heights overlooking central Harlem as far south as 130th Street, had moved north to 160th Street, and had begun to settle as far south as 110th Street, where their neighbors were not white, but Spanish-speakers from Puerto Rico and the Caribbean.

But if the influx of Southerners and West Indians made most

of Harlem black, it was scarcely a homogenous place. In addition to the areas in which better-off blacks made their homes (Strivers Row on West 139th Street and, late in the 1920s, Sugar Hill on Edgecombe Avenue), there were other distinctive neighborhoods in Harlem. Climbing the stairs from the 135th Street subway station brought new arrivals and commuters on to Lenox Avenue. Crowded, dirty, and noisy, the avenue was the site of the Savoy Ballroom and Harlem Hospital, but otherwise its businesses were small and less reputable. To the east, the blocks between Lenox and Fifth were among the most densely packed residential streets in the entire city. All Harlem's cross streets other than 135th Street shared this solidly residential character, if not the population density. That did not mean they were indistinguishable. Migrants and immigrants clustered together; the tenants in particular buildings often came predominantly from the West Indies, or from Georgia or North Carolina or Virginia.

It was also on these streets that many black organizations and churches were located. Harlem boasted a rich fabric of voluntary organizations. Hundreds of small clubs gathered in apartments or small meeting rooms to socialize, play cards, and to organize dances, lunches, and excursions. Fraternal orders such as the Prince Hall Masons and the Elks, which set up a dozen or so lodges in Harlem, had more elaborate buildings, with auditoriums and rooms in which members could meet and where their renowned orchestras and bands could practice. Religious organizations outnumbered even the many voluntary groups. Scattered throughout the neighborhood were forty-nine churches and hundreds of storefronts and apartments converted to house worship. Each was "much more besides a place of worship," wrote James Weldon Johnson in 1930. "It is a social center, it is a club, it is an arena for the exercise of one's capabilities and powers, a world in which one may achieve self-realization and preferment."[8] The largest churches organized athletic clubs (particularly basketball teams), classes ranging from vocational training to art, choirs and musical groups, and social clubs.

To see the grandest of Harlem's churches, one had to exit the subway to the west, and walk past the businesses located below the apartments on 135th Street, and the landmark Young Men's Christian Association building, to Seventh Avenue. Christened the "Black Broadway" by writer Wallace Thurman, the wide avenue was Harlem's main street. Here were the best stores, theaters, and churches, and a constant stream of black pedestrians either frequenting shops or houses of worship or simply promenading along the generously broad pavements. Spend enough time strolling on Seventh Avenue, it was said, and sooner or later one would see everyone who was important in Negro America. But to step off the avenue and into the stores was to enter a rather different world, one in which whites owned and staffed almost all of Harlem's businesses. Most black enterprises were to be found not in the district's storefronts, but in apartments on its residential streets, where women operated beauty salons. To the west of Seventh was Eighth Avenue, shrouded in dirt, noise, and shadow by the elevated train line that ran its length—a street, as Thurman put it, "to cross hurriedly in order to reach places located east of it."[9]

Photographs of the streets and avenues from the 1920s and 1930s capture a sea of black and brown faces, snapshots of a striving Harlem conscious that it was on display. Much of Harlem life was lived out on its streets and avenues. Today, when one looks at images of Seventh Avenue or any other Harlem street, what catches the eye is how respectable and well-dressed all the people were. Every morning, thousands of black residents poured out of their apartment buildings, walked to the station, and caught the subway to their jobs downtown as janitors, elevator operators, maids, cleaners, and laborers, for employment in Harlem itself was hard to find. Decades later, Arthur Davis, a professor of English at Howard University, would recall that such men "seldom went downtown to *work,* but to *business.*" And that each one carried "not a lunch pail but his overalls and lunch in a *brief case.*"[10] There was a similarly striving air to the way black women dressed, whether they were off to work downtown or merely ducking around the corner to do the market-ing. Newcomers from the South quickly learned that in Harlem one did not sit on the front stoop in a housecoat or head rag. It was as if the whole race were constantly being judged, not just by any passing whites but by blacks themselves. There was a palpable sense of the pride that African Americans took in the Black Metropolis.[11]

Harlem was a beacon attracting migrants and immigrants from all across the South and the Caribbean, but there was another, less well-known area of New York City that was also home to many blacks. Throughout the nineteenth century a combination of the exponential expansion of the city and white racism, often on the part of recent immigrants, had pushed African Americans farther and farther north, from Greenwich Village, to the Tenderloin (on the West Side between the Thirties and the Fifties), and eventually to San Juan Hill. This district, a few blocks between Sixtieth and Sixty-Fourth streets and west of Broadway, was the African Ameri-can neighborhood in New York around the turn of the century, just before large numbers started to trek uptown to Harlem in the 1910s. It had originally been called Columbus Hill, but acquired its new name from the famous battle of the Spanish American War because many black veterans of that conflict settled there, and also because interracial battles constantly erupted on its streets.[12] Eventually, many of its inhabitants would be displaced by the construction of Lincoln Center in the 1950s and 1960s, but in the 1920s and 1930s San Juan Hill remained a lively black neighborhood—not as important as Harlem, yet still a very lucrative market for numbers bankers.

Some numbers runners went around knocking on apartment doors in Harlem and San Juan Hill to pick up bets from their clients; others operated out of stores; and many stationed themselves on the city's streets and avenues, accepting business from passing pedestrians. Runners worked on commission, skimming off 20 percent from their total receipts before they conveyed the day's bets and takings to their banker. Moreover, if a client's bet hit, the individual gambler was obligated to pay the runner 10 percent of her or his winnings, effectively reducing the winning odds from 600:1 to 540:1. In the 1920s many runners were making $20–30 a day, and it was not unusual for some to make in excess of $50. But of course it was the bankers who had the largest opportunity to make money. It was they who were successful who became the Kings and Queens of Harlem.[13]

The Clearing House numbers game existed for almost exactly a decade. It began in 1920 or 1921 and ended when the Clearing House, never particularly enthused about its links with the denizens of San Juan Hill and Harlem, apparently came under increasing pressure from insurance companies and credit businesses to stop publishing the statistical information on which the game depended. It was hardly surprising, therefore, that, as of December 31, 1930, the New York Clearing House ceased publication of the daily figures.[14] Some people initially surmised that the end of the Clearing House numbers would lead to the "extinction" of the game, but this was little more than wishful thinking.[15] Bankers quickly came up with alternative ways of generating a daily number, and, over the next decade, figures taken from the New York Stock Exchange, from the pari-mutuel totals paid out on horse races at various tracks throughout the country, and, for a while, even from the Cincinnati Clearing House were all used to fuel the city's gambling racket. None of these sources ever quite had the cachet of the New York Clearing House or its reputation for being unfixable, but, regardless, numbers continued to expand at an exponential rate during the years of the Great Depression.

The Clearing House numbers game was far too good an idea for it to remain confined to New York City for long. Very soon after it was established and began to take off there, the game was exported to nearby cities with substantial black populations. In the 1920s, Atlantic City, Philadelphia, Washington, D.C., Atlanta, and a host of other places on the Eastern Seaboard adopted the game wholesale, even to the extent of using the New York Clearing House as the source of the numbers on which players would bet. The game even penetrated beyond the major cities, catching on in some small towns that were home to concentrations of African Americans. According to the black New York newspaper the *Interstate Tattler,* in the summer of 1927 Asbury Park on the New Jersey shore was "'number' mad." Indeed, "Harlem, in the days of its wildest orgies," the reporter wrote, "could not approach the passion of the Jersey-ites to get two cents down on 726 and a nickel on the bolita." Apparently, "most of the shopkeepers in the sepia section of the town have purchased standardized placards on which they display the winning number in their windows." More than was usually the case in the bigger cities, the telephone was the instrument by which many of the black residents of Asbury placed their bets. The *Tattler's* correspondent concluded not only that the bankers and runners were "living in clover of course," but also that the telephone company was "cashing in rich on the gamble."[16]

Chicago, though, was different. The Clearing House numbers never caught on there, or in the nearby midwestern towns and cities in its orbit, and blacks living on the South Side carried on playing policy. Policy in Chicago was based on using what was called a "wheel"; in fact, this was usually a barrel containing seventy-eight numbered balls from which, in the game's simplest form, twelve numbers were drawn. Gamblers bet on various possible combinations, the most common being the first three numbers drawn; for example, a gambler could take a "gig" on, say, 7-10-11 being the first three numbers drawn (this was, according to local dream books, the gig for "William," on which there was a plunge after comedian Will Rogers's death in August 1935). Policy, as we shall see, was also first developed in New York as a way of betting on the numbers being drawn in lotteries, or "insuring the lottery"—hence the name "policy." The game was run by whites, was endemic there for almost the entire nineteenth century, and died out very early in the twentieth century. Events took a rather different trajectory in Chicago. There, policy began to take off only in the 1880s and 1890s; furthermore it was run by blacks, such as "Policy Sam" Young and John "Mushmouth" Johnson.[17] In New York in the very early 1920s, the new game of the Clearing House numbers filled a vacuum, but at the same time in Chicago policy was still a thriving business, and blacks on the South Side persisted with it, unwilling to try anything new. As a consequence, there were, from the 1920s on, rather different systems of illegal gambling in New York and Chicago, and these differences would be an important factor in the contrasting ways in which the South Side and Harlem were linked to political authorities, and gangsters, in their respective cities.

Right from the start, in the very early 1920s, artists working in a variety of genres recognized the centrality of numbers to an urban black culture now being transformed by the Great Migration, and used it as a vehicle for ruminating about African American identity. For instance, gambling, policy, and numbers were grist for the mills of many of the blues singers who recorded in the 1920s and 1930s. Plays such as Wallace Thurman and William Jourdan Rapp's *Harlem: A Melodrama of Negro Life in Harlem* (1928), which had ninety-three performances on Broadway, and the less successful musical *Policy Kings,* which first surfaced in 1932 and was finally staged, fleetingly, in 1939, also featured numbers as a prominent part of Harlem life. Harlem Renaissance luminaries Langston Hughes, in *Little Ham* (1935), and Georgia Johnson, in *Starting Point* (1938), likewise wrote plays that were centered on the role of numbers in black life.

Novelists, too, recognized a rich vein when they saw one. Carl Van Vechten, a writer and photographer who knew at least parts of Harlem as well as any white man, made the Bolito King—a thinly veiled depiction of Casper Holstein, the putative inventor of numbers—an important character in *Nigger Heaven* (1926), his controversial depiction of the Harlem that he visited, loved, and promoted. From a rather different perspective, the ever-elusive Rinehart, one of the major figures in Ralph Ellison's *Invisible Man* (1952), was identified by others as a Harlem preacher, pimp, and numbers runner. Several black writers have based entire novels on numbers or policy. Lewis A. Caldwell was born in 1905 in Chicago, where he completed a master's thesis at Northwestern University entitled "The Policy

Game in Chicago." Employed as a probation officer at the Cook County Juvenile Court in 1941, he used his knowledge of Chicago's black underworld to write *The Policy King* (1945), a novel that laid bare the workings of policy on the South Side by following the fortunes of the fictional Marshall family. From 1967 to 1979, Caldwell served in the Illinois House of Representatives, where he would oppose the introduction of the State Monopoly Lottery on the ground that lotteries would quickly kill off policy and, as a result, would undercut entrepreneurship in minority communities. Julian Mayfield's novel *The Hit* (1957) traced one day in Hubert Cooley's obsessive search for a way out of Harlem by winning the numbers. Robert Pharr's *Book of Numbers* (1969), set in 1935, detailed the travails of Dave Green as he introduced numbers for the first time to a southern town. But probably the best-known today of these novels is Louise Meriwether's *Daddy Was a Number Runner* (1970), set in Harlem in the 1930s—a book that has proved to be enormously popular with adolescent readers. Much the same interest in the numbers also permeated the fledgling and always precarious black film industry. Films such as *Dark Manhattan* (1937), *Policy Man* (1938), and *Moon Over Harlem* (1939) are known only to a few film *aficionados* today; but when first released, they were popular in theaters in the black areas of northern cities, largely because they featured all-black casts and depicted through their portrayals of numbers in Harlem at least one version of what it meant to be black, urban, and sophisticated.

In order to appreciate the role of numbers and the centrality of the game to black life in the 1920s and 1930s, we must place the game in the rather different context of black business history. The fact that numbers was illegal is important, but it should not be allowed to mask the essentially economic nature of the whole enterprise. Dismissing or even demonizing numbers simply as criminal or deviant behavior is the wrong approach. Writing, from the vantage point of 1939, about numbers in the period up to 1931, Richard "Dixie" Davis, lawyer to the gangster Dutch Schultz, made it clear that "the policy bankers were not mobsters." He continued: "They were merely gamblers running an illegal business, on a very peaceful, non-violent basis." Davis exaggerated the benign nature of numbers, but his essential argument—that "there is a distinction, very real, between ordinary law violators and the public enemies of the organized underworld"—was valid.[18] On this point, Dixie Davis was an expert. More than just about any individual, he was responsible for enabling the entry of Dutch Schultz and the mob into Harlem numbers in the 1930s.

In June 1933, at the height of the struggle between Dutch Schultz and the black bankers over control of the numbers in Harlem, a man identified only as a Black King gave a remarkable interview to the *Amsterdam News* in which he declared, "You know this is a Negro game in a Negro neighborhood and it has been carried on by Negroes for twelve years without outside groups."[19] To a slightly lesser extent, this was also true of a score of other urban areas, mostly in the northeast of the United States. In the nineteenth century, "insuring the lottery," or "policy," had been played extensively by blacks although the game was run almost entirely by whites. But in the 1920s, with the advent of large and rapidly growing urban black populations, a host of black entrepreneurs in many different cities latched on to the novel idea of the Clearing House Number and began building their empires. Starting from nothing in 1920, in a few years they created a multi-million dollar business. By 1926, the estimated turnover of numbers in Harlem alone was some $20 million.

What makes this performance all the more remarkable is that numbers was one of very few black businesses that took advantage of the dramatic changes wrought by the Great Migration. Black newspaper editors in Harlem and elsewhere continually lamented the fact that black residents in most American cities spent the vast majority of their money in stores that were owned and staffed by whites. In 1937, Claude McKay, a West Indian by birth and a key figure in the Harlem Renaissance, almost despairingly wrote of Harlem that "the saloons were run by the Irish, the restaurants by the Greeks, the ice and fruit stands by the Italians, and the grocery and haberdashery stores by the Jews. The only Negro businesses, excepting barber shops, were the churches and the cabarets."[20] Marcus Garvey, charismatic founder and leader of the United Negro Improvement Association—the mass movement of ordinary blacks, with several thousand members in Harlem, devoted to racial unity and uplift—energetically championed the idea of black business and economic independence. His organization published a newspaper, the *Negro World,* and established two restaurants, three grocery stores, a printing press, a laundry, and a millinery store, which manufactured the UNIA's elaborate uniforms and insignia, as well as fashionable clothing. All these endeavors paled in comparison with the founding of the Black Star Line, a shipping enterprise designed to move goods and people between America, the Caribbean, and Africa, thus linking literally and symbolically Africans and descendants of Africans, an event that was one of the signal black achievements of the post–World War I years, even if its foundering would eventually lead to Garvey's deportation. For all the hoopla, though, the most successful black business of the 1920s and 1930s was neither the Black Star Line nor any other similarly grandiose scheme; it was, rather, an enterprise driven by the nickels and dimes of scores of thousands of ordinary African Americans. The police, legal authorities, and various outraged newspaper editors and disapproving race leaders may not have liked it, but the simple fact was that numbers was *the* black business.

White gangsters knew a lucrative enterprise when they saw one. The great misfortune of the Black Kings and Queens, as well as their thousands of employees across the country, was that the early history of numbers coincided with the years of Prohibition. This was so on two counts. First, more than their fair share of speakeasies, nightclubs, and other outlets for illegal alcohol were located in black urban areas all across the nation: it was not just Harlem that attracted "slumming" whites in search of drink, jazz, and an erotic frisson that they could not find in their own neighborhoods.[21] As a result, white gangsters, who ran most of the clubs and supplied most of the alcohol, had front-row seats as numbers became a craze, and were unlikely to be fooled into dismissing the new game as "nigger pool." Second, Prohibition firmly established criminal gangs as a prominent part of the terrain of modern American cities. A combination of the enormous profits made from bootlegging and, from the mid to late 1920s, the appalling prospect that the "noble experiment" of Prohibition was going to end and their income stream dry up, forced the white gangs to diversify—to move into and take over prostitution and various other rackets. For the gangs, usually well-connected to the police and politicians, an illegal game being run by a few blacks and Cubans appeared to be a rich prize just waiting for the taking.

The overall pattern of what ensued is clear enough, even though the details varied from city to city (it should be added, however, that New York was the preeminent market and new developments usually first occurred there). Sometime from the mid-1920s on, occasionally even as late as the 1930s, white gangs moved into the black areas of cities, set up as rivals, and attempted to take over the numbers game. This prompted considerable resistance from African Americans, usually a mixture of independent black bankers forming some sort of association or union and attempts to enforce boycotts of the intruding white bankers. For example, in 1928 a group of white gangsters, mostly Jews from Cleveland, did their best to oust the blacks running the numbers in Detroit.[22] They almost succeeded. In the end, what saved the black bankers and their employees was that they united to form the Associated Number Bankers, an organization that both protected its members and, in ensuing years, regulated the racket in Detroit. Blacks may not have owned many businesses in American cities, but the strength and persistence of their opposition to white interlopers demonstrated clearly that the one business they did control—numbers—was highly valued, not just by the Kings and Queens who made all the money, but also by ordinary African Americans keen to gamble on their gig with a banker who was a compatriot and imbued with the new spirit of race consciousness, pride, and militancy that characterized urban black America in the 1920s and 1930s. In these years, black men and women came together not only in Garvey's UNIA, but also in the National Association for the Advancement of Colored People (NAACP), more radical groups such as the African Blood Brotherhood, and unions such as the Brotherhood of Sleeping Car Porters. They thronged the streets to celebrate the achievements of black athletes such as Jack Johnson and Joe Louis (heavyweight boxing champions of the world), to protest, and to parade, resplendent in lodge or UNIA regalia; turned to the courts to contest their treatment by landlords; and claimed places in nightclubs, on streetcars, and in the ranks of the municipal officials, police, firefighters, teachers, nurses, and doctors who served their communities.

In city after city, the most active and often strident of the race men and race women—terms that referred to individuals with a reputation for proudly defending blacks from attempts to make them subordinate—turned out to be numbers Kings and Queens. Partly, of course, their championing of black business was self-serving, but it was also usually more than that. As was often the case with race men and women, personal beliefs and self-interest merged seamlessly. Interestingly, later, in the 1930s, much the same tactics that were used against white gangsters would be adapted and used against white storeowners who refused to employ black help. A wide spectrum of black organizations came together in these campaigns to boycott businesses under the banner, "Don't Buy Where You Can't Work." Helped by court decisions allowing picketing and the imperative provided by the riot in Harlem in 1935, these activist groups succeeded in reversing the long-prevailing absence of black staff, so that by 1944 the majority of the neighborhood's salespeople were black.[23] In the case of numbers, after an uneasy coexistence that occasionally lasted years, white gangsters and black bankers eventually reached some sort of accommodation. As a result, day-to-day operations in the black areas were left mostly in the hands of African Americans, and there was at least some room for independent black bankers, but a good proportion of the revenue from numbers ended up in the coffers of usually mobbed-up white gangsters.

By now the story of love and theft, of white appropriation of things created by blacks, is a familiar enough part of African American history. Even as Americans have celebrated black cultural achievement, they have sought to control and subdue it.[24] White artists and entrepreneurs—almost invariably better funded and, above all, having access not just to the relatively small black market, but to the full gamut of American consumers—for centuries have raided African American culture, borrowing and remaking dance steps and a host of musical forms. Whether it was apocryphal or not, Sam Phillips's comment, reportedly made before he "discovered" Elvis Presley, that "if I could find a white man who had the Negro sound and the Negro feel, I could make a billion dollars," encapsulated a wisdom that was common in the American entertainment industry.[25] Indeed, this blackening is one of the most noticeable and oft-written about features of the making of American popular culture. At least part of what makes the history of numbers such a compelling story is the extension of this familiar tale from the cultural arena to the new territory of American economic life. For not only did white gangsters do their level best to take over the black business, but by the end of the 1930s they had expanded the game's market dramatically through the selling of numbers to white gamblers. In the case of New York, what had been confined essentially to African Americans in Harlem and San Juan Hill in the 1920s was, by the middle of the 1930s, not only a commonplace but a lucrative business servicing whites in all five boroughs. The legacy of the successful expansion of numbers is still obvious today, for eventually, in the 1970s, the states would replace the illegal gambling game with their own legal lotteries and reap a windfall of hundreds of millions of dollars. Although state governors are certainly unaware of the fact, the genius of Casper Holstein, combined with the entrepreneurial skills of the Black Kings and Queens of the 1920s and 1930s, has, three-quarters of a century later, made balancing their budgets a whole lot easier.

A close look at numbers also clearly reveals that, contrary to the usual depictions, Harlem was not an area peopled solely by African Americans that existed in some sort of splendid isolation. Harlem was an integral part of New York City. This was obvious in the mornings and evenings, as thousands of blacks who traveled to and from work downtown crossed paths with a stream of whites making the reverse trip, in what (if anyone at the time had noticed) must have seemed a slightly surreal moment. But there were still other, more surprising links, of which many contemporaries were only dimly, if at all, aware. Not only was numbers difficult for outsiders to understand, but the game itself received only the most cursory coverage in the nonblack press before the late 1930s. That scores of thousands of African Americans concentrated their minds on the New York Clearing House on Cedar Street every morning at 10:00, or that some newspapers, such as the archetypically white tabloid the *Sun,* sold several thousand extra copies every day in Harlem to black readers anxious to check the day's number, may well have startled many of the residents in other parts of Manhattan had they ever found out. Indeed, what was quite striking about numbers in New York in the 1920s and 1930s was who, precisely, was involved in running the game. Few of the people who participated had been born and raised in New York. Initially, people of color dominated numbers. Those arrested ranged in skin color from white through brown to black; they were often men and women whose first tongue was Spanish, and who hailed from Puerto Rico, Cuba, and elsewhere in the Caribbean, as well as migrants from the British West Indies and from all across the U.S. South.[26] Later on, as whites attempted to control the numbers, Jews (mostly from eastern Europe and often denominated as Russians) and Italians featured prominently in the court records. To a considerable extent, numbers became the vehicle by which members of many different groups succeeded in becoming Americans. More than that, numbers was a harbinger of what America would one day have to become. The mélange of ethnicities and racial groups involved in numbers suggested not so much the race relations of the past, trapped in the simple binary opposition of black and white, but rather a possible multi-ethnic and more fluid future.

And finally, there are the gamblers themselves. Little attention has been paid to these, the ordinary men and women of Harlem, and when they are mentioned—fleetingly—whether as members of Garvey's UNIA, participants in race riots, or numbers gamblers, they have, until very recently, usually been treated as passive ciphers, manipulated by their charismatic leaders. On top of this, social scientists have tended to dismiss gamblers either "as hopelessly stupid or to posit some unconscious masochism as the root cause of their folly."[27] Neither was the case with blacks betting on the numbers. If we return to Lester Walton's *New York World* article on the first public speaker in the spring of 1928, Walton was in fact offering the mostly white readers of his newspaper a point of entry into a rather different Harlem from the milieu of speakeasies, clubs, and fancy parties attended by Harlem Renaissance writers—a milieu with which they may have had at least some familiarity. Probably, most of the *World* readers skipped quickly to the sports pages, but that is no reason we should ignore the insight of this long-term Harlem resident. Understanding the world of Black Cat Dream Books and the Clearing House numbers provides the basis for a rather different, and more inclusive, perspective on the Black Metropolis, allowing us to see in new ways why so many thought of Harlem as the Negro Mecca.[28]

I

HISTORY

Four, 'leven and forty-four,
Four, 'leven and forty-four.
Goin' down this mornin'
'Cause I got to go.
But if I hit this gig,
Ain't gonna bust these suds no more!
—"The Washwoman's Gig," from *Gumbo Ya-Ya:*
A Collection of Louisiana Folk Tales (1945)

Although there were elements in the Clearing House numbers game that were strikingly new, the practice of gambling on the chance that a number or series of numbers would turn up had a history that went back to the colonial period. In the second half of the eighteenth century, lotteries were a commonplace in the colonies and later the United States. Ticket receipts in the early years of the nineteenth century in New York were in the region of $2 million a year, a very large sum, given that the population of the city was less than 100,000. Ostensibly, lotteries, which had to be authorized by the local legislature, existed for the purpose of funding internal improvements, items such as canals, roads, and hospitals that were beyond the reach of the cash-starved public purse. Indeed, the lottery has legitimate claims to being the forebear of private banking and stockbroking, facilitating, as it did, the accumulation of a large number of very small amounts of money into real capital. The lottery was one of few ways in which the wealth of ordinary Americans could be transformed into investment. By the early decades of the nineteenth century, lotteries had become a huge business. Although the number of schemes shrank, drawings increased in frequency, and the amount of money spent on tickets and the size of prizes increased in an almost exponential fashion. Also in these years, lotteries were transformed from amateur affairs run on an ad hoc basis into a professional business: ticket brokers and contractors, in return for their cut of turnover, assumed control of the day-to-day running of the lotteries. In 1819 there were sixty lottery offices in New York; by 1827 there were 190. Little wonder that a writer in the *New York Evening Post* wryly noted that a stranger might suppose "one half of the citizens get their living by affording the opportunity of gambling to the rest." One historian of the lottery in America concluded, with only slight exaggeration, that early nineteenth-century lotteries were "the genesis of American big business," since much that was innovative and of value in the way lotteries were promoted and organized would be taken up and developed in ensuing decades.[1]

Occasionally, free blacks, and even slaves, managed to scrape together the few dollars necessary to participate in what was fast becoming an American craze; some even bought winning tickets and managed to collect large sums. Most famously, Denmark Vesey, a Charleston slave, was able to use part of his windfall from a city lottery in 1799 to buy his freedom. Vesey's eventual rendezvous with the hangman's noose for his role as the chief conspirator in an abortive uprising in Charleston in 1822 did little to quiet the fears of those who worried about the disruptive impact on society, should members of the lower orders, be they black or white, suddenly acquire significant sums of money. Yet for all the worrying implications of the Denmark Vesey case, there is little evidence that many blacks were able to purchase lottery tickets.

African Americans were, however, very closely linked to a related form of gambling—one known as "insuring the lottery," or "policy"—that had developed alongside lotteries. For a small sum, usually a fraction of the cost of a lottery ticket, individuals could "insure," or "take a policy on," a number with a broker or agent; in other words, they could bet on the chance that that particular number would be drawn in a lottery on a given day. Money raised through the actual lotteries financed any number of capital works, such as roads and bridges, but the whole enterprise of policy was parasitic—a side wager on the lottery, as it were, with no benefits either to the economy or to state or federal authorities. It was also illegal. Furthermore, as all manner of commentators repeatedly pointed out, those who gambled on policy tended to come from the poorest stratum of society, which meant that in the cities of the Northeast there was a close association between African Americans and "insuring the lottery."[2]

Almost invariably, the indictments for insuring the lottery in New York that are contained in the district attorney's Closed Case files for the 1810s and 1820s are cases where white agents refused to pay free blacks who had "hit." By 1820 more than 95 percent of the city's black residents were finally free: at the time of that year's census, there were only 518 slaves left in the city. In April 1815, Peter Seaman, a colored man living at No. 9 Anthony Street, "purchased a policy as it is generally called" from Benjamin Haskins at his shop on the corner of Nassau and Little George streets. Seaman paid three shillings and sixpence, so that if either 125 or 57 was drawn in the Board of Health lottery, he would be paid five dollars for each number. On April 5, Seaman deposed that "the number 125 did come out of the wheel yesterday after the first hundred numbers were drawn," but that when he had called upon Haskins the agent had refused to pay, offering instead two shillings if his black customer would quietly go away.[3] Of course, taking welching white policy agents to court meant that wronged blacks relinquished any chance of collecting their winnings, or indeed of even getting their initial bet returned, but if the case was prosecuted effectively, such action did offer the possible solace of revenge.

Scandals about the way in which lotteries had been conducted, usually over the drawing of the numbers, regularly piqued the interest of newspaper editors, but the reputation of lotteries was pristine compared with that of insuring the lottery.[4] From about 1815 through the 1820s, New York's economy was not only expanding and developing with considerable vigor, but it was also essentially a free market, with very little regulation or control. Even in the most respectable counting rooms in town, there was a very fine line between normal business practice and bankruptcy, fraud, and disgrace. In this period, policy was still only a marginal activity, a minor offshoot of the lottery business, and the people who controlled this form of gambling were the city's bottom-feeders. Almost anything went. Agents were forever coming up with excuses for not paying up on hits or even simply refusing to meet their obligations, and gamblers reciprocated by doing anything they could to get inside information on what the day's winning numbers would be. In February 1818, the *New York Evening Post* editorialized about "this detestable nuisance" that was such a "pernicious and ruinous practice" among gamblers, who were "all of the poorer class." The piece went on to explain to readers, many of whom were probably unaware of the details of this form of gambling, that policy was carried on not "in the more reputable lottery offices," but "in petty shops, set up in the more obscure parts of the city." Things had now reached the ludicrous point where each morning the Union Hotel, where the drawing of one lottery took place, was surrounded "by hundreds of servants and poor people, black and white," anxiously awaiting the results. Some members of the crowd would have horses at the ready, "and as soon as the first drawn number is called out, they jump upon the saddle and ride off at full speed to some distant office, and get the number insured." Exploiting the need for agents to keep their books open as late as possible in order to maximize their turnover, and managing to bet on a known winner, was called "pigeoning." The *Post* was hardly sympathetic to the conned agents, noting that "this, to be sure, is only to bite the biter," and concluded: "What a system of morals must exist in the community where such things are openly practiced, and no notice taken of them."[5]

Early lotteries were complicated affairs—often it took months for all the prizes to be drawn—and in the 1820s, in an attempt to make the system more efficient and to curb policy insurance, the "ternary combination principle" was introduced. From a pool usually consisting of the numbers one through seventy-eight, twelve were drawn. The lottery ticket bearing the first three numbers, drawn in order of appearance, won first prize (for example, 72-14-64 could be the winning ticket); the fourth, fifth, and sixth numbers won the second prize; and so on. Tickets with two drawn numbers, or even one, garnered smaller prizes.[6] It was an ingeniously simple system enabling the sale of tens of thousands of chances in a lottery, whereas the paraphernalia required to draw the winners was limited to a barrel with seventy-eight numbered balls. This system was used well into the twentieth century; indeed, "wheels" with twelve numbers drawn from the first seventy-eight would remain the basis of policy on Chicago's South Side. The new method of drawing lotteries did save time—winning lottery numbers were now determined in a matter of minutes—but it made no discernible impact on the business of policy insurance.

Of rather more moment for policy was the gathering sentiment in the 1820s, particularly in New England, Pennsylvania, and New York, that lotteries were an unabashed evil, little more than a corruption on the body politic. The lottery abolition movement was part and parcel of the reform impulse that was galvanizing America in the 1830s, as groups ranging from temperance and prison reform to the abolitionist and women's movements attempted, with a considerable degree of urgency, to get things right before the new nation became set in its ways. In the wake of yet more scandals, the movement succeeded in banning all lotteries in New York State as of January 1, 1834. Unfortunately for the reformers, however, New Jersey and most southern states did not follow the lead of their northern neighbors. The entirely unintended consequence of the abolition of lotteries in New York was a very sharp increase in the amount of money gambled on policy. By the late 1830s and 1840s, every weekday, thousands of New Yorkers were insuring numbers on the Delaware Lottery, whose results came in to Manhattan at 1:00 P.M., or on the Jersey Lottery, whose results arrived at 4:00 P.M.[7]

Insuring the lottery was also illegal, but spread throughout the city were hundreds—by some accounts thousands—of policy shops and agents willing to take bets.[8] Recognizing one of these establishments was a simple matter. In 1856, "Phil," a self-confessed "man about town" intrigued by all the talk about the plague of policy offices in the city, spent ten days engaged in a "discovery" of parts of town he had never seen before. In a letter to the *New York Daily Times,* he claimed that there were at least a thousand such offices, not infrequently "as many as four on one block." They were everywhere. "Whenever you see a store window whitewashed, or a white curtain suspended on the inside, in ninety-nine cases out of a hundred, it is a policy shop." Similarly, the word "Exchange" on the shop window or on a sign over the door was a fairly good indication that one could place a bet inside. But the most obvious giveaway was a constant stream of ordinary New York workers beating a path through an establishment's doorway. "If you stand in front of a cigar store a minute or so, and see a poor German, a negro whitewasher and a woman enter, you may depend upon it that in a room behind the store they do a lively business in selling policies."[9]

On July 1, 1848, the *National Police Gazette* printed an illustration showing the interior of an exchange office. In the image, a heavy curtain prevents the curious on the street outside from seeing through the window, an arrangement that "Phil" pointed out was a commonplace. On the wall there are two posters, one probably detailing results from the Pokomoke Lottery, which was drawn in Delaware, and the other interestingly emblazoned with the words "Policy Dream Book." Dream books were a genre that had its origins in Europe, but in their American incarnation they were increasingly being made over, in the years before the Civil War, into publications that disseminated an African American view of the way the world worked. Short and cheap, they provided a guide for interpreting dreams and converting them into numbers that could be backed. Virtually every policy shop in New York had a well-thumbed copy of at least one of these books on the premises—indeed, some unscrupulous agents apparently charged for a glance at the black gamblers' bible.[10] Something of the way this worked is conveyed in the illustration's caption. Joe has dreamed about weakfish, a species which had just returned to New York Harbor after an absence of some years, and the agent tells him that the number for that is eleven.

It was more than just the artist's desire to pun on "lights and shadows" that led him to depict a caricatured black as the customer. Most of the surviving detail about the way policy worked involves African New Yorkers. In August 1839, Joseph Ten Eycke, a black man, visited a policy shop on Bayard Street, near Orange Street, that was run by a black woman named Jeanette Parker. Parker was an agent for Josiah Paine, a white broker, who insured numbers in the Wilmington Lottery. Ten Eycke picked 7-54-24 as a "gig" (three numbers); had "saddles" (two numbers) on 7-54 and on 24-7, and also bet on 24 as a "day number." All in all, the African American gambled $20, and should have received the substantial return of $625 when several of his bets "hit," but Paine refused to pay up, causing the black man to have him charged. What is particularly fascinating about this and other accounts is how many features of numbers in Harlem in the 1920s and 1930s—not just the betting on numbers or even the way dreams so often provided the inspiration for the wager, but also the language (the use of terms such as "gig," "saddle," and "hit"), as well as the fact that the banker had welched when a large sum of money was involved—were already in place a century earlier. Ten Eycke claimed that he had "spent hundreds of dollars in purchasing tickets and insurances on these lotteries," and he was hardly the only African American plunging heavily on policy.[11] There were scores of cases in the court records and newspapers in the 1830s and 1840s that involved the insuring of lottery tickets by blacks.

The visibility of blacks in policy was out of all proportion to their representation in New York's population, let alone their position as the poorest inhabitants of the metropolis. By 1850, there were slightly more than half a million residents in the city, and only 13,815, or 2.7 percent, were black. Yet according to the editor of the *Ram's Horn,* a black newspaper, in the mid-1840s, $2,500 out of the estimated $10,000 expended every day on policy came from blacks.[12] White newspaper editors railed against the havoc wreaked by what they viewed as a contagious and addictive vice. The *National Police Gazette* claimed, in May 1846, that "there is no such thing as trusting a negress as a domestic servant at all any more," since every sum of money that went through her hands was tithed a few pennies "for the purpose of feeding her passion for policy gambling." A few weeks later the newspaper urged anyone hiring servants to inquire *"whether they play in policies,"* and, if they did, to reject them out of hand. Policy mania was seen as being little short of a plague, and many whites had no doubts as to its source. "We found that the alluring infection had spread from its Negro victims to the poorer white classes of the city," claimed a writer for the *Police Gazette.* Indeed, when he had "looked into the prisons" it turned out that two-thirds of incarcerated petty thieves ascribed "their recent pilferings to the ungovernable cravings of a morbid appetite for policy gambling."[13]

Time after time in the 1840s and 1850s, white commentators indicated they believed that almost every black on Manhattan Island gambled regularly on policy. In October 1845, the editor of the *Police Gazette* claimed that "out of a colored population of more than ten thousand souls, nine tenths are its victims." Two and a half years later, totally exasperated by the seeming inability of the police to do their job and "to eradicate these pestilent dens from our city," the

Gazette's editor proposed that more drastic measures be taken. "Any Negro going along the street" should "be subpoenaed at random," as almost certainly a quick rifling through her or his pockets would turn up numerous policy slips. Indeed, "any magistrate who feels disposed to enter into an independent investigation of the policy abuse, may take enough evidence in this way in ten minutes, from the dusky wayfarers upon the very sidewalk of the Tombs" (that is, the city's prison), to put fifty or sixty miscreants behind bars.[14]

Doubtless there was some exaggeration involved in such claims, but there is little reason to question the assertion that a large proportion of African New Yorkers were avid aficionados of policy. Coincidentally, what had happened was that slavery had finally ended in New York, on July 4, 1827, just as policy had begun to take off. Abolition was always going to be more disruptive and difficult for whites in New York and its surrounds than anywhere else in the North. For most of the eighteenth century, the city had ranked second only to Charleston, in British mainland North America, in the number of slaves held by its inhabitants. In 1790, one in every five white households contained a slave, and in the neighboring areas, within ten to fifteen miles of the metropolis, the figure was four in every ten households, a rate of slave ownership higher than that found in Virginia or South Carolina. Holdings were generally small, with very few whites owning more than one or two slaves, but slave ownership was widespread and was not confined to the elite. In 1799, the New York Assembly legislated to end slavery, but the measure was a compromise that demonstrated both the power of the slaveholding interests and the respect accorded property rights, even if the property was human beings. The bill freed only those slaves not yet born, and they had to serve a lengthy apprenticeship. Those who were still slaves on July 4, 1799, were abandoned to their fate; not until 1817 would the legislature finally agree to free such persons—and even then, they would not actually be freed for another decade, on July 4, 1827. The legislature had ensured abolition would occur at a pace that could only be described as glacial. In the event, many slaves took things into their own hands and negotiated individually with their masters. Most of the advantages in such transactions still lay with the owners, but for once the deck was not stacked entirely against the slaves, and many played their cards very skillfully indeed. Not only was slavery in New York doomed, but the city's free black population was increasing rapidly, making the successful pursuit of runaway slaves much more difficult. Implicit in every negotiation was the threat that if some arrangement was not agreed upon, the owner would be left with either a sullen, refractory slave, or, if the slave decamped, nothing at all. Some owners accepted money, or the promise of money, while others extracted pledges of good behavior for three or five years; but most eventually made a deal with their slaves and took what they could get for their human property. To a large extent, then, the details of slavery's demise in New York City were worked out on an individual basis. By their own initiative and hard work, most New York slaves managed to achieve freedom well ahead of the lackadaisical timetable set in place by the legislature.

In the early decades of freedom, the material realities of life for most of New York's black inhabitants were grim. To be sure, there were African Americans who managed to get ahead—individuals such as Thomas Downing, who, for decades, ran an elegant, upmarket oyster establishment just off Wall Street that catered to whites. But most New York blacks were forced to piece together an existence from short-term jobs, usually as domestic servants if they were female, or as day laborers, often around the docks, if they were male. Even here, they were increasingly squeezed out of these meagerly paying jobs by the poor Irish migrants who were flooding the city. But for all the problems of life for blacks in antebellum New York, the most important fact was that, mostly through their own efforts, they were no longer slaves. For the first time in American history, there were a great many black city dwellers who were free and who had some money in their pockets and purses—certainly not much, but rather more than had been the case when they were slaves.[15] Policy, a game that tantalized with the dream of transforming very small sums of money into large ones, was designed to soak up not just the spare pennies of the poor but also, as its critics vehemently and repeatedly pointed out, their hard-earned wages that should have fed, clothed, and sheltered their families. It was a game tailor-made for people in the position in which African Americans found themselves in antebellum New York.

Policy and dream books certainly had English origins; but African New Yorkers seized on these practices, transformed them, and made them an important part of the urban black culture they were beginning to forge on the city streets in the early decades of their freedom. Right from the start, astute observers discerned that there was something distinctive about the ways in which many blacks approached the business of betting on policy. Hitting a number was considered less a matter of luck than a matter of fate or destiny; hence the importance of dreams, and their interpretation, in each person's effort to divine the correct numbers on which to bet. When "Phil" did his ten-day tour of the policy offices in 1856, he could not help noticing some of the differences between black and white players. In one particular establishment, a stream of "Negro whitewashers" all "seemed to put their money on 4, 11, 44." This particular combination was known as the "washerwoman's gig" because of its popularity among blacks and the fact that a large number of black women eked out a living by washing clothes; 4-11-44 would assume a prominent role in the African American lore of policy over the ensuing century. "Phil" also paid careful attention to the various reactions of the bystanders when the numbers were announced. "It was pitiful to behold the faces" of some of the white gamblers, "Phil" observed, "while others cursed their luck dreadfully." According to this onlooker, blacks reacted differently, seeming "to take it the easiest." Perhaps that was because, for most blacks, lamentations about having backed today's winning numbers yesterday, or in one lottery but not another, were totally beside the point. If your number was going to come up, it would. One of the blacks who prompted "Phil"'s observation chanted, "I plays my money on forty-four / And if it comes I works no more." And that was pretty much the way things were for blacks in antebellum New York.[16]

The caption that accompanied the illustration of the policy office also pointed to one of the keys to understanding this form of gambling. Although Joe bet only four cents on number 11—a trivial, almost laughable amount—the entire business of policy was based on the fact that many, many wagers of pennies quickly added up to surprisingly large sums of money. Throughout the history of this sort of gambling, it has always been difficult for the police, courts, and lawyers to maintain much enthusiasm for pursuing poor people when the individual transactions involved, say, a mere four cents. Almost all of the cases of "insuring the lottery" that wound up in the court records, or that made the newspapers, were instigated not by the police but by aggrieved gamblers who had not been paid off for a hit. Policy was a deceptive business, all too easily dismissed by those not in the know as being of little note.

The people who ran the policy business in New York in the 1840s and 1850s certainly appreciated that thousands of dollars was being wagered every day, and they were almost entirely whites. There were a few blacks running policy shops, but they were relatively rare. More commonly, whites would employ blacks as agents in an effort to maximize custom from African Americans. In 1839, Josiah Paine, a white man, "employed negro wenches as *policy agents*," as the *New York Herald* italicized. When Joe Ten Eycke (mentioned earlier) hit to the tune of $625, Paine refused to pay, on the grounds that "his agents had exceeded their commission"—a claim that, according to the *Herald,* made the black man "as wrathy as a bottle of ginger pop" and induced him to seek revenge in court. Usually, though, the agents were male. Charles Vultee, a white grocer, employed Abraham Caldwell, a black, as an agent, and allowed him 18 percent of all the policies that he sold. When Vultee was hauled in front of court for welching on a black man's hit, he was not only found guilty but also given a very public verbal flaying by the judge. What Vultee had done was illegal and fraudulent; "he had, moreover, practiced this traffic among a portion of our population the least able to bear such losses—the poor and ignorant black." Insidiously, as far as the judge was concerned, he had sought out one of "their own color" to employ as an agent, "the better to carry on this illegal and (to them) ruinous business."[17] Whatever the court's qualms, however, at least some whites thought it made sense to employ blacks to cater to black customers.

There were occasional dark mutterings in the more legitimate press about the people who were involved in the policy business. In June 1846, the *National Police Gazette* claimed that "we have in our possession a list of over two hundred of the names of these dealers, and of a still greater number of witnesses or players against them—

some of whom are among the wealthiest brokers and speculators in the community." But it was the flash press, wearing its lack of legitimacy as a proud badge, that decided to begin naming names. The flash press was a group of weekly newspapers with titles such as the *Flash*, the *Whip*, and the *Rake*, which burst onto the New York scene in the years 1841–1843. Brash, provocative, trenchant, and offering a titillating cocktail of gossip about prostitutes, theater, and the like, these ephemeral rags provided a guide for sporting men to the pleasures of commercialized leisure in the city. They also pushed the boundaries of what a newspaper could publish; their editors were constantly being dragged into court on charges of libel or obscenity.[18] It was all a winning combination; even today, these newspapers dating back more than a century and a half remain a lively and enjoyable read. In February 1843, the *New York Sporting Whip* railed that "every penny broadside published has teemed with long windy articles upon the propriety and impropriety, honesty and dishonesty of policy vending; but there they have stopped." The *Whip*, however, "hope[d] to be the instrument of bringing these gents to justice," a desire that prompted the editor, with his usual pun on his paper's title, to write that "annexed are a *few* of the fellows who are doomed to some five or six hundred lashes each" and to list the names and locations of seventeen policy shops, the last of which, run by Mackay & Farrar on Park Row, had twenty-eight agencies.[19] The *Flash* and the *Weekly Rake* ran similar exposés of the lottery and policy business. There was always more than a hint of extortion to these stories—the suggestion that unless consideration was forthcoming, more names would be exposed in the next issue; and indeed blackmail was one of the sources of revenue that helped make these short-lived publications very profitable. The *Whip*, however, vigorously denied the insinuation "that our object in giving publicity to the names of the scoundrels who deal in policies was to extort hush money from them." Similarly, some six months earlier, the editor of the *Flash* lambasted some "unprincipled scoundrel" who had written to every lottery office demanding five dollars as a charge to suppress their name from a list to be sent to the grand jury and had "had the impudence to affix the initials of persons connected with this journal to his scurvy missives."[20] Such denials should probably be read with even more skepticism than the rest of the contents of the flash newspapers.

New York's flash press revealed well the "deceit and counterfeit" that were everywhere in the city in the 1840s. According to historians of these newspapers, this was a place "where attractively innocent young women turn out to be sexually available, where respectable men young and old lead double lives and fear exposure, where swindlers and cheats abound among the lowlife and the elite—where things, in short, are seldom what they seem."[21] It is difficult to convey a sense of both the liveliness and danger of New York's streets at this time. The population was expanding at an exponential rate, surpassing half a million people by the end of the 1840s, and the city was awash with men and women on the make, confidence artists of all stripes, and their victims. "Burners," usually blacks, lured gullible whites up alleys on the pretext of settling a bet and then relieved their marks of their pocketbooks; the operators of the fake auction system, known as "Peter Funks" in the local slang, continued to make money despite the press's warnings to the public; and decoy houses, or "touch houses"—brothels where disguised partitions allowed secreted criminals to rummage through the client's clothes while he slept—were common.[22] Even something as simple, nowadays, as paying for an item was often fraught with difficulty: most banks, both well known and obscure, issued their own notes, counterfeits were ubiquitous, and everyone was anxious to unload the fake banknotes that they had mistakenly accepted. This was a time and place that could have coined the phrase "caveat emptor." As a historian of Wall Street has noted, this was a "modern, commercial civilization that seemed fraudulent at its core."[23]

If New York City of the 1840s was permeated by deceit and counterfeit, we should not be surprised to discover that an enterprise that was illegal and therefore hardly regulated by law, that was largely patronized by the most powerless members of society, and that turned over tens of thousands of dollars every week was indeed rotten to its very core. The intense rivalry for business between the competing policy shops meant that individual agents carried on selling insurance on the various lotteries up until the last moment before the drawing, "for the purpose of catching all the chance custom." As a consequence, a considerable amount of human ingenuity was invested in devising ways of transmitting the results of the drawings in Delaware, Maryland, and New Jersey to Manhattan ahead of the official notification. If this could be achieved, then obviously bets could be placed on guaranteed winners, numbers that had already been drawn. Sometimes this was done by using carrier pigeons; indeed "policy pigeoning" became a generic term for this type of fraud, no matter how it was committed. Con artists also tampered with the clocks in policy shops, allowing bets to be placed after the results had arrived in New York. On at least one occasion, the *Subterranean* reported that "a policy seller who relied upon St. John's time piece" was "duped to the tune of $50 by the hands of that clock being set back ten minutes."[24]

This, of course, was all fairly petty stuff. It paled into insignificance compared with what went on in New York in 1842 and 1843, where the level of complexity and chicanery of the fraud brings to mind, for readers of a certain vintage at least, George Roy Hill's film *The Sting* (1973). Stations were set up about every thirty miles atop whatever prominent features of the landscape were available between Wilmington and New York for the Delaware Lottery, and between Baltimore and New York for the Maryland Lottery. A set of what were called Bengola lights was then used, with a red light standing for tens and a white one for units, and the numbers were flashed from hilltop to hilltop. To prevent this valuable information from being available to all, a code was used, so that while "one red light and six white ones might appear to indicate sixteen, it may mean forty five." Incredibly, results of the Delaware Lottery reached New York in twenty-five minutes; and the Jersey numbers were known in the city one minute after they had been drawn. The result of all this was chaos on the city streets. Several policy agents were involved in this system "out of self protection and those who are in the secret retaliate upon the players, by spreading a report that eight or any other, is a pigeon number, to induce players to buy, when sixteen as they already know, is the real number." This, as the *Subterranean* commented, was "a game of rogue fleece rogue and the poorest and most stupid go to the wall." "Crowds of poor, ignorant negroes who imagine they have got a pigeon number manoeuvre to appear unconcerned while buying it," as knowing agents pocket their money. "It would appear incredible to the uninitiated," this newspaper pointed out, if they could see "the extent to which this system of juggling is carried." There was "hardly a steeple in the city but what is used as a look-out for lights and scarcely a negro goes along the streets who is not dreaming what will be first in the Jersey tomorrow."[25]

Inevitably, in a system that was rigged to this extent, it was those at the bottom of the heap who were the most exploited. The word "pigeon," meaning someone who was swindled especially in gaming, had a history that went back at least to sixteenth-century England, but it took on a new American resonance in the New York of the 1840s. Not only were blacks duped with fake pigeon numbers, but even if they beat the odds, interpreted their dream correctly, and picked the right number by themselves, "pigeoning" was used as yet another excuse for not paying them their winnings. As the *Herald* noted in March 1842, there were thousands of "poor blacks and whites" addicted to policy, but even "if one of them should be lucky enough to make 'a hit,' as it is called, they are then cheated of their dues by an allegation on the part of the policy office keepers, that they have been 'pigeoned.'" A few months later, as part of his campaign to denounce and name individual policy agents, the editor of the *Flash* excoriated one Hiram Marsh of 118 Chatham Street as being "the most notorious of this class of swindlers." The *Flash* then detailed one case where a black "had *hit* Marsh for sixty dollars" but was "done" out of both his winnings and his original stake. When the black man had fronted up for payment, "he was accosted by bully Marsh with 'Well, you d—d black rascal, you *pigeoned* me last night, eh? Now walk out of my office, and if I ever catch you here again, I will blow your black head from off your shoulders.'"[26]

This was the free market, untrammeled by almost any regulatory authority. Yet what is most intriguing is the extent to which blacks, the most exploited group in the whole corrupt affair, were the ones most likely to try to play by the rules and to call in the police. This is part of a broader pattern where, to a surprising extent in the antebellum years, aggrieved blacks used the law in an attempt to solve their problems. In the summer of 1840, William Vanness, "a fat, jolly looking colored man, with spectacles on his nose," played a "saddle" and "hit" in the Delaware Lottery; but William Coursen, the black agent who had taken the bet, refused belligerently to pay the twenty shillings he owed his client. Coursen told Vanness that he "might go to H—," and that "if he wanted anything better he might take it out in fighting." This offer Vanness "declined," "preferring," the *Journal of Commerce* noted, "to push this prosecution for his satisfaction."[27] As far as we can tell from the newspapers and court records, most blacks who found themselves in Vanness's position followed his example and surprisingly few resorted to violence. Partly, this almost touching faith in the American legal system must have been pragmatic: this period was midway between the horrors of the 1834 race riot and the murderous 1863 draft conflagration, and it was not a time for African New Yorkers who valued their lives to get involved in violent struggles with white policy agents. But it does seem to have been more than this; Vanness, after all, declined to fight a black, not a white, welcher. As we shall see, this reticence would soon change. By the twentieth century, faith in the law had certainly dwindled, and few Harlem blacks had any hesitation whatsoever about using the razor or the revolver to sort out the nonpayment of a hit.

The association of African Americans with this form of gambling continued throughout the second half of the nineteenth century even though, for most of this period, the black share of New York city's population had dwindled to between 1 and 2 percent. According to James McCabe, writing about New York in 1868, "the negroes of the city are great policy-players." Everywhere "they live you will find dingy little lottery offices, patronized mostly by them." Jacob Riis, in *How the Other Half Lives* (1890), his now classic investigation of New York's underbelly, made a similar observation. According to Riis, policy was "the meanest of swindles, but reaps for its backers rich fortunes wherever colored people congregate." A combination of the "closely allied frauds" of the fortune teller and the policy shop resulted in the squandering of "the wages of many a hard day's work . . . by the Negro." Riis also noted that blacks maintained a remarkable and "undaunted faith" that they would hit the right numbers. And "when periodically the negro's lucky numbers, 4-11-44, come out on the slips of the alleged daily drawings, that are supposed to be held in some far-off Western town, intense excitement reigns in Thompson Street and along the Avenue, where someone is always the winner."[28]

By the 1890s, the twin gods of the dream book and policy were an established part of New York life. As Jacob Riis had witnessed, when a popular number hit, it reinvigorated the poorer areas of town; not only did celebrations spill out into the streets, but also (and this Riis failed to mention) angry unpaid winners searched high and low for agents who were skulking, or perhaps holidaying in warmer climes. In late August 1893, 9-19-29, the "dead gig," was drawn from the barrel that decided the lottery results. According to the *New York Times,* this combination of numbers had gained this sobriquet "because the policy dream book states that it is to be played on the death of a great man, or when the player dreams of a dead man." When "such a favorite and consistently played 'gig'" came up, the result was a financial disaster for policy agents; on this occasion the reporter estimated that, in New York State, they had lost a million dollars. The *Times* wasted little sympathy on the "policy backers," however, as they would soon recoup their losses; it was, after all, little more than "throwing a mackerel to catch a whale." For African New Yorkers, working out what number to back was often a sociable and very public affair. In late March 1892, a white passer-by on Thompson Street eavesdropped on "several negroes deeply absorbed in what another was telling them." The conversation was about policy. "Well, I'se goin' to play 9-19-49," one of the blacks explained. According to the *Times*, "the speaker had evidently had a dream and upon consulting his dream book had found that 9-19-49 was the number that the dream book told him he must play." Inevitably, sharing information about dreams, ruminating at length about which numbers to back, caused a clustering of bets on certain particular combinations. As the *Times* somewhat disdainfully noted of this area characterized by a concentration of African Americans, when one of these "lucky series of numbers comes out, Thompson and Sullivan streets go crazy about it."[29]

Throughout 1894 the Lexow Committee, formed by the New York State Senate, though eventually funded by the Chamber of Commerce, a body whose desire to expose the corruption of Tammany Hall and the Democratic administration in New York City caused it to dig deep into its pockets, investigated the police department. More than 10,000 pages of testimony from some 678 witnesses provided a graphic snapshot of New York's underworld, a picture of police excess and sleaziness that made newspaper headlines across the country. What makes the committee's report a particularly intriguing window onto policy in the 1890s was the fact that most of its members were neophytes when it came to what they undoubtedly viewed as the more sordid aspects of life in the city, and their very bafflement compelled the witnesses to give detailed explanations of the way things actually worked. Asked what class of people "indulge in this policy business," Thomas Boese explained that sometimes it was "prosperous people," but "downtown, it is the poor class, the Jewish people, and uptown it is the negroes," and over in Little Italy it was the Italians. One member of the committee was especially puzzled by the fact that it was the poorer sections of the city that were the most profitable for the people running policy. Boese reaffirmed that "they are [the] best districts; the very best," and went on to explain that "they do not play such big amounts, but the quantity more than covers that." Witness after witness explained that there were hundreds of policy shops all over New York. As Charles A. Beeck vividly declared, "On Seventh Avenue you can find them in every block; just follow a nigger woman and you are sure to find one."[30]

Not only did the testimony before the Lexow Committee reveal in depth the way policy worked—the rates of commission, how much the police were paid off, the meaning of the game's distinctive argot—but various witnesses also explained, from the perspective of white men involved in running the whole enterprise, how the ordinary gamblers worked out what to back. "Everybody has a dream," Patrick Ryan testified, "and next morning they come in and tell them to the policy writer, and the policy writer gives them a gig for it." As he pointed out to his inquisitors, "there are thousands of gigs; any three numbers make up a gig." Named gigs included the working gig (14-26-42) and the sick gig (10-20-30). As well, there was the Irish gig, the beer gig, the Wednesday gig, the police gig, and innumerable others. Thomas Boese explained to the committee that there were at least half a dozen different police gigs and that "they play them in different parts of the city, different gigs." Whenever anything happened to "a policeman everybody plays a police gig—any policeman is discharged or drunk, somebody goes in and plays a police gig." A slightly perplexed member of the committee then asked, "You mean to say if a policeman ran up against the Broadway cable car and got the worst of the collision, you mean to say the people would run in and play the police gig?" Boese patiently replied that "they would take the police

gig, take the number of the car and run the combination." Once
the committee had reached an understanding of policy, its members seemed disappointed to discover that there was no "Lexow
gig," perhaps some sort of an indication that they were not having
quite the impact they had anticipated on the city's underworld. Be
that as it may, there was little in what the committee was told
about New York City that could have provided much reassurance.
One witness was asked how long a policy shop could be open without the police knowing. His answer was "about twelve hours." And
that, of course, was the rub, for there were hundreds of policy
shops and the police were taking thousands of dollars in bribes to
leave them unmolested.[31]

The Lexow Committee was told frequently that the person in
charge of policy in the city was Al Adams. The following exchange
occurred between one of the committee and a Vincent Majewski:
"Q. And what is he called?" "A. The king; they call him king."
"Q. King of the policy dealers is it?" "A. Yes, sir."[32] Adams was not
the first New York Policy King. Zachariah Simmons had been acknowledged as holder of this position by the end of the Civil War,
but Adams was the best-known and probably the most crooked, as-
suming the title of "Policy King" around about 1880. A decade later,
when Jacob Riis made his veiled reference to "alleged daily drawings, that are supposed to be held in some far-off Western town,"
he was referring to Adams's operation. By this time, most states
had banned the running of lotteries; policy in New York had to rely
on the drawing of lotteries which took place twice each weekday in
Frankfort and Louisville in Kentucky. Supposedly, the numbers
were picked out of a barrel by a blindfolded child. In fact, what happened with some degree of regularity was that Adams and his
bookkeepers totaled all of the bets placed at his numerous shops in

New York, worked out which combination of numbers was least heavily backed by gamblers (thus making him the greatest profit), and then telegraphed the winning numbers, in code, to Kentucky. In due course, the results of the "drawings" were telegraphed back to New York City, and Adams would make even more money than usual on that day. Adams amassed a fortune from the business. Eventually, however, the authorities succeeded in catching and convicting him, and in April 1903 he was sentenced to twelve to eighteen months in prison. Apparently, he emerged from his incarceration a broken man who made no attempt to start over in policy.[33]

In the aftermath of Adams's fall in the first years of the twentieth century, policy in New York seems almost to have slipped into abeyance; from the perspective of the 1920s, a writer in the black newspaper the *New York Age* claimed that Adams's demise "was the final blow that killed policy in this town."[34] Certainly, there was little trace of the game in the 1910s. The authors of this book examined all of the district attorney's Closed Case files for the second half of 1916 and the whole of 1917 for all of Manhattan, but turned up only a handful of policy cases, and they suggest that, unsurprisingly, policy had splintered into various ethnic groupings.[35] There were a couple of arrests in Chinatown. In March 1917, a young man named Chu Gum (and it is difficult not to imagine that an immigration officer somewhere created that name with a sardonic smile on his lips) was arrested for possessing "Chinese policy slips." Sometimes the arrests came from further afield in the city: in October 1917, Knita Genaka, a thirty-four-year-old butler and Japanese national living on Lexington Avenue, was picked up by the police in the Hudson Terminal with "sixty-two slips of paper with Chinese figures of a policy drawing." In both cases, this game was probably Gee Far, an import from China that involved betting on one of thirty-six symbols drawn by the Sin-shang, or head man, and that mostly catered to Chinese and other Asian Americans.[36] Little Italy was another important center of policy. Beginning very early in the twentieth century, Italian lotteries, drawn in eight major cities including Rome, Turin, and Venice, were used to generate the winning numbers, obviously a cumbersome system. By 1917, Frederico Valentino, a forty-two-year-old Italian, had made his living out of policy for at least the previous dozen years, and was widely known among Italians living in Lower Manhattan as the Policy King. According to the police commissioner, he was "one of the principals of the group which controls the Italian Lottery Policy." Although there had been the occasional murder, putatively linked to this small cabal, it had a small-time air about it.[37] There was also an arrest or two on what is now the Upper East Side, the suspects usually being Spanish-speaking and Cuban.[38]

In retrospect, it is difficult not to see that the stage was set for something new, a way of gambling that would consume the pennies, nickels, and dimes of the city's myriad poor, entranced by the chimerical hope of making easy money. And for all the Clearing House numbers' links to the past, it was still new, a simpler, more streamlined game than policy, and one that paid better odds. Once the Clearing House numbers became known in Harlem, the game spread like wildfire.

2

Beginnings

Sugar Lou: "That's one thing I sure miss in Europe, the numbers.
They don't seem to know how to play 'em over there."
Ham: "They started in Harlem, didn't they?"

—Langston Hughes, *Little Ham* (1935)

The precise origins of the practice of gambling on the Clearing House numbers are shrouded in myth. More than was the case with most endeavors, numbers was fueled by publicity. Indeed, it was the most oral of activities, though inevitably some of those spoken words made it into the written record. Rumor, gossip, and innuendo about who had just had a hit, what number was going to turn up at 10:00 A.M. the next day, who had been arrested and who had not, which banker had left town rather than pay off a hit, and the lifestyle of the Kings and Queens of the business reverberated around Harlem, eagerly listened to and retold by ordinary residents and, of course, the newspapers and the police. Stories accreted to numbers like bees to a honey pot, making it hardly surprising that there was more than one version of how the business began.

For the Jamaican-born Harlem Renaissance poet and novelist Claude McKay, writing in *Harlem: Negro Metropolis* (1940), the founding of the "numbers industry" occurred in the 1910s, as blacks made the "big trek" up to Harlem. The migration also included Puerto Ricans and Cubans, some of whom established barber shops in the black belt. The game of "bolita" or "paquerita," which the British West Indians called numbers, had its start in these Spanish establishments. According to McKay, the first prominent figure, a man nicknamed Catalan, inspired by his knowledge of the way the Spanish lottery worked, created a method of gambling that used figures taken from the New York Stock Exchange. Shortly after the end of World War I, Catalan retired to Spain, handing over his business to his offsider, a Cuban black whom McKay named as Messalino. If Catalan had been a quiet and unassuming man, his successor was anything but that. Messalino had "a flair for extravagance," employing liveried chauffeurs to drive his ostentatious cars and developing a presence in Harlem that helped excite interest in the fledgling form of gambling. According to McKay, "he was the first of the dazzling line of numbers kings."[1]

In January 1925, the *New York Age* ran a story, based on "well-authenticated information," that also located the origin of numbers in the activities of Caribbean migrants, specifically the large numbers of Cubans who worked in tobacco factories and warehouses. On Mondays and Saturdays these workers played "bolita," a game in which 100 numbered balls were placed in a bag, chances were sold at a dollar apiece, and usually a young child drew the winning number that secured the ninety-dollar prize—which later, as the organizers became more avaricious, shrank to eighty dollars. The banker made ten dollars or twenty dollars on every draw. The system had its shortcomings. As far as the banker was concerned, his "take" was certain but limited; and from the gamblers' perspective, there was the possibility that the drawer would use substitute balls and that either the banker or a confederate would win the prize. Consequently, the racket took a new form. A series of cards numbered 0 to 999 were sold at twenty-five cents each. The winning number, taken from the thousands column of the stocks and bonds sales as reported in the *New York Sun,* paid $25, a return of 100:1. Furthermore, if the number on the gambler's card had the correct final two digits, it was a "bolita" and paid $2, or 8:1. This system, too, proved to be flawed: apparently, there were occasions on which someone was "bought off," and the number printed in the newspaper turned out to be more favorable to bankers than the actual figure had been. This prompted a move to the system of using the Clearing House numbers. Gamblers could now choose the number they wished to back, rather than just buying a card on which a random number was printed.[2]

Other writers agreed that numbers had been imported from the Spanish-speaking world. Writing in the *New York Times* in 1937, Henry Lee Moon, who had previously worked for the black newspaper the *Amsterdam News,* admitted that there were "contradictory theories as to the origin of the game," but claimed that in Harlem "it is generally believed to have been introduced from Cuba, either directly or by way of Key West, Fla."[3] The following year, in the well-known African American newspaper the *Pittsburgh Courier,* Edgar T. Rouzeau and Jack Pelayo gave the most specific account, claiming that it had all started in New York in 1914. According to them, the game began as a "more or less harmless pastime for the 5,000 Porto Rican, Cuban and other Spanish-speaking tobacconists" working at the Schwartz Brothers tobacco factory located at Eighty-First Street and Avenue A. Initially, the workers had played bolita, but the presiding genius of this form of gambling, a white Spaniard known as El Catalan (whom the *Pittsburgh Courier* reporters identified as Florentino Hernandez, claiming that this was the first time he had been named in print), invented the new game of numbers. Rouzeau and Pelayo also outlined the rise of Marcelino Cardenas[4] (whom McKay, almost phonetically, would label "Messalino"), "the first Negro numbers millionaire." In Cuba, Marcelino had been a skilled cabinetmaker, but—and this would be the case with many of the future Numbers Kings and Queens—his color barred him from using his considerable talents in his chosen field. Struggling to make enough money to live on, the young black migrant was offered work by El Catalan: "You are a fool to keep on suffering like that. Come work for me and I will give you $40 a week." Marcelino, hesitating, asked "if the game wasn't against the law." El Catalan shrugged and pointed out that the game was akin to the stock exchange. "The white man takes your money, gives you a piece of paper which he dignifies by the name of stocks, and you gamble on your luck. If the value of your stock goes up you make money. If it goes way down you lose everything." Somewhat disingenuously, Catalan continued: "I don't see where this is any more unlawful than that." El Catalan's rationale may have been flawed, but it was more than enough for Marcelino, who enthusiastically launched himself into his new business. Within a year or two Marcelino's style and extravagance had become a byword in Harlem for the good life, proof that the dreams of at least some poor blacks could come true.[5]

There were other possible sources of inspiration for numbers that were also aired publicly. In July 1924, the *Age* printed a story claiming that numbers in Harlem was a modification of the New England Clearing House Lottery, which had been in operation for about five years. In the New England game, however, "a series of tickets [was] issued, numbered serially," and 420 prizes were on offer each day.[6] What was different about the game that developed in New York, though, was that gamblers could pick any number on which they wanted to bet and could wager any sum, from one cent upward. These were crucial differences.

According to Saunders Redding, a black author and literary critic, writing in the *North American Review* in December 1934, although no one knew where the numbers game started, "the most authentic tradition" located its origins with Casper Holstein, a black, born in 1876 in what was then the Danish West Indies. Having emigrated with his mother to the United States in 1894, Holstein graduated from a Brooklyn high school and then held a series of jobs, ending up as a Fifth Avenue store porter sometime around the end of World War I. According to Redding, what differentiated Holstein from other black porters was that he combined "an eye for the stock market reports" with "the shrewdness of a race-track tout." Inspiration struck while Holstein was sitting in an "airless janitor's closet, surrounded by brooms and mops," whiling away the hours "studying" the Clearing House totals printed each day in a year's worth of newspapers that he had "saved religiously." As Redding memorably wrote, "The thought that the figures differed each day played in his mind like a wasp in an empty room." Six months later he came up with his scheme: two digits would be taken from the first total published by the Clearing House and one digit from the second, and if the gambler hit, he or she would be paid at the rate of 600:1.[7]

These different stories are not necessarily contradictory. What seems quite possible is that early versions of numbers were established by the time of World War I and were popular with migrants from Cuba, Puerto Rico, and the British West Indies. But around

1920 or 1921, someone—and Casper Holstein is a very likely candidate—possibly even in part prompted by the New England Clearing House, had the flash of genius that allowed for the invention of the Clearing House numbers as it was played throughout the 1920s. We use the word "genius" advisedly. Numbers was such a wonderfully elegant scheme. There was no need for the expensive procedure of drawing numbers out of a bag or barrel, and then having to publicize the results. Instead, every morning the respectable, indeed staid Clearing House released figures that gamblers could check at any newsstand in Harlem in the afternoon papers and then use to compute the winning number. As Claude McKay wrote, "To the uninitiated it was an extremely puzzling thing; to the players who were given the key, it was simple."[8] For ordinary residents of Harlem, numbers was a game of chance that seemed to be transparently fair and that offered the tempting possibility of converting a ten-cent bet into the substantial sum of $60. Setting up as a banker was easy. The Clearing House inadvertently supplied and publicized the winning number every day; all the banker had to do was to take bets. And unlike earlier schemes, where there was a fixed number of tickets sold and a set return to the bank of 10 or 20 percent, the possible returns were limitless. Quite conceivably, a banker could accept, say, 10,000 bets on a given day and not one of them would require a payout. If a popular number did hit, however, the odds of 600:1 meant that a banker might easily be unable to pay. These two features—the possibility of a banker's making staggering amounts of money and the constant threat of his or her ruin—combined to create a very unstable system, and that instability would help shape life in Harlem in the 1920s and 1930s.

As the game of numbers was refined and perfected, from the

drawing of balls out of a bag to the total reliance on the Clearing House numbers, it attracted little attention from those in authority. People of color, often speaking Spanish or English with a West Indian lilt, living in or near Harlem, betting pennies or nickels on an opaque game of chance, hardly seemed of much import when rival gangs were warring with each other to determine who was going to supply Prohibition New York with alcohol. In the early years of the 1920s, numbers was often cavalierly dismissed with the epithet "nigger pool."[9] But right from the start, those pennies and nickels added up. According to the *Age*, the first banker to operate in Harlem was Carmalita (who most likely was the person we have already referred to as El Catalan, though the *Age* claimed he was Cuban and not Spanish), who monopolized the business of the earlier version of numbers popular among Hispanic immigrants. By the late 1910s, he had made a "large fortune" and retired to Spain. Sometime in 1922 he visited New York in order to buy some cars. When asked if he was going to resume his earlier occupation, he replied, in the bowdlerized translation that the *Age* was able to print: "No, no. When I played the game that virgin was a lady. Now she has become a wanton."[10] This may or may not have been true, but what was beyond dispute was that the shift to using the Clearing House numbers had indeed transformed everything, most particularly by allowing bankers to make even more money. By 1924, Marcelino controlled much of the gambling by Spanish-speakers, employed more than 100 agents, cruised up and down Lenox Avenue to collect his bets in his $12,000 chauffeur-driven limousine, and lived in a "veritable palace" on Striver's Row, the famous three-storey brownstone houses on 139th Street. He imported three chandeliers costing $1,000 each from Cuba, purchased a baby grand piano for

$5,000, and was fond of showing off to his friends his specially built safe in which he kept $50,000 in cash. He was only one (albeit a conspicuous example) of more than thirty bankers who, the *Age* claimed, were thriving in Harlem.[11] But it was Casper Holstein, likely inventor of the modern version of numbers, who did best. According to Saunders Redding, within a year of his moment of inspiration "he owned three of the finest apartment buildings in Harlem, a fleet of expensive cars, a home on Long Island and several thousand acres of farmland in Virginia."[12]

Although numbers was being played in the early 1920s, knowledge of the practice remained limited and the police made few arrests. There were occasional fleeting references to numbers in the black press in Chicago. In September 1922, the *Chicago Defender* ran a brief article about a plunge on the number 400, resulting in bankers being unable to pay and "approximately $50,000 [being] won by Harlemites that could not be collected." A few months later, in February 1923, the *Defender* published a three-paragraph story referring to "the great sucker game of clearing house numbers that for a time seemed to grip all Harlem and still has a strangle hold on a large number of Harlemites"; but the game received only the most cursory coverage in the New York newspapers.[13] One of the earliest occasions on which a New York paper devoted more than a line or two to numbers occurred after Patrolman William H. Cox, in late January 1923, arrested a suspected banker who lived at 450 St. Nicholas Avenue and who was carrying an envelope full of numbers slips. In court a few days later, a skeptical magistrate questioned the policeman: "How do you know they're Wall street slips?" "I played them myself—twice, a year ago." "Did you win anything?" Cox had to admit "to the loud laughter of the court that he didn't get the

$12 he had expected for his two pennies."[14] Not only was the terminology incorrect—the Clearing House was not on Wall Street—but the incident was played for laughs, both by the curious magistrate and also by the more knowing *Amsterdam News*, which printed the exchange.

Seemingly, sometime in early 1924, somewhere in the universe a gear shifted and everything changed. Suddenly, numbers in Harlem became less a minor vice and more a full-blown craze. The number of gamblers willing to place daily wagers of pennies and dimes increased exponentially, and the vogue for numbers became a story demanding attention from the black press.

Fred Moore, crusading editor of the *New York Age*, was quick to stake out his paper's position. Moore had been born in Virginia in 1857, had been raised in Washington, D.C., and had begun his working life in the U.S. Treasury, eventually ending up as personal messenger to the Secretary. In 1887 he moved to New York, assumed the editorship of the *Colored American Magazine*, and then, in 1907, with the support of Booker T. Washington, founder of Tuskegee University and the most influential black man in America, was appointed editor of the *Age*. By the 1920s, the newspaper was directing most of its attention to Harlem. The *Age* ran stories about successful black businessmen and businesswomen, and supported boycotts of white establishments in Harlem that refused to employ blacks. As with Harlem's "hooch joints" (establishments selling illicit and usually poor-quality liquor), which Moore crusaded against, numbers was an issue tailor-made for his moral concerns—concerns that had been shaped by the philosophy of Booker T. Washington. In May 1924, the *Age* warned that playing the "Clearing House Numbers" had "assumed proportions that constitute a distinct menace to the moral and economic life of the race." The following week a lurid headline in the paper blared: "Bankers and Their Runners Lead Sleek and Unctuous Lives, While Poor Suckers in Game Are in Debt, Trouble and Squalor." Two months later, Moore, his anger and frustration still barely controlled, claimed with admirable sibilance that "this invidious, insidious and pernicious form of gambling has spread its tentacles into almost every strata of race life in Greater New York."[15]

Commencing in the spring of 1924, numbers evolved from an activity carried out, furtively and almost unnoticed, in a few Spanish-speaking barber shops, into something that was mainstream and obvious on every street in the Black Metropolis. According to a reporter for the *Age* in May 1924, "the casual stroller along Harlem thoroughfares can hear, without conscious effort at eavesdropping, comment from almost every group of two or more which he might pass concerning some phase of the 'Numbers' playing game."[16] Numbers became part of the rhythm of Harlem street life, so that, until December 31, 1930, when the Clearing House ceased publishing the clearance figures and the basis for numbers changed, a flurry of early-morning activity leading up to the 10:00 closing off of bets put a hum in the air. Partly, this busyness resulted from the rush to place bets. As one reporter noted, "Every morning, until around 10 o'clock, scores of men and women may be seen flocking into these places to make their daily play on the 'numbers.'"[17] And partly, it was a product of the way in which Harlem blacks transformed the individual act of putting a nickel or a dime on a number into something that became a social event. It was "a common sight, of mornings," according to one observer, "to see two or three individuals, and they are not always of the lower strata, putting their heads together over slips containing presumably the numbers they have played and looking for either a straight hit or a 'bolita' on the day's outcome."[18] As some newspaper editors lamented, publicly and often, it was all very obvious. A piece in the *Age* in July 1926 noted that runners and collectors "employed by the bankers are on a regular schedule each morning, picking up their collections, and there is nothing clandestine or hidden in their movements." Whether walking "boldly and openly along, picking up the slips with the money from the players on the street, or being handed an envelope with money and slips" already tabulated by storekeepers or others acting as go-betweens, numbers runners were larger-than-life denizens of Harlem's streets and avenues.[19]

As Winthrop D. Lane wrote in *Survey Graphic* magazine in March 1925 (a special issue devoted entirely to Harlem and its Renaissance), "All Harlem is ablaze with 'the numbers.'" The game, Wallace Thurman declared, was "Harlem's most popular indoor sport." There was "ample evidence," the *Age* reported, that "addicts" were "to be found in all ranks." This newspaper, in particular, delighted in relaying gossip about rich undertakers allegedly playing as much as $50 a day, or about some person or other who was "able financially" to gamble $2.25 on one special number every day. The *Age* also printed dire warnings about people who were so addicted to what its editor viewed as "the racket" that they gambled away rent and food money. In 1928, the *Interstate Tattler* alleged that it was common to see children as young as three waiting in line in the morning to place bets, presumably for their parents.[20]

But most press attention focused on the fact that an unusually large number of black women were gambling on the Clearing House game. A collector for a Harlem furniture company complained to the *Age* that his receipts were plummeting because, wherever he went, "including some of the best homes in Harlem, it is a common sight to see a group of women gathered around a table doping out figures to be used in playing the 'numbers.'" Rather than being paid what he was owed, the collector was asked for a number, and "told that when a 'hit' is made he will be paid something on account." Black women were often depicted as being even more gullible than black men. The headline to a story in the *Age* in March 1925 blared: "Collectors Play on Credulity of Women Addicted to 'Numbers' Habit and Keep Them in Game When They Would Quit." As one woman lamented, "We try to get rid of the fever. We can't pay our legitimate bills." Another story run by the *Age* revealed some of the detrimental effects that numbers was having on families. It began with a vignette of a black woman hunched over a table in an apartment, concentrating with furrowed brow as she wrote on a piece of paper. She was not, however, laboring on a "best seller" or a "wonderful poem, or anything of the sort," and when her husband entered and asked, "Why is there no breakfast?" she answered, "Because there is no money. The 'numbers' collector has just been here and I've got a 'gig' that's bound to win, so I gave him all the money I had to play that number, and now if you want any breakfast you had better get out and find some for yourself."[21] Probably the story was apocryphal, but it still signified the way in which, for Fred Moore and the *Age,* the Harlem numbers game was turning the world upside down.

It is difficult to convey the extent to which the numbers game permeated the sights and sounds of Harlem in the mid to late 1920s. For the most part, the blues, particularly recorded blues, was associated with Chicago rather than New York. Gambling in all its many forms is one of the major preoccupations that runs through the blues, although the dominance of Chicago meant that the main emphasis was on policy, the game still played on the South Side. For all that, as early as April 1924, Clara Smith recorded her "Clearing House Blues" in New York City.[22] In June 1926, Elvira Johnson sang that she had "Numbers on the Brain." According to the singer, she was "hitched like a horse to the carriage, trying to beat the game," and she had "numbers on the brain, I see them I dream them, they're driving me insane."

> I put my money on 1-22,
> Now what in the world am I goin' to do?
> I just have numbers on the brain.
>
> I picked those numbers the other day,
> The man with the money done gone away,
> I just got numbers on the brain.
>
> Nothin' in the ice-box, nothin' in the trunk,
> I don't use a needle, and I like junk,
> I just have numbers on the brain.
>
> Lost my money playin' *bolita*,
> I went home, robbed my gas meter,
> I just have numbers on the brain.[23]

The following year, in June 1927, Bobby Leegan, in his "Nobody Knows When You're Down and Out," sang: "I thought I'd play some numbers, like most colored people do," and no one with any knowledge of Harlem was likely to argue with him.[24]

It was not only blues singers who wrestled with the difficulty of picking the right number. In March 1925, the *Amsterdam News* printed a poem sent in by one James Haywood Olphin:

> Those Numbers
>
> I take a heavy pencil and I clutch it doggedly.
> Before I've even washed my face or had my breakfast tea
> I ponder and consider (some tell me that I frown),
> As I carefully select . . . and set my numbers down.

Geology, biology, science and the like
I have performed with perfect ease, and calmly termed them
  "pike."
I've even had theology, elaborate but pure.
I've worked a world of crossword games, though they possessed no
  lure.

So now I've turned my ample mind to those which bards
  condemn,
And alas, it's difficult to rule and master them.
But I cast my lot, and I sent them in at eight o'clock or nine.
And when the *Sun* or *World* appears, I am not the last in line.

Then anxiously, yes, nervously, I turn and tear the news,
Quite happily oblivious to the wise men and their views,
Till I spy the column "Clearing House" . . . my feathers fall, I
  frown,
I had the proper number, but I failed to turn it round![25]

For all its limitations as poetry, this piece contains a power of its own, representing, as it does, the effort of one seemingly ordinary Harlem resident to set down on paper the everyday experience of probably a majority of the city's African Americans.

The *Age* was hardly the only institution that was spreading stories about numbers. At least some of the buzz surrounding numbers amounted to self-serving advertising put out by workers in the industry. As the *Age* noted in May 1924, if a player made a "hit," it was "such an important event that news of it spreads through the ranks of thousands upon thousands of players with the rapidity of wireless radio." "Every banker, every runner, and every collector of money from the 'numbers' players becomes a courier of information and every client is promptly told of the fact that one 'Mrs

Brown' or 'Paul Smith' . . . has either won a 10 cents three-number play . . . or has won a *boleta*." And, of course, in a place as large as Harlem, there was no particular reason why the player who had just had a hit had actually to exist. When collections began to fall off, a favorite ploy of runners was to invent a fictitious player—someone "who has been playing without winning for a long time but his play had finally come through netting a considerable profit." This story was told to players who were losing enthusiasm for the game, in order "to bolster up courage" and to ensure that they continued to play their lucky number, for if ever they lapsed, that number was sure to hit.[26]

As the craze for numbers became all-consuming, New York blacks began to look at their surroundings in new ways. For some, Harlem was the City of Refuge, but, as many more discovered, the Black Metropolis was also a city of numbers.[27] Numbers were everywhere: on subway cars and license plates, and in the form of baseball scores, commodity prices, telephone numbers, even hat sizes—all of these sources and many more supplied gigs, or three-digit numbers, that could be backed. One onlooker noticed two men meeting on the street and exchanging their addresses. "'Ah'm gonna play it! Ah'm gonna play it!' says one, as he takes down the address of the other."[28] At church on Sundays, some "listen intently for the reading of the numbers of hymns to be sung or the chapter verses of scriptures that are read, and from these figures work out 'numbers' to be played during the ensuing week."[29] With proper help, perhaps from one of the figures loitering around Lenox, a number could be extracted from just about any event, even, most particularly, from dreams. One man's wife dreamed of "a white veil on a black child" and "the dream book says that both a white veil and a black child means number 267"—whereupon the husband knew to outlay "fifty cents a day on number 267."[30]

Some sources were known to be especially lucky. As the *Interstate Tattler* noted in 1929, any numbers runner "who is arrested and has the presence of mind to eat up his slips before the policeman chokes him, and thus escape conviction, can increase his collections after his release by giving his clients the shield number of the officer who nailed him."[31] And sometimes individuals would read the signs correctly, and of course theirs are the stories that passed around and have survived. According to the *Age* in November 1926, the pastor "of a certain large and influential congregation" in Harlem told his flock that there was a "pressing need" for a large sum of money. Then he said, "Now, here is a number that might come out, so you had better put it down and play it tomorrow for the church." He then proceeded to announce the number of a hymn. Reportedly, that number hit, but, as the newspaper dryly noted, there was no record of any profit for the church fund. In March 1930, on the famous radio serial *Amos 'n' Andy,* Amos called up his girlfriend in Chicago, asked the operator the cost, which was $2.45, and, aghast at the expense, refused to speak to her. By then, however, quite a few people had scribbled down "245." The following day they played the number, and of course it hit.[32]

In a few years, and out of almost nothing, the numbers had created an enterprise with the largest number of employees and the highest turnover in Harlem. Estimating the dimensions of what was an illegal, albeit often winked-at business is notoriously difficult, but, for varying reasons, many in the 1920s and 1930s were prepared to make the attempt. As early as May 1924, the *Age* estimated that there were at least thirty bankers in Harlem, many of them Cuban, and that many of them employed between twelve and twenty collectors. The following month, the newspaper declared that Marcelino, the largest banker, employed more than 100 agents as runners and collectors.[33] Writing in the late 1920s, Wallace Thurman opined that there was "no possible way of checking up on the number of runners" who were drumming up business, but he guessed that "there must be in Harlem over a thousand number runners daily collecting slips from 100,000 clients." In June 1926, the *Age* estimated that the daily turnover on numbers was $75,000, an amount which would have created an annual turnover of around $20 million.[34] Testifying before a bail bond inquiry in March 1935, attorney Richard Davis, counsel for the gangster Dutch Schultz, who himself was heavily involved in illegal gambling, claimed that in 1931 numbers was "played only by the colored people in Harlem," and the daily gross was $300,000, that is, roughly $80,000,000 a year.[35]

No doubt some of these figures are exaggerated, but it is still clear that simply staggering amounts of money were being gambled on the numbers game in Harlem every day. As befitted an industry that was illegal, margins were very high and profits for bankers could be enormous; as early as December 1924, the *Age* noted that it was "freely reported" that some of Harlem's bankers "show a weekly profit of from $10,000 to $15,000, or even more."[36]

Investigations by city and federal authorities turned up other sets of figures, which allow a more detailed glimpse into individual bankers' lives. Wilfred Brunder, for instance, was one of the more important Numbers Kings. In February 1928, Brunder, then aged thirty and living on fashionable Edgecombe Avenue, was convicted of being a numbers banker and sentenced to a brief stint in the penitentiary. At the conclusion of his trial, probation officer Jacob Lichter claimed, in his report to the court, that Brunder "had been running the game for years and that his collectors brought in $3,000 and $4,000 a day." Brunder himself was reputed to be worth more than half a million dollars.[37] Three years later, in December

1931, a federal grand jury indicted Brunder for income tax evasion, claiming that he had failed to file returns on income of $1,000,009 earned in 1929 and 1930. Realizing that his time was up, Brunder had fled to Bermuda some months previously; but after the government put a lien on Harlem property and bank accounts held by the Rednurb (read it backward) Corporation, he negotiated a return to New York for payment of a $45,000 fine.[38] In 1935, Brunder was hauled in front of the bail bond inquiry. By then, Brunder, described by an *Amsterdam News* reporter as being "plump" and "well dressed," had retired from the numbers racket, but he was still prepared to wax eloquent about the old days, giving "his hearers a gleaming of the tremendous profits of the 'number' game." He claimed, for instance, that for three consecutive years he had grossed over $2 million. According to the former King, he personally had made more than $200,000 in one of those three years—but expenses had been horrendous, he'd had a run of "bad" numbers, and the arrest of over thirty collectors a month in 1927 had cut into his take.[39] It should be emphasized that in a business in which the common coin was brown paper bags stuffed full of cash, and in which bankers dispensed largesse from thick wads of banknotes that they carried with them, any figures taken from bank accounts and the balance sheets of corporations are likely to be understated.

What all this meant, in Harlem, was that the evidence of numbers was everywhere. Everyone knew a numbers runner; most also knew who the bankers were as well; and probably well over half of Harlem's residents put at least a few cents on a number with some degree of regularity. Only churches attracted comparable sums of money. Fourteen congregations, including Metropolitan Baptist Church and St. James Presbyterian Church, had the tens of thousands of dollars necessary to purchase large buildings from white

Christian and Jewish congregations, whose members were in the process of abandoning the neighborhood as blacks arrived. Nine other congregations, including St. Philip's Protestant Episcopal Church (the wealthiest in Harlem) and the Abyssinian Baptist Church, built equally imposing edifices of their own. In addition to houses of worship that seated from several hundred to several thousand, these buildings included community houses incorporating auditoriums, gymnasiums, and meeting rooms. Writers in the *Crisis* and the *New York Age* joined James Weldon Johnson and others in complaining that most of the resources gathered from members were earmarked for expensive buildings of one sort or another, but many churches also developed social, recreational, and community programs, ranging from aid to the needy, adult education, and daycare, to concerts, excursions, and sports teams.[40]

Across the enormous variety of faiths that could be found in Harlem's churches—Baptist, African Methodist Episcopal, Presbyterian, Congregationalist, Catholic, Seventh Day Adventist, African Orthodox, Holiness, Apostolic—members heard a broadly similar message of respectability, sobriety, and thrift. Nonetheless, church attendance and playing the numbers did not belong to different worlds, as a story doing the rounds of Harlem in the summer of 1924 made clear. A well-known black minister harangued his flock about the need for a decent-sized collection, claiming that at least $200 was needed. He added a rider to his plea: he wanted no money tainted by "numbers" in his church's plate. The collection was very quickly added up—and it came to $8. The minister then changed tack, stating that he wanted $200 and did not care where it came from. The plate went around again, and this time it was piled high with more than $400 in notes and coins.[41] Money touched by the numbers racket in some way percolated to every corner of the Black Metropolis.

3

DREAMS

A dollar and a dream, that's all you need.
—Joseph O'Neill, *Netherland* (2008)

The principal selling point of Casper Holstein's scheme was the use of the Clearing House figures to generate the day's number, a number that would therefore be random. Unlike the situation with policy in the 1840s, when gamblers and agents alike were duped by pigeon numbers, or, in the 1890s, when Al Adams ran a system that on some days was totally rigged, the Clearing House numbers gave everyone exactly the same chance—one in a thousand—of coming up with the winning number. Given the amount of money gambled and the size of the potential winnings, it is hardly surprising that tens of thousands of New Yorkers, mostly those living above 125th Street, dreamed of proving Casper Holstein wrong. Some came up with all manner of schemes to manipulate the daily number, so that they would be betting on a sure thing; others were content to try to discern a pattern in the winning numbers, in order to show that in fact the numbers were not random at all.

It was a brilliant stroke on Holstein's part to link numbers to the New York Clearing House. Lotteries in the nineteenth century had

had an increasingly suspect reputation, but that of the Clearing House was beyond reproach. In the early 1960s, the Clearing House moved from Cedar Street to a new building on Broad Street, and even today the premises of this institution exude its augustness. Wood paneling, Victorian furniture, and, lining the walls, the somber portraits of past pillars of the financial establishment, now totally forgotten but still impressive in their collective rectitude—all suggest a time when New York was unequivocally the center of world capital, and when the financial establishment employed blacks solely to man the elevators. The link between the Clearing House and the ordinary African Americans living in Harlem and San Juan Hill has now been totally forgotten.[1] When one of the authors of this book made his way to the Clearing House in order to use the archives (not one of the more often visited resources in the city) and explained his purpose, he was greeted with a certain amount of disbelief. Could the colorful stories that this historian—an Australian at that—was telling about their past be true? A quick check in the *New York Times* for the 1920s turned up a number of items showing that there was at least some basis for his claims. As it happened, there was very little from the 1920s left in the Clearing House archives; probably, when they had moved from Cedar Street, the records had been purged of almost everything but the bare bones of the minutes of the Clearing House Committee meetings. Before leaving, our intrepid researcher was given a tour of the premises by the very generous archivist, a tour that included a meeting with two senior executives who run the modern-day Clearing House. They too were taken aback to hear that their institution was intimately linked to the everyday life of Harlem in the 1920s. It turned out that the wife of one of these men collected Clearing House memorabilia on eBay; but even so, the fact that their institution was mentioned in novels, plays, and blues lyrics, and that acres of print in both the black and white press had been expended decrying the Clearing House numbers, was news to them and to everyone else who worked there.

Things were rather different back in the 1920s. As numbers expanded exponentially in 1923 and the spring of 1924, employees of the New York Clearing House did not know what had hit them. For the next six years, until the institution ceased publishing the daily figures on December 31, 1930, the switchboard and mailroom of the Clearing House received a constant stream of inquiries every day from gamblers wanting to lay their hands on the figures just a little bit early. As a writer in *Time* magazine noted as early as March 1924, "Clearing House officials were constantly [being] telephoned regarding the likely outcome of their activities by people who could not possibly tell the difference between a clearing house and a dry cleaning establishment." Sometimes the callers—and the calls came from all over the country—pretended that they were financial reporters who needed the figures early for a deadline. Even more embarrassingly for the Clearing House's reputation, officials were called by people who innocently assumed that the institution ran the numbers and wanted to place their bets at the source rather than with their agents. It all seemed very bizarre. The Clearing House had been publishing the daily clearances since 1853, but, as the *Time* reporter somewhat archly commented, it was not until the early 1920s that "the Clearing House statements possessed this vivid interest to hoi polloi."[2]

As we have already seen, gambling on the numbers was the most verbal of activities. Stories of the game were constantly circulating on the streets of Harlem, and many of them centered on people who supposedly knew in advance what the day's number would be.

In August 1924, the *Age* breathlessly announced that "at last the biter has been bit!" The article continued: "Players succeeded in getting hold of advance information as to the figures which were to appear in the Clearing House balances, and this information carefully handled was played by such a large number of individuals that the aggregate losses to the bankers assumed formidable proportions." A few months later, in June 1925, the *Age* reported that some bankers were "suborning certain individuals connected with either the Clearing House forces or the daily newspapers so that the true numbers shown in the Clearing House reports each day are juggled, and players are deprived of even the slim chance they ordinarily have to win." Sometimes the rumors were more specific. In March 1925, "three or four shopkeepers in the Columbus Hill section" (or the black neighborhood San Juan Hill) gained "advance information as to the Clearing House reports for a certain day about two weeks ago," played the number 318 with three local bankers, and won $36,000.[3]

To a large extent, it did not matter whether advance information was circulating around Harlem or not. It was enough that many people believed that it was. Plunges, or heavy betting, on certain numbers and occasional big wins combined to induce at least some bankers to behave in a skittish fashion, closing off their books early, at 9:00 A.M. rather than 10:00 A.M., to avoid being cleaned out by gamblers with inside knowledge. Here was a perfect situation for con men to exploit; and it should be remembered that the 1920s was the golden age for black con artists and that Harlem was the center of their activities. In March 1925, Harold Bancroft, a thirty-four-year-old Jamaican who had been living in America for fifteen years, hooked and landed one John Nairne, who lived on West 64th Street in San Juan Hill. Bancroft had convinced his mark that he possessed a contact in the Clearing House named Mr. Bacon. There was in fact a Mr. Bacon working as an assistant manager at the Clearing House, but he had no idea of the way his name was being bandied about up in Harlem. Bancroft convinced Nairne that if they both put up $1,750 and paid Bacon $3,500, the supposedly bribed official would arrange to "have a certain set of figures appear in the day's 'clearings and balance' as published in daily papers." Nairne dutifully handed over the money, at 132 West 122nd Street. After a week in which the arranged numbers failed to appear, Nairne demanded his money back, and received a check for $1,750. The check, of course, was returned by Nairne's bank, stamped "No account."[4]

In reality, though, the weak link in the chain lay not in the Clearing House but in the transfer of the figures from the Clearing House to the newspapers. There were several failed attempts to subvert this process. In August 1929, two white men, aged twenty and twenty-two, were arrested outside the Clearing House. They had twice attempted to bribe a sixteen-year-old messenger of the Financial Bureau of the Associated Press, who was carrying the just-released figures back to the Wall Street office. They had offered the lad $50 and later $75 to change the figures to ones that suited their employers. The *New York Times* reported that the two arrested men supposedly "had been employed by a negro named Williams in Harlem to bribe the boy," and, more worryingly, "that they had previously bribed eight other messengers."[5]

For sheer chutzpah, though, it was unlikely that anyone could match the spectacular attempt to hijack the Clearing House figures that had occurred nearly a year earlier, in December 1928. By this time, the Clearing House figures were being posted in Cedar Street at 11:30 A.M., not 10:00 A.M., as had previously been the case. On December 5, at precisely 11:28 A.M., "a well dressed young man walked quietly up to the board and posted a set of figures purporting to represent the previous day's exchanges, balances and Federal Reserve credit balance." On completion of this task, he quickly and unobtrusively slipped out of the door. Reporters and press association representatives wrote down the figures and were just about to begin sending them out, when a Mr. Arthur Harman, who really was an employee, arrived with the correct figures, at which point everyone realized what had happened. The fraudulent figures were: Exchanges, $1,9**09**,000,000; balances, $16**3**,000,000; Federal Reserve credit balance, $156,000,000. This would have resulted in a winning number of **093**. The correct figures were: Exchanges, $1,9**06**,000,000; balances, $16**1**,000,000; Federal Reserve credit balance, $156,000,000. The real winning number was thus **061**. What was startling to all observers was the similarity between the fake and real numbers. According to the *New York Times,* the Clearing House had also noted how similar the figures were, for such closeness did at least raise the possibility of inside involvement. The *Times* concluded its story by pointing out that it was "believed that those responsible for the attempt wagered heavily on 093 in the hope that they could collect their money before the substitution was discovered."[6]

Yet for all the rumor and innuendo about insiders, and even the occasional failed attempt to infiltrate the process of generating the daily number, the reputation of the Clearing House in Harlem and San Juan Hill remained unsullied throughout the 1920s. It was certainly the case that—by comparison with what had occurred in the nineteenth century, and what would happen later in the 1930s after the Clearing House ceased announcing its daily figures—the system of using the totals of the exchanges and the balances to work out the winning number was as pure as the driven snow. Indeed, for all the ingenuity and flamboyance displayed by various con men as they attempted, and mostly failed, either to control or obtain early information on the winning number, it should be remembered that they constituted an infinitesimally small percentage of those trying to beat the odds. The real action lay elsewhere. One could not walk twenty paces in Harlem without hearing about some scheme to come up with the winning number. Innumerable African Americans were convinced that the daily numbers were not random and that a pattern could be discerned if one looked closely enough. A multi-million dollar industry was built on this premise.

For some with a mathematical bent, the key to future winning numbers lay in the past. Although the Clearing House had no idea of its existence, some enterprising individual published a pamphlet entitled "N.Y. Clearing House Exchanges & Balances," which listed the figures for every workday from January 1920 to November 1924. In May 1925, when Silas Holt, who ran a restaurant, was arrested in a store on Lenox Avenue, he had in his possession eight policy slips and a copy of this booklet. A few months later, according to the *Age,* cigar stores all over Harlem had advertising placards in their windows promoting "the 1926 Clearing House Book at 50 cents per copy," another publication of which the actual Clearing House was totally ignorant.[7] In November 1930, Harlem newspaper sellers were for some time puzzled by "an unprecedented demand" for "a certain out of town weekly." It turned out that the magazine contained "a tabulated record of the number hits produced by the clearing house reports for last year." As the *Age* somewhat incredulously noted, "Some ingenious and industrious soul had tabulated these figures by days and months, showing the three digits that were money winners on the respective dates." What the article revealed was that three numbers had hit three times and that twenty-six numbers had come out twice. As the *Age* reporter wryly observed, "We do not see much to gamble on in that dope."[8] Of course, as long as the number is random, it makes no difference whatsoever if a given number has come out five times in the previous year, or has not come out at all for three years. It still has exactly the same chance—one in a thousand—of winning. Unlike many card games where a system can improve one's chances of winning, there is no system that can improve the odds of one in a thousand in numbers. But that did not stop countless people from trying to devise one.

It was not merely the unsophisticated who tried to beat the system. Carl Van Vechten, the white novelist and photographer, was an habitué of Harlem and the most prominent champion of many of the Renaissance writers and artists; Langston Hughes, poet and novelist, was the most gifted of the Harlem Renaissance writers, a man whose letters sparkle with wit and acuity and to this day remain a delight to read. In a letter to Van Vechten in January 1931, Hughes wrote: "I came near hitting the other day with your Shetland pony numbers—but I am scared of Lindy Hoppers with razors! I'm boxing the Shetlands today."[9] "Boxing" meant betting on all possible six combinations of any three digit number (i.e., betting not just on 123, but also on 132, 213, 231, 312, and 321). Typically, Hughes's aside combines a jesting tone with enough of an underlying hint of seriousness to make one wince even to imagine what conceivably could have been the basis for the Shetland pony system. At any rate, Hughes and Van Vechten's surviving correspondence details no notable success in their backing of the numbers.

Langston Hughes, though, was one of a kind. And if few Harlem blacks had a circle of friends that included ultra-sophisticated whites such as Van Vechten, it was still the case that they had other resources on which they could rely. Scores of thousands of ordinary black New Yorkers made their decisions about which number to back on the basis of an array of traditional beliefs that had been developed and refined over at least a century of African American involvement in what we might call games of chance. It cannot be emphasized too strongly, though, that for perhaps a majority of black participants in the 1920s and 1930s, numbers was neither a game, nor did it involve chance. Indeed, for thousands of African Americans the daily number was not random, and hitting it did not depend on luck. As early as June 1923, a writer in the *Age* noted that "by all imaginable methods these bettors pick the numbers that they are to play the next day." Distancing himself from his fellow citizens with a dash of condescension, the *Age* journalist continued: "They are mostly superstitious and almost any odd incident may be interpreted as a tip by them."[10]

On June 23, 1926, Malcolm Wright, a thirty-five-year-old porter who had been living at 127 141st Street for some eight months, was languishing in cell 200 in the Tombs on Center Street, accused of grand larceny. With time on his hands, Wright decided to pencil (pens not being allowed) a letter to Joab Banton, the district attorney, explaining that, far from running the confidence scheme of which he had been accused, he and his friends had been playing craps and "the game was on the level." The whole sorry tale had started on the morning of Tuesday, June 15, "in the beer saloon at 139th Street and Lenox," an interesting admission to the city's chief legal officer in the middle of Prohibition. Wright and several other black porters had been "talking the numbers" when someone pointed out that if they had played "the hunch," they would have made a lot of money. It turned out that what he was referring to was the fact that "the number of the first hymn that little 14 year old girl preacher sang Sunday June 13th was hymn 329, [and] that was the number came out Monday June 14th." There is no recorded response from Banton in the file, but there can be little doubt that this was all somewhat removed from the milieu in which the district attorney was accustomed to move.[11]

For the knowing and observant, there were signs everywhere in the city that could guide the numbers player; but for African New Yorkers, the most common and most powerful "incidents" providing a "tip" were dreams, for, if interpreted correctly, dreams foretold winning numbers. In February 1933, a white probation officer paid his regular home visit to one of his Harlem clients. The probationer was a regular attendant of the Abyssinian Baptist Church, and it was also his custom to read a chapter of the Bible every day, believing that he could find the solution to his problems there. As the probation officer typed up later in his case notes, the probationer's conversation at this meeting "revealed his simple nature." The elderly black man, who was sick and owed a considerable amount of money, told his probation officer that he "has been waiting for a dream in which he hopes to have a number revealed to him," and that, when this occurred, he would place a wager and clear his debts. Apparently, in 1932, his dead father had "revealed" a number to him and he had won $20. The probation officer drily ended his brief account of the meeting with the notation, "P.O. advised him against such procedure."[12] Undoubtedly the P.O. was well-meaning, but in the end his notes "revealed" little more than his incomprehension of the way his probationer made sense of the world.

Talking about dreams became ubiquitous among African Americans in the mid to late 1920s and 1930s. It is difficult to convey the extent to which dreaming and the recounting of dreams to family and friends saturated urban black life in these years. Some were not prepared to be quite as patient as the elderly probationer waiting for his dream to occur. In the mid-1930s, blacks could buy the "Dream Pill," a capsule "guaranteed to make anyone taking it dream lucky numbers which are sure to hit." According to the *Chicago Defender*, these pills were sold for "fancy prices" but, on examination by experts, proved "to be filled with ordinary baking soda put up in attractive boxes."[13] In August 1926, Mme. Sarah Washington devoted one of her regular *Amsterdam News* columns entitled "Beauty Secrets" to the topic of "Dreaming the 'Numbers.'" "Beauty is dependent solely on health," she began, and health was dependent on sleep, "nature's greatest rejuvenator." Furthermore, the "character of sleep depends largely on the mental attitude on going to bed." But, increasingly, there was a problem bedeviling her African New Yorker readers. Some were "so absorbed" in "playing the 'numbers' and doping out their slips before going to bed that they carry their worries to sleep with them and are robbed of proper rest because of dreams." It had even reached the point where a few of Mme. Washington's acquaintances "kept a pencil and pad at their bedside and during a course of dreams would actually awaken and jot down the 'dream numbers.'" There was, however, a cure. The beautician recommended that "if you are worried or have been giving considerable thought to the "numbers" it is a good plan to read something diverting, but not exciting just before retiring." Doubtless authors the world over took cheer from her advice that it was "often abstruse books that require great mental concentration" that would "prove serviceable in quieting the mind and inducing sleep."[14]

Few, if any, societies can ever have expended so much time and energy on the recollection, analysis, and discussion of the details of dreams. Sigmund Freud would have had a field day in interwar Harlem or San Juan Hill. About 6:30 A.M. on the morning of May 15, 1930, Gurnie Roberts, superintendent of the building at 149 West 134th Street, was sweeping the hall when he noticed a fellow standing on the street out front with a numbers pad in his hand. The numbers runner asked him, "You got change of a quarter?" Roberts went out to the street and gave him change for his quarter, after which they had the following exchange:

"Fellow ain't you playing?"
"No, but I had a dream last night."
"What did you dream."
"I saw a clock and the hands of the clock, one hand on five and the large hand on eight."
"Yea. You ought to play five eighteen."
"I don't play numbers but give me 18, I'll play a combination. Five and five is ten and eight is eighteen."

Then one of the tenants in his building who did play came downstairs and Roberts inquired about the reputation of the numbers runner, adding: "I hope to hit, I ain't played in a good while." As fate would have it, his number did hit, but the numbers runner's banker went broke and Roberts never received the $16.50 he had coming to him.[15]

It was unusual for a specific number to be embedded in a dream, but a veritable industry sprang up around the numbers game, the object of which was to help players interpret their dreams, and to translate images of, for example, white veils on black children into specific figures on which to bet. This returns us in much greater detail to dream books.[16]

This genre had been common enough in the nineteenth century, but in the 1920s and 1930s a tidal wave of these publications swamped Harlem and other black centers throughout the nation. Some, such as *Aunt Sally's Policy Players Dream Book,* carried on much as before and continued to sell well in Chicago and other midwestern cities that retained daily drawings and policy wheels. But the Clearing House numbers, with its new format, required one three-digit number rather than a sequence of three or more numbers between one and seventy-eight. Thus, if someone dreamed of "coffee" in Chicago, he or she could thumb through *Aunt Sally's* and learn that it was "a sign of misfortune" and that the combination to back was **11, 12,** and **39;** but the same dream in Harlem, according to *Policy Pete's Dream Book,* meant that the dreamer should put money on **098.** The market among African Americans for dream books was now split between two different systems: policy in Chicago and the Midwest, and numbers in New York and other cities on the Eastern Seaboard. There was soon a fistful of publications catering to those who wished to gamble on the newly created Clearing House numbers.

Uriah Konje's *H.P. Dream Book,* copyrighted in 1926 and 1927, was one of the more successful in Harlem. Konje began his ninety-six-page publication by claiming modestly that "it has been my desire for many years to produce a dream book of one hundred per cent efficiency, and I have succeeded in doing so." Indeed, "never in the history of the world has there been such a book." Throughout, there is an almost ethereal, otherworldly quality to Konje's writing. "The Beautiful little flower by the wayside we often overlook, and go in search of the wild one. This beautiful little book is real and genuine, and there is no reason why you should pass it by." On the next page is a list of holidays, each with a recommended number: "Christmas **250,**" "Lincoln's Birthday **564,**" "Independence Day

469." The bottom half of the page contains more of Konje's opaque, semi-mystical prose: "Some say that there is no tomorrow. But I say that there is a tomorrow; for every yesterday has its tomorrow, and every tomorrow its yesterday. So we go on in this world, from day to day, like automatic fools, until we sink down into our dusky graves. **868.**"

What then follows is a sixty-five-page list of words in alphabetical order, each with its Clearing House number: "bomb" was **010,** "car" was **414,** and "leaky pipe" was **562.** The range of items covered in this list is truly impressive: Konje even gave a number, **700,** for dreams abstract enough to be encapsulated by the phrase "capitalistic production." Then follow pages and pages with headings such as "Ladies' Names," "Gentlemen's Names," "Days of the Week," "Months of the Year," "States of the United States," "Important Cities of the United States," and the like, all with a three-digit number attached to each word in the lists. Toward the end of the book, Konje devoted another page to his thoughts, entitled "To the Colored People of the World." "I am appealing to you not in rhythm or Rhyme but in simple language," he began. "I beseech you to wake up, and teach your children trades and professions of all kinds." He continued: "There is no pleasure in digging a ditch. But there is much pleasure in using a typewriter, there is much pleasure in painting a landscape, especially when the golden sun is on its edge and the silvery skies are illuminating with ever glittering stars peeping out, here and there on a mid-summer's day."

Konje concluded by asking his many readers "not to fight for social but political equality." Once the latter had been gained, "there is nothing to prevent you from obtaining social equality." *The H.P. Dream Book* ended with several pages of advertisements seeking agents and storekeepers willing to sell dream books of all sorts. It was a curious mixture of black uplift and social conservatism, dressed up in the pious language of self-help. After all, "love is the only supreme agency in the guidance of man's career and self-determination of his ultimate destiny," and, doubtless, after purchasing and using this dream book, readers would hit on the numbers and achieve the American dream.

Dream books were the key to unlocking the city of numbers. For the modern reader, perhaps the most noteworthy feature of this genre is the emphasis on violence in the city. Not only did these guides allow their readers to convert the images from their dreams into a three-digit number, but they also performed the same function for the incidents of everyday Harlem life. In *The H.P. Dream Book* (1927), readers were informed at the beginning of one section that "the following are not dreams, but things that you naturally see, hear or happen." The list began with "To see a race riot **291**," and continued through such sights as "To see a funeral procession **976**," and "To see a person bleeding **815**." Similarly, *Policy Pete's Dream Book* (1933), under the heading "Dreams and Happenings," itemized "A Murder Committed **217**," "A Cutting Affair **801**," and "A Gang Fight **389**." "Harlem Hunches for This Year," in *Rajah Rabo's 5 Star Mutuel Dream Book* (1933), was another litany of mayhem and violence: "To see a riot, **222**," "To see a gang fight, **228**," "To see cops chasing bandits, **299**," "To see two men fighting, **797**," and "To see two women fighting, **798**." The actual listings for dreams likewise suggested a world suffused by violence and sudden death. To judge from the dream books, blades and blood certainly haunted the sleep of a large number of residents. *Policy Pete's Dream Book* listed, among others, "bayonet **100**," "blade-razor **786**," "blood **584**," "carving knife **045**," "cutthroat **517**," "cutting **270**," "dagger **802**," "knife **397**," "murder **183**," "murderer **219**," "murderess **527**," "razor **047**," "razorblade **726**," "stabbing **676**," "stabber **147**," and "stiletto **278**."

There was good reason for such an emphasis in the dream books. Without doubt, Harlem was a violent place. In April 1932, the reporter Henry Lee Moon wrote a three-part series on Harlem in the *Amsterdam News*. Moon found that in 1931, blacks were only 12 percent of New York County's population, but made up one in three of its homicide victims. One hundred African Americans in New York County and 122 in Greater New York City were murdered in 1931, yet in England and Wales, with a combined population of some 40 million, there were only 109 homicides in the same period. And the violence was sharply increasing: in 1920 the murder rate was 22.09 per 100,000 blacks; in 1931 it was 44.5. Bringing everything back to the personal, Moon pointed out to his readers that they had one chance in 2,247 of being murdered that year. Indeed, in terms that everyone in Harlem would understand, "Your chances of being slain are something less than half as promising as your chance of 'hitting the numbers.'" Moon was at some pains to point out that the razor was not used by blacks as frequently as was commonly supposed, but whatever his intentions, the figures were still quite striking. In New York City in 1931, fifty-nine of the homicides among blacks were caused by cuttings, and fifty-two by firearms; among whites, in contrast, 214 individuals were shot and only 115 died from stabbings. Dream books mirrored a sobering reality: the murder rate among blacks was at least three times higher, and probably closer to four times higher, than the murder rate among whites.[17]

For a large number of residents in Harlem in the 1920s and 1930s, a dog-eared dream book was accepted as a necessity if one wished to ensure success in playing the numbers. Like businessmen, numbers players used calculations to arrive at figures and then acted on those figures. Bettors, however, were basing these calculations not in the rational realm of profit and loss, but on the completely unquantifiable content of dreams. In addition, interpretation is always a difficult art: dreams are slippery entities, seldom reducible to just a single image, meaning that readings were always open to debate. To complicate matters further, it was very unusual for any two dream books to agree on the number any particular object represented. Yet, for all that, a myriad of blacks swore by these, what must have seemed to outsiders, mysterious guides to their world.

By the 1920s and 1930s, dozens of different dream books, including *The H.P. Dream Book, The Lucky Star Dream Book,* and various volumes by Aunt Sally, the Gypsy Witch, and Professor Konje, were for sale at stationery stores and newsstands all across Harlem. Dream books were a lucrative, bestselling genre, one that most New Yorkers had little or no knowledge of. In addressing an all-white jury in a corruption case in August 1938, Thomas Dewey—the district attorney and, in 1944 and 1948, Republican Party candidate for president—breathlessly orated: "There are, in fact, books, a substantial number of different books, incredible as it may seem to you, which have a large sale in the City of New York to the superstitious or people who believe that if they dream of seeing a cat at night they will get up in the morning, look in the book, find 'cat,' and find that 'cat' means a certain number, and then bet their money on that number."[18] Even those more in the know were often taken aback by how popular these books remained with ordinary black New Yorkers. A writer in the *Amsterdam News,* almost with an air of embarrassment, claimed in 1937 that dream books "are still listed among the bestsellers in the Harlem stationery stores."[19] No sales figures exist, but, clearly, dream books sold by the truckload. Some indication of the stakes involved in the dream book business can be discerned from other sources.

In 1938, Herbert Parris, "publisher of several dream books which are on sale on Harlem newsstands," outbid two other interested parties to purchase what the *Pittsburgh Courier* described as "the pretentious estate of the late Charles G. Stoneham, former owner of the New York Giants." The "ritzy home" in Westchester County reputedly cost more than $40,000, a sum beyond the wildest imaginings of the blacks who bought his dream books.[20] Similarly, the doings of Professor Uriah Konje were regularly reported in the black press.[21] Yet perhaps the most revealing incident occurred in 1930.

Early in that year, Konje noticed that sales of his dream books, which, according to the *Tattler,* had previously done "a rousing trade," were starting to fall. Stymied in his attempts to find out what was going wrong with his sales, Konje turned to Herbert S. Boulin. Boulin, a denizen of 135th Street, was one of Harlem's larger-than-life characters. Born in Jamaica, he had arrived in the United States in 1909, and, in 1930, was forty-two years old. By the time of the 1920 census, he was running a business making black dolls, but later that year he embarked on a new line of work, as an informant for the Bureau of Investigation (the forerunner of the FBI) who was paid to spy on Marcus Garvey and the United Negro Improvement Association. The only operative to file detailed daily reports, even when he had no information to offer, Boulin clearly relished undercover work, and when the Bureau dismissed him after thirteen months, he set up his own detective agency. Seeking to establish his credentials, he effectively outed himself as an informer by advertising that he was "formerly with the Department of Justice."

Harlem in the 1920s was a city where everyone was on the make, a place of dizzying movement, with migrants pouring in and almost everyone constantly shifting residence. Business, especially divorce work, flourished, prompting J. A. Rogers, writing in the *Amsterdam News,* to describe the black private eye as the "nemesis of unfaithful husbands and wives." Whether it was barging into bedrooms in the early hours of the morning in search of evidence of an adulterous relationship, or engaging in a brawl on a street corner with one of the many aggrieved subjects of such investigations, Boulin managed to establish a reputation for himself as a man of action. His aspirations, though, ran less to preying on wayward spouses and more toward finding a respectable niche in Harlem life. Undoubtedly, the title Rogers gave to his piece in the *News*—"Harlem's Sherlock Holmes"—pleased the black private detective immensely. Uriah Konje offered Boulin an opportunity for further such work, engaging him to, in the *Tattler's* words, "ferret out the matter" and establish exactly why sales of Konje's dream books were plummeting. The investigation, which took Boulin and his employees to several states, demonstrated that Konje's *H.P.* and *Lucky Star* dream books were being plagiarized by a group in Philadelphia, who had previously been Konje's agents. Konje promptly brought a civil action against the Philadelphians, claiming that they "were flooding Philadelphia, New York and other cities with pirated copies of his dream books." He sought the considerable sum of $50,000 in damages.[22]

Dream books were hardly the only source for predictions about the next day's winning number. As Lester Walton had noted in the *World* particularly from the summer of 1927 on, Harlem streets were full of people claiming to be in the know. A decade later, in August 1937, Ken Jessamy, a reporter for the *Amsterdam News,* decided that the ease with which ordinary African Americans were being fooled by what he called "Harlem's fakers" was all "a throwback to the days when their foreparents believed in voodoo gods and the magic to be found in the application of roots and herbs." On every Harlem avenue, Jessamy declared, "there are men, some with their heads wrapped in turbans, others wearing snakes around their shoulders, who can give you the lucky number for the morrow. The price for the information ranges from ten cents to one quarter." Furthermore, Jessamy continued, in most of the herb and root stores which were all over Harlem, "one may also purchase incense, which after burning, will leave in the ashes the lucky number for the week and one's lucky days." What the reporter found amazing was the number of people who managed to "reap a fair livelihood" from supplying these sorts of services to their fellow citizens.[23]

For Harlem residents who were dubious about purchasing, from some street huckster, a number written down on a slip of paper, a more personalized service was readily available. Droves of African Americans consulted various spiritual guides, desperate for the edge that would score them a hit in the numbers. In March 1925, a young black janitress explained to Fred Moore, editor of the *Age:* "I certainly do believe in spiritualism." She had paid a fifty-cent fee for each one of her daily visits to her spiritualist preacher, who dispensed advice about the numbers. "I couldn't possibly live on the pay I get as a janitress, and what I win on the 'numbers' helps me to get along." The advice she had obtained had been good, the woman declared, and "I am ahead of the 'numbers' game right now."[24] Many African Americans, like this woman—often, but not always, recent migrants from the South—were desperate to believe that there was an easy, inside path to success in the Promised Land.

A decade and a half later, in early May 1940, Marvel Cooke, a reporter for the *Amsterdam News,* walked the streets of the Black Metropolis investigating what her newspaper headlined as Harlem's "Million Dollar Take." Cooke estimated that there were some 200-odd spiritualists, and perhaps as many again card readers, crystal gazers, and their ilk, reaping "nearly $1,000,000 from approximately 50,000 or more Harlemites passing through their doors annually." This was one of the "few businesses in Harlem which has actually flourished during this latest period of economic stress." Spiritualists, fortune tellers, and the like were "usually housed in dimly lit, smelly railroad flats in sections where they are not apt to be hounded by the police who periodically declare war on them." There were two issues that these modern "miracle workers" were called on to resolve: "Am I going to find work?" and "Am I going to hit the number soon?" It will come as no surprise to discover that the vast majority of customers, though by no means all, came from the ranks of the unemployed and the poorest of Harlem's residents.[25]

It matters little whether these people were genuine spiritualists and fortune tellers or out-and-out con men and women. The underlying principle behind any business of selling "winning" numbers was the same, and it was very simple. Success was a function of getting out as many numbers as possible every day. For example, if an individual built up a client base of 100 people, he or she would give them each a separate number to play. Each client would be told to "box" the number and then, provided that each number had three different digits and as long as there was no overlap with a combination of someone else's number (for example, you had to avoid giving 123 to one person and 321 to another), then there would be 600 numbers in play, giving a much better than one-in-two chance that a client would hit.

In addition to paying a fee for each number, clients knew very well that if they won, they were expected to give their benefactor a cut—anything from one-quarter and one-half of their winnings. In his remarkable fieldwork in Detroit in the mid-1930s, Gustav Carlson spent a considerable amount of time observing this part of the numbers racket. In Detroit, a clientele of 100 was about average. Of the approximately fifty clients who won and whom Carlson managed to observe, only two failed to share their winnings. Indeed, he knew of cases where "the confidence man demanded as much as three-fourths of the winning and seemed to have no trouble in collecting." Clients had no desire to offend the golden goose, expecting to get more good numbers in the future. Unfortunately, there is no ethnographic study of numbers in Harlem, let alone anything that comes close to matching the brilliance of Carlson's insights into the way the business worked, but it seems unlikely that on this point things differed greatly between Detroit and Harlem.[26]

A milieu such as this, where large numbers of black men and women believed that there was an insider's way to success, offered an opening a mile wide for all manner of charlatans and con men and women, ranging from small-time hustlers selling numbers for quarters to rather bigger predators. Black confidence tricksters were particularly adept at sensing the fault lines in the society and in an individual's makeup. The stories they told relied on, and played with, the culture of their fellow blacks, and the cruel elegance of their schemes laid bare the fears and foibles of their victims. In their own way, the confidence men and women, and their schemes, were often as creative as the much-studied poetry, short stories, and novels of the Harlem Renaissance itself—and sometimes they were even more revealing of the culture of the vast mass of Harlem citizenry. Confidence men and women were attracted to the numbers game as were iron filings to a magnet.

Over the course of several months in the first half of 1930, Arthur Millwood, a.k.a. Jake Williams, born in the British West Indies, and his accomplice, Victor Davis, originally from Cuba, fleeced several Harlem residents of somewhere in excess of $10,000. It was, a writer in the *Amsterdam News* commented, "an amazing story of superstition and simple credulity," but the newspaper was exaggerating just how unusual the case was, and underestimating how convincing the glib-tongued Millwood had been as he sold his scam. Millwood and Davis were caught and charged with mulcting Olive Dean, a laundress living on West 119th Street, of $2,311. The two policemen concerned told the *Age* that this was "one of the most important arrests of their career." The affair had begun when Victor Davis entered into conversation with Olive Dean, telling her that he had just won $13,000, thanks to the assistance of a Hindu priest. The following day the Hindu priest (in reality Millwood), who supposedly needed Davis as an interpreter because he could not speak English, came and visited Dean. Millwood took out a sheet of paper and "went into alleged religious rites, holding the paper over a lighted burner on the gas range. Before long, some writing appeared: "My Dear Daughter: You can trust these men. They will make you wealthy. Do as they say. (signed) Your Dear Dead Mother." Dean was then instructed to withdraw all of her money from the bank in order that the serial numbers on the bills could be written down; if given this information, the Hindu priest would be able to work out the next day's winning policy number. The con men then placed the $2,311 in an envelope, performed another religious ceremony, tied the envelope to the woman's back, and left, warning her not to move herself or the envelope for two hours. Just to be safe, Olive Dean waited three hours before stirring. Needless to say, when she eventually opened the envelope, it contained only cut-up newspaper.

The arrest of Millwood and Davis brought to light a series of other cases. Herbert Reid, an expressman living on West 127th Street, had been approached by Millwood, who claimed to know "a certain African who was making white men rich." As if to demonstrate their versatility, it was Davis, on this occasion, who posed as the African, claiming to be in contact with Reid's dead father. Reid dutifully went off to the Union Dime Savings Bank, where he withdrew $1,450. On his return, Millwood wrote down the serial numbers on the notes, in order, so he said, to work out the winning policy number. Reid was told to wait two and a half hours with the envelope on his back, but in fact he delayed until the following morning, at which point his fed-up wife tore open the envelope and emptied out nothing but strips of newspaper. According to the *Age* and the *Amsterdam News,* other victims of the pair of con men included David Brown, who lost $853, Elmer Jordan, who lost $2,537, and Abraham Harris, who was swindled out of $4,000.[27] It is worth remembering that, as the *New York Age* and others were fond of pointing out, "You cant trim a 'sucker' unless he's got larceny in his heart."[28] Olive Dean, Herbert Reid, and scores of other African New Yorkers who were conned knew perfectly well that they were engaged in an illicit enterprise and that someone somewhere was going to lose a large sum of money; but they thought that, for once, they were on the inside and did not suspect that they were the ones being duped. Millwood and Reid played their victims pitch-perfectly and took them for every cent they had managed to scrape together in this world.

In 1928, Wallace Thurman, the *enfant terrible* of the Harlem Renaissance who, tragically, drank himself to death in his early thirties, collaborated with William Jourdan Rapp, a white writer, to pen *Harlem: A Melodrama of Negro Life in Harlem,* a play that was performed ninety-three times to sold-out houses on Broadway and had runs in Chicago, Detroit, Toronto, and Los Angeles. Unlike so much of the writing of the Harlem Renaissance, *Harlem* was concerned less with black uplift and more with the gritty texture of everyday life in the Black Metropolis, and consequently numbers was an important feature of the play. Early in Act I, a character named Basil Venerable ventured his opinion on numbers: "Some people are lucky but there's really no way to beat that game. These guys that sell tips on the number are a bunch of fakers. Why it's calculated from the daily Clearing House Report and there's absolutely no way of telling ahead of time what that's going to be."[29] And that, of course, was perfectly true. But as Thurman was very well aware, by that time the numbers was all but impervious to such rational pinpricks. For the vast majority of residents, the numbers was a vital part of the new urban black culture that they were creating in Harlem in the 1920s and 1930s. As they did with most facets of their culture, blacks took the "play" in "playing the numbers" seriously, and made the game itself into a performance. Everything, from the way in which groups of black women "doped" out their numbers, through to the insouciant swagger of the numbers bankers and runners as they patrolled the avenues and streets, and even the spiels of the spiritualists and black con men as they ensnared their marks, was infused with a sense of black style. Partly that style was derived from the African American past, in both the South and in New York itself, but much of it also was a response to the new circumstances in which African Americans found themselves in the Black Metropolis. Yet we should be careful not to mistake any of the elements of this style for a lack of seriousness about numbers. African New Yorkers did not gamble on the numbers for a thrill; they were only in it to win. And all it took was a dollar and a dream.

4

TURF WARS

Kidnapped **419.**
      —Uriah Konje, *The H.P. Dream Book* (1927)

Given the amounts of money involved in the Clearing House numbers, there was, right from the beginning, an inevitable jostling over territory. In the early 1920s, divisions often tended to run along ethnic lines. According to the *New York Age* in 1924, West Indian bankers were said to "operate mostly among their own West Indian folk," an observation that the newspaper thought was "in keeping with a characteristic trait of the migrants from the Caribbean." Much the same was true of other groups, be they Spanish-speakers or black migrants from the American South (the relationship between the runners and the gamblers was critical here), but by the mid-1920s some of these parochial divisions were beginning to dissolve. As the *Age* noted, so far as West Indian bankers were concerned, "the money of American players is not despised or rejected." Indeed, in July 1924, the talk on Harlem streets was of the "Numbers Kings' rivalry" between the established Cuban Marcelino and the newcomer Joe Tanner. Born in Brooksville, Florida, Tanner learned cigar making in Key West before coming to New York in 1901. In a letter printed in the press, Tanner's lawyer explained that his client had been successful in the real estate business, owned ten properties in the city, was as honest as the day is long, and had nothing to do with the numbers racket. The *Age* claimed, however, that Tanner was using various poolrooms that he owned as collecting points for his betting slips, and was rapidly closing in on Marcelino as the most important banker in Harlem. Tanner was also behaving like a Numbers King, "disport[ing] himself in a handsome and costly car, said to be a 'special' Lincoln, costing way up in four figures."[1] Such struggles over turf between established Numbers Kings and Queens were an almost expected part of conducting an illegal business. Much more important in the long run, however, were two concerted attempts by outsiders in the 1920s and later in the 1930s—in both cases white underworld figures attracted by the very large sums involved—to take over the whole numbers industry.

The first of these attempts occurred in the mid-1920s. In late 1924, only months after the game took off in New York, the black press began printing stories about a disreputable group, led by Moe Immerman, "one of the most notorious of the Jewish bootleggers operating in Harlem," that was making a determined effort to run black bankers out of business and so monopolize the "enormous profits" generated by numbers. Others involved included Al and Sam Redd, Greenfield and Goldberg, and, most importantly, Hyman Kassell, "one of Harlem's king bootleggers operating at one time as many as a dozen speakeasies."[2] Through their extensive activities in Harlem, controlling the sale of alcohol and running most of the clubs there, these men were very well aware that, far from being something that could be dismissed with the epithet "nigger pool," numbers was in fact an extremely lucrative pursuit. All the bootlegger bosses were also well aware that Prohibition, which had made them rich and powerful, would not last forever, and they were keen to position themselves strategically for its repeal. To a group who had few scruples about breaking the law and who were well-connected with the police and politicians, the numbers business—being run, as it seemed, merely by a few blacks and Cubans—looked like easy pickings.

It was hardly surprising that the white newcomers played to their strengths, attempting to shift the locus of numbers from the apartment block and the street to small stores. Notoriously, such stores in Harlem were not run by African Americans. Small-time shopkeepers were enticed into writing numbers slips with the promise of money—in late 1926, some were taking as much as $400 a week in commissions on numbers—and those who resisted the gangsters' blandishments were pressured with standover tactics (threats of violence). In the spring of 1926, Hyman Kassell opened a chain of stationery stores in Harlem. These were staffed by Kassell's relatives and, as everyone knew, were fronts for taking bets on the numbers. Reputedly, Kassell had collectors working for him in every cigar and stationery store, butcher shop, and ice cream parlor on Lenox and Seventh avenues.[3] It was also a matter of some local humor that the purchase of a cigar or an ice cream in one of these shops during the morning before the Clearing House numbers came out could take a while.

White newcomers also targeted the runners and collectors for established black bankers, making "seductive offers" for them to bring across their clients and their daily collections. When, one day in July 1925, a mistake occurred with the publicizing of the daily number, and two winning numbers were in circulation, most of the black bankers refused to honor their slips. White bankers, however, paid off on both numbers, attempting thereby to win the favor of black gamblers. According to the *New York Age,* this was just part of the strategy designed "to push the colored bankers out of business," and it was one that was beginning to succeed, as many players "switched and are now putting their money with the Jews."[4] Moreover, using their connections with the police, the newcomers had their black rivals harassed and constantly raided.

The struggle for control of the numbers took some time to sort out. For a while it looked as though the days of the Black Kings and Queens were over: the *Age* repeatedly ran headlines such as "Combination of Jews Seeks Monopoly of Game, Trying to Hog Profits" and "'Hymie,' Former Bootlegger King, Now Wants Title of 'Numbers' King."[5] Interestingly, the black press was reporting this struggle as one in which the white interlopers were interested less in attaining a share of the market than in total domination of numbers in the Black Metropolis, forcing their African American competitors right out of the business. In ways that mirrored the larger structural problems of Harlem, it seemed that the blacks who controlled the streets and the residential collections were being slowly excluded by gangsters operating out of mostly white shopfronts. Anyone conducting business on the street was either moved along or arrested, but, allegedly, the white stores had cards with printed insignia placed inconspicuously in their windows—Kassell used a yellow bird printed on a white background, and another banker used an owl—that warned police to leave them alone. Furthermore, bankers who had come to an arrangement with the police furnished their runners and collectors with a card, bearing "a cabalistic emblem of some sort," that was flashed at any policemen taking too keen an interest in what the numbers operatives were doing. Those that the *Age* labeled "the big Jewish bankers" put aside their differences (there had been little love lost between some of them) and presented "a solid front in the fight to crowd out the Negro and Spanish operators." In late July or early August 1926, the white numbers bankers held a secret conference, a gathering that prefigured the much better-known meetings between gangsters that constituted some of the modern mafia's founding moments, in order to control and regulate the numbers business.[6] Yet for all the advantages Kassell and his cohorts had, the obituaries being written for the days of the Black Kings and Queens would turn out to be premature.

The main reason the white attempt to take over the numbers failed was the strength of black resistance. Fred Moore and the *New York Age* made such a fuss about what was going on in Harlem, even to identifying names and addresses where numbers slips were being written, that eventually police arrests became a serious inconvenience for the white bankers. Just as importantly, many black residents of Harlem did not like dealing with white collectors and were certainly chary about the fact that their money was going to white bankers. In Harlem, in August 1926, there were at least thirty white men and women working as collectors, making daily house-to-house rounds; and reputedly, in order to win custom, some of these collectors were not deducting the usual 10 percent commission from winnings. But for all that, there was resistance and resentment among many black residents when black runners were replaced by whites. As the black writer Claude McKay noted, "Colored folk are not comfortable with whites penetrating into their homes." Indeed, not a few blacks were quite unhappy with the way in which Harlem itself was yet again being penetrated by whites, bent on making money out of people they regarded as their inferiors. One black Harlem resident and, as he claimed, soon-to-be ex–numbers player, questioned by an *Age* reporter in a "tonsorial establishment" on 135th Street, stated: "As for me, I've quit; made my last play; no more will I be the sucker contributing to the bank accounts of these Jews, Cubans, and others who are riding around in their big, powerful cars, living in fine houses, and using hundred dollars bills as cigar lighters."[7]

Not all the cars filled with well-dressed whites that increasingly traveled Harlem's streets conveyed numbers bankers. From the mid-1920s, "Harlem at night," James Weldon Johnson noted, saw "lines of taxicabs and limousines standing under the sparkling lights of the entrances of the famous night-clubs." They disgorged so many white thrill-seekers that the black physician and writer Rudolph Fisher, returning in 1927 to black cabarets he had frequented five years earlier, found himself "lost in a sea of white faces." "Uncomfortable and out of place," Fisher reacted by becoming an infrequent customer. His was a broadly shared reaction among Harlem's black residents. Rather than be "stared at by white folks," "non-theatrical, non-intellectual Harlem" increasingly opted "to have a get-together of one's own," Langston Hughes observed.[8] Apartments provided the favored venue for such gatherings, which took the form either of periodic rent parties or of buffet flats. Rent parties are better-known nowadays, but buffet flats were more widespread and more central to black nightlife. They did not charge admission, as the hosts of rent parties did, nor did they advertise widely; they were ongoing concerns that offered privacy (as parties did not), in addition to alcohol, music, dancing, prostitutes, on occasion, gambling, and, less often, rooms to which couples could retire. When Raymond Claymes, a black schoolteacher working undercover for the Committee of Fourteen, a private anti-vice organization, sought out buffet flats in 1928, he found the proprietors and patrons of buffet flats were almost exclusively blacks.[9] So too were their counterparts in more respectable forms of leisure such as basketball games, lodge meetings, and social and bridge clubs.

Black residents had fewer options for avoiding whites in other aspects of daily life, but demonstrated a similar resentment of their presence in Harlem. The white faces that can be glimpsed in images of the crowds that thronged Harlem's streets generally belonged to police officers. Black organizations campaigned for the hiring of black officers, but in 1926 the New York Police Department counted only forty-nine in its ranks. As a consequence, white officers did much of the policing of Harlem, a situation to which residents regularly took exception. In April 1920, for example, the sight of Officer Peter King using his billy club to subdue Al Gilbert as he arrested him for pawning stolen goods at a shop on Lenox Avenue attracted a crowd. "Threatening remarks" directed at King, and an off-duty officer, Herman Guran, who had come to his aid, escalated as they took Gilbert down 135th Street to the police station, until King reported hearing someone in the crowd yell, "Come on boys, get out your knives and don't let those white livered mother fuckers take our friend in!" A man behind King slashed him with a razor. Guran grabbed the assailant, William Smith, only to have four men in the crowd push the officer away, forcing Guran to pursue Smith and shoot him as he fled into a building on 136th Street. While this was occurring, two other men grappled with King trying to free Gilbert and, indeed, continued their struggles with the police officer right up to the station door.[10] Blacks directed similar outbursts at whites who owned and staffed the neighborhood's businesses. In July 1930, the screams of a black customer drew an angry crowd of several hundred to a hat-cleaning and shoe-shining store on Lenox Avenue. She had been arguing with the white proprietor, Philip Nasselbaum, over some ribbon missing from a hat she had cleaned, when he allegedly struck her. As the crowd besieged the shop, a police officer on the scene was forced to summon a squad in order to arrest Nasselbaum and protect his store.[11] Given the limited numbers of black businesses, and of black police officers, Harlemites had no option but to continue dealing with white store-owners and police. But when they played numbers, as when they sought entertainment, many could, and did, go out of their way to shun whites.

Toward the very end of 1926, the tide began to turn against the white bankers. Inspector Lewis Valentine—"head of Police Commissioner George McLaughlin's confidential division," according to the *Age,* and someone free of any links to the Harlem police—brought in "squads of headquarters men" and began trying to clean things up. Valentine and his men were "making daily intensive drives against the cigar and stationery shops, grocery stores and other 'numbers' collecting headquarters." Key to the success of the lightning raids made by these outside forces was keeping knowledge of them a secret from both the Harlem police and the numbers runners. A *New York Age* reporter writing about one such expedition pointedly began his account by noting that Valentine had proceeded "without informing even the captain in charge of the local precinct." In this case, in mid-November 1926, a squad of police "swooped through Eighth avenue on Wednesday night" and "before the astonished 'numbers' operatives could get themselves together, a half-score or more places had been ransacked, bushels of policy slips captured and proprietors and clerks taken into custody."[12]

These raids sent shock waves through Harlem and began to inconvenience severely the smooth operation of the numbers racket. One of the distributors of the *Age,* on his rounds delivering bundles of the newspaper, found that a number of shops were shut, "closed tight as wax with all of the folks gone." On the door of one of these establishments was a hastily scrawled sign: "Gone To a Wedding, Be Back Tomorrow." Even when he gained admission to some of the stores, the *Age* representative "ran into incidents that illustrated the unrest and anxiety rampant among the 'numbers people.'" Delivering his newspapers to one stationery store, he overheard a conversation between a customer and the proprietor's wife, to whom she was trying to hand her numbers slip. The shopkeeper "threw up her hands in horror, exclaiming 'No! No! we don't take no numbers—we don't take no numbers! Never took no numbers!'" "Astounded," the customer "gave every evidence of being handed the surprise of her life. 'No numbers. Are you crazy? Aint I been playing here every day. What's the matter with you?'" By now, the shopkeeper was almost shouting. "Believe me, we don't take no numbers!" and she continued to refuse to accept either the slip or the money.[13]

On top of the police crackdown, the problem that always bedeviled numbers bankers occurred: a hot number came in. Most of the time, running a numbers bank was a license to print money; but if and when a heavily backed number came in, bankers had to be able to lay their hands on a large amount of cash very quickly. In November 1926, **510** came out in the Clearing House numbers, and "it was soon discovered that the number had been played to the limit." There were rumors all over Harlem that Hymie Kassal "had been hit for from $35,000 to $40,000, and was 'broke' as a result of 'paying off.'" Moe Immerman "was hit for $15,000 to $20,000, and just 'cold turkeyed' his customers, telling them to 'try and get it.'"[14] If not quite prepared to announce victory, Fred Moore and the *New York Age* certainly were not shy in claiming a prominent role in the way events were panning out. "The long campaign waged by *The New York Age* against the pernicious and harmful 'numbers' gambling game," Moore believed, was now taking effect. There was "a good deal of 'numbers' playing still going on," but "many of the strongest and most important of the bankers have quit." Reportedly, storeowners were not even willing to lend customers a pencil, fearing that the police would subsequently believe they were accepting bets on the numbers.[15] The following week, the *Age* claimed triumphantly that "the stores have practically gotten out of the game."[16]

In December 1926, District Attorney Joab Banton announced that "the policy ring which operated for so many years in Harlem has been broken up." Police Commissioner McLaughlin pointed out that "for years legal technicalities prevented prosecution of the players and operators, but last spring the Legislature amended the law, and war against the policy kings was declared." In effect, the crime of gambling on policy was reclassified from a felony to a misdemeanor, so that the accused would be tried not by a jury of citizens, seldom interested in sending someone to prison for numbers, but only by a judge, who felt little compunction about incarcerating anyone who broke the law. Both the district attorney and the police commissioner agreed that "the new laws have frightened away many of the policy operators who formerly did a business of several hundred thousand dollars a year." Since July 1, 1926, when the legislation had come into effect, the police had arrested 964 bankers, collectors, and players. Of these cases, 534 went to trial, and in every single instance the prosecution had secured a conviction.[17] This was a remarkable turnaround from what had occurred in earlier years, testimony perhaps to what was possible if the city was able to rely on the opinion of a judge rather than a jury. Bailing out operatives, paying legal fees, and serving three-month sentences in the Welfare Island workhouse were all extremely expensive, and the onslaught on numbers began to take its toll. What was happening was that numbers was shifting away from the stores—and the emphasis in all the news stories was on the closing down of numbers in cigar, candy, and stationery shopfronts—back to a myriad of numbers runners making their rounds of Harlem's apartment buildings. A cynic would claim that it was all a question of who was paying the most money to the police at any particular time. We, unfortunately, have no specific evidence about that. But what is clear is that police action decisively tilted the balance in Harlem away from the white interlopers and toward the black bankers.

The dissipation of the first white attempt to take over and control the numbers was followed in the late 1920s and very early 1930s by several halcyon years, in which the business was largely left in black hands. According to Claude McKay, these were "unbelievably fabulous, gold-years." Writing of this period from the vantage point of the bail bond hearings in 1935, a reporter for the *Amsterdam News* claimed that it was during this time that "the royal raiment of Policy Kings was draped around the shoulders of Casper Holstein, Wilfred Brunder, Alexander Pompez, Henry Miro and others."[18] And this, too, was the time when Stephanie St. Clair, one of the most extraordinary figures ever to set foot in Harlem, established herself as a Numbers Queen.

Inevitably, success came at a price. It was impossible to make money on the scale that the Black Kings and Queens were doing in the Harlem of the late 1920s without attracting some sort of attention. The most dramatic sign that things were beginning to change—and it is difficult not to see it as a harbinger of what would descend on the Black Metropolis in the ensuing decade—was the kidnapping of Casper Holstein. On his way home from the Turf Club, which Holstein owned, on Thursday night, September 20, 1928, he stopped off to visit a married woman, Mrs. Gomez Whitfield, on West 146th Street. It was late, a few minutes before midnight, and seeing that "the boy who works for me" looked "pretty tired," Holstein told him, "Well I don't want to keep you." "You take the car to the garage and I will walk back." The Numbers King then strolled through the courtyard of 225 West 146th Street and stepped into the vestibule, where he was approached by a white man who claimed to be a policeman detailed to pick Holstein up and take him downtown to headquarters. Holstein replied, "All right; I will go anywhere; my sheets are clean." They went back to the street where the supposed police officer and three others bundled Holstein into "a small car about the size of a Ford sedan." Once in the car, they headed east and then uptown instead of downtown. Immediately, Holstein started to struggle, but he was hit on the head with a pistol, subdued, blindfolded, and driven to a hideaway. Once there, Holstein was tied up, dumped on the floor, and told, "We are going to hold you for ransom." Seventy-two hours later, at about 12:30 A.M. on Monday morning, Holstein was let out of a car at the corner of 140th Street and Amsterdam Avenue. He caught a cab back down to the Turf Club on 136th Street, where a crowd of well-wishers, alerted that his release was imminent, welcomed him home.[19]

Holstein's kidnapping was a big event. At least forty members of the police force had spent the weekend searching for him. The investigation was headed by Samuel J. Battle, who, in 1911, had become the first African American patrolman in New York City and, in 1926, some two years previously, had been appointed as the first

African American police sergeant. Holstein's disappearance made the front page of the *New York Times*. Stories about Harlem very seldom attained that sort of prominence, though it should be added that the details of the *Times* article, perhaps reflecting a lack of experience with the goings-on above 125th Street, differed from those in the black newspapers and from Holstein's own statement to an assistant district attorney, which we have relied on in our account.[20] As well as being newsworthy, it was also a puzzling case—the headline on the front page of the *Amsterdam News* blared, "Mystery Surrounds the Kidnapping & Return of Holstein." The confusion was not helped by the fact that Holstein initially tried to protect the married woman he was visiting by suggesting that the kidnapping had occurred a couple of blocks away. A terse Detective Sergeant Battle set the *News* straight on that score: "Regardless of what Holstein said he was not kidnapped near his home at 8 West 144th street, but was taken from the hallway of 225 West 146th street, where Mrs. Whitfield lives. We have two eye-witnesses who saw the kidnappers take him away."[21]

At first, there was some skepticism surrounding Holstein's account. The *Amsterdam News*—still reeling from the $100,000 libel charge that Holstein had brought against them for linking him to the numbers game, and that was slowly wending its way through the maw of the legal system—had to be extremely cautious, but still seemed to be hinting that something else was going on. The *News*'s man on the spot had to walk a knife's edge in his reporting. One sentence in one piece began by mentioning "the tense period of his absence," before going on to detail that "it was persistently reported by those supposed to be in 'the know' that 'everything is alright,' 'he is in good hands,' 'yes, he has been heard from and he is in good health.'" Another sentence noted that Holstein's appearance on his release was "quite unkempt," and then slyly slipped in "but he appeared to smile a little too brightly for a beaten man without food for three days." The following week, though, the *Amsterdam News* printed that "those closest to him who were skeptical of the genuineness of the kidnapping now believe that it was on the level."[22]

The focus of the skepticism soon shifted from the issue of whether or not it was a genuine kidnapping, to that of whether Casper Holstein had arranged for the kidnappers to be paid the ransom. Holstein was adamant that he had paid no money and that he was unable to recognize anyone in any of the police lineups. The police had charged Michael Bernstein with kidnapping and four others with being accomplices, but Holstein was unable, or unwilling, to help the prosecution. Within days, the cases against the conspirators were dismissed by the magistrate, as would have been the case against Bernstein if he had not skipped bail.[23] As part of the attempt by Assistant District Attorney Aurelio to put Bernstein behind bars, he interviewed Casper Holstein. The eight typed pages of interview provide some detail about the kidnapping, but when it came to identifying the perpetrators Holstein was unhelpful. It must have been a frustrating experience for the assistant district attorney. Asked to identify the nationality of his kidnappers, Holstein replied, "Well, some Jewish fellows look like Italians. Some are swarthy and some are fine featured. There were some swarthy men in the group, and a couple of them were rather refined; and this fellow, Bernstein, he is a Jew they say, but I would take him for a Greek or Italian, from my own judgment." Holstein had repeatedly assured the kidnappers that he did not have plenty of money and that their informer, "a colored fellow" named Brown, was wrong. In response to the question, put to him twice, of whether he had paid any money to the kidnappers, Holstein answered, "Not one penny, sir," and "Not one penny." Asked the crucial question of why the kidnappers had freed him, Holstein replied, "I cant tell." He then added, "I believe it was on account of the activity of the police; and one of the men, one of the ringleaders, said to me, he says, 'We got a wrong steer on you, Casper,' and he says 'That dirty, black rat gave us the wrong steer and we are going to let you go, because we believe you are telling the truth.'" When Bernstein was eventually caught, he pleaded guilty to Assault in the Second Degree and was sentenced to eighteen months to three years in state prison.[24]

Then, as now, the idea that the kidnappers had simply released Holstein seemed unlikely. The Bolito King's own actions suggested that he was playing some sort of game. An article in the *New York Times* described Holstein the day after his release as "suave, beaming and tailored to the last crease," with "nothing but kind words for the kidnappers who held him prisoner." According to the *Times*'s man, when another reporter asked if he recognized any of his captors, "a smile overspread Holstein's face. 'Well, you know how it is,' he said. 'I could'—a slow wink went with this—'but I can't.'" A week later, the *Amsterdam News* was rather more blunt. The paper explained that a $50,000 ransom had been demanded. "As it was, the kidnappers got at least $25,000 out of Holstein and dared him to open his mouth, it is reported." The writer then added, "Behind Holstein's smiling countenance there lurks a grim terror, his friends say." According to the paper, this explained Holstein's remark at the police lineup: "I could [identify them], but I can't." On page two of the story, the *News* reported that, on the Saturday night, Charles King, secretary of Holstein's Turf Club, "is said to have displayed that alleged ransom money to a girl friend, consisting of $30,000 in $1,000 bills and $8,000 in $500 bills." Admittedly, this was gossip from the streets of Harlem, leavened with a generous helping of the passive voice, but nevertheless it seems likely that Holstein had paid the ransom. Some two decades later, when Mayme Johnson heard what had happened, undoubtedly from her husband Bumpy Johnson, it was a simple fact: Holstein had handed over $50,000.[25]

What was important in all of this was not just that Casper Holstein's kidnapping made the *New York Times,* but that information about an apparently wealthy black made page one of the city's paper of record. If not a first for the *Times,* this was certainly an unusual occurrence. Holstein, the paper reported, "is considered among the wealthiest negroes in Harlem," owning an apartment and an expensive car and employing a chauffeur; at the time of the kidnapping, he was wearing a diamond ring and a watch and chain, collectively valued at somewhere between two and three thousand dollars, and was carrying a similar amount of cash. In addition, Holstein was "reported to have bet more than $30,000 on the races at Belmont Park one day during the past week."[26] This was behavior from a New York black that would have been shockingly new to almost every reader of the *Times.* What was potentially the most impressive fact of all was not reported in the press. If Holstein had indeed paid his ransom, then Holstein's employees had been able to raise $50,000 in cash over the weekend with little apparent trouble, even though all the banks were shut. The press may have studiously avoided mentioning that Holstein was a Numbers King, but the city's underworld knew how he made his money. And now it had been made perfectly clear to them as well just how much money he made. No longer was it possible for anyone to dismiss numbers as "nigger pool."

Stephanie St. Clair began to make her mark on Harlem a year after Holstein's kidnapping. St. Clair was born in about 1890 in Martinique, though she often claimed to be French, and migrated to New York in 1912. She set up as a numbers banker early on, in 1922, with capital of $10,000. Apparently, St. Clair never spoke about where the money had come from, but Mayme Johnson, Bumpy Johnson's widow and someone disinclined to miss the opportunity to make a negative comment about another woman, pointed out that "her detractors snidely reminded people that her title was, after all, Madame." Through most of the 1920s, St. Clair maintained a low profile and established a successful numbers bank, though it was by no means one of the larger or more prominent ones. Writing in December 1930, T. R. Poston, author of the "Harlem Shadows" column which ran in the *Pittsburgh Courier,* summed it all up by stating that "she didn't really catch the eye of Harlem until the fall of 1929." As Poston explained to his Pittsburgh audience, "readers of the *Amsterdam News* were puzzled to note that a new kind of ad was appearing" in the newspaper: "it consisted of a two-column cut," or picture, of St. Clair, under which was a paragraph or two of her views on some matter or other. "The first two or three of these messages set the old Black Belt agog."[27] Then suddenly the content of her "messages" changed and she began accusing the Harlem police of corruption and discrimination. As Poston noted in his column, "Harlem stopped wondering": "When you attack the Law, the average Harlemite knows better than to wonder about you—for he knows one thing definitely then. You are going to get yours." Toward the end of December 1929, St. Clair was arrested and charged with being in possession of numbers slips. The following week, in her paid advertisement on page two of the *Amsterdam News,* she began: "Well, folks, I have been arrested. Yes, arrested and framed by three of the bravest and the noblest cowards who wear civilian clothes." In March 1930, she was convicted and sentenced to an indefinite term in the penitentiary. She was released from the prison on Welfare Island on a

Wednesday in early December. The following Monday she went downtown voluntarily and testified that she was a numbers banker; indeed, "she modestly admitted that she was the Queen of the Policy Racket." Sensationally, as the *New York Times* reported, she detailed that "she had paid $7,100 to a police lieutenant and to plain-clothes men of the Sixth Division for 'protection,' and that the police had 'welshed' on their bargain."[28] Once again, numbers had made the front page of the *New York Times*—publicity that those who ran numbers, and those whom they paid off, hardly welcomed. Stephanie St. Clair would continue to demonstrate her flair for the dramatic and make headlines throughout the 1930s.

Yet for all the drama of Holstein's kidnapping and Stephanie St. Clair's strident claims of police corruption, the most important feature of numbers in the late 1920s and very early 1930s was that the money, huge sums of money, kept on rolling in. Indeed, these years were so profitable that the banks grew like Topsy and the various organizations reached the point where they had to be restructured. This being the case, the Numbers Kings created a new position, that of controller, as a buffer between themselves and their collectors or runners. In 1931, Henry Miro, a Numbers King and the largest banker in Harlem at the time, testified that he had six controllers, each looking after twenty or more collectors.[29] The controller was responsible to the banker for his collectors, and in return he received a small percentage, usually somewhere around 10 percent of the turnover which he handled. This new position would prove to be of some importance during the 1930s.

More obviously fundamental, though, was the change to the way the daily number was worked out. By the end of the 1920s, the New York Clearing House was well and truly fed up with its links to the denizens of San Juan Hill and Harlem. Not only were employees of the Clearing House continually being harassed by attempts at bribery, or annoying phone calls from people all across the United States who were attempting to discover the winning number a few minutes early, but it was also the case that, particularly with the onset of the Depression, the institution came under increasing pressure from insurance companies and credit businesses to stop publishing the statistical information on which the game depended. So successful was the game, and so all-consuming, that far too many residents of Harlem were gambling on the numbers, using whatever surplus money they had, and were frankly telling the agents who came knocking on their door "that they will pay up their installments or insurance when they make a 'hit.'" Furthermore, with the growth in importance of the Federal Reserve Bank, economists and financial analysts now found other indices to be of more use. Essentially, the institution realized, to its chagrin, that the New York Clearing House was publishing its daily figures for the sole benefit of numbers bankers and gamblers. It was hardly surprising, therefore, that as of December 31, 1930, the New York Clearing House ceased publication of the daily figures.[30]

Some initially surmised that the end of the Clearing House numbers would lead to the extinction of the game. The *Negro World* editorialized that it hoped "no substitute for these "numbers" would be found," suggesting that, instead, African Americans should "save their earnings judiciously," a move that would make them, "even economically, a great power to be reckoned with."[31] But this was little more than wishful thinking. To be sure, a week's notice that the basis of the Clearing House numbers was about to be abolished, and at Christmas at that, was hardly ideal. On December 24, 1930, the *Amsterdam News* speculated that the effect of the cessation of the publication of the figures was going to be "staggering to the men who have long mulcted Harlemites and thousands in other cities, of their earnings through the gambling scheme," and at least initially there must have been some considerable confusion. At the end of January 1931, the New York Stock Exchange announced that in future it would release the daily turnover figures of trades on the exchange only rounded to the nearest 100,000—this in what proved to be a vain attempt to discourage numbers bankers from latching on to them, in the same fashion as they had to the Clearing House. Over the ensuing decade, different banks would use a variety of sources, including figures taken from the New York Stock Exchange, the Curb Exchange, and even the Cincinnati Clearing House figures, to work out the daily number, but the most important proved to be derived from the mutuel payouts on race meetings from all across the country.[32]

The new method of working out the number, which at first glance looks quite complicated, is best seen by working through an example. In the first race, Royal Link won and the mutuel machine paid off, on the $2 ticket, at $7.20 for the win, $3.40 for second place, and $2.80 for third. A horse named Instead was second, paying $4 for the place and $2.40 for the show. Grandeem was third, and paid $3.40 for the show. The total odds for the race are the sum of all of these figures, here the number being $23.20. Similar calculations were then made for every race on the program. For example, at the end of the day's racing at Thistledown Park, an Ohio track, on August 3, 1938, the following results were compiled:

First race	36.40
Second race	33.40
Third race	24.80
Total three races	94.60
Total five races	233.80
Total seven races	299.80

The first number to the left of the decimal point in the totals for three, five, and seven races were then used sequentially to make up the winning number, in this case, **439**.[33] To an outsider, it all looked rather baffling, but numbers aficionados could work out the daily number in seconds. What made it all the more easy was that, even though the totals of money paid off on three, five, or seven races were of no conceivable use to anyone but a numbers gambler, newspapers published these figures on their sports pages. In the highly competitive market of New York City, newspapers would leave no stone unturned in their attempt to boost circulation figures.

Although this way of working out the daily number was hardly as elegant as the old Clearing House scheme, it at least fulfilled the function of generating a number that was both random and looked as though it could not be fixed. What is most intriguing is the question of how the details of the new regime were worked out, an issue on which the usual sources are silent. Saunders Redding, a black man of letters, wrote in 1934 that within days of the decision of the Clearing House, "the chief bankers from Richmond to Boston met in impressive conclave in New York." According to Redding, the meeting quickly "took on the nature of an N.A.A.C.P. conference," with one participant declaring that "white demagogues had squelched their means of livelihood because they were loth to see Negroes acquiring wealth," and others similarly bemoaning their fate, before "a mild-looking little man," the secretary of a New England banker, raised the idea of using the racetrack figures. The suggestion of links between numbers bankers in different cities and at least a certain level of organization, a development very occasionally hinted at in the newspapers, is certainly intriguing. Yet Redding's factual inaccuracies (he seems to suggest that the Clearing House stopped publishing figures in the summer of 1929 rather than December 31, 1930), combined with the arch tone of his writing (there are references to bankers having "pulled their kinky hair" and "worked themselves into a lathering rage"), militate against placing any reliance on his claims.[34]

Similarly, we have very little idea of what was occurring on the street. As it happened, Langston Hughes was in Cleveland for much of January and February 1931. In one of his informative letters back to Carl Van Vechten, he wrote that "the poor numbers writers are having a hard time here, the way they have to change from one basis to another." A "young gangster friend" of Hughes had told him "about a recent shooting two days before it came off," and also that "the Hearst papers have fallen off in sales by three car loads a day here, since the New York clearing house stopped giving out their totals." In Cleveland, they were "using the Detroit clearing house now, but nobody believes in it much." Indeed, things were so chaotic in Cleveland, that policy, or the game played in Chicago, was beginning to make inroads in the city.[35] Eventually, stability would return with the use of the mutuel payouts on the horse races as the basis for numbers, but Langston Hughes's letter gives some idea of the confusion that reigned on Cleveland streets at least initially. And, of course, gamblers hate unpredictability.

Much the same was probably the case for Harlem. Given that numbers was at least nominally illegal, how did bankers and runners educate somewhere in excess of 100,000 people about the new system in a matter of days? For nearly a decade, Harlem residents had played the Clearing House numbers; now they were being asked to place their faith in, and their nickels and dimes on, something novel. There must have been even more talk than usual from runners in January 1931. It also seems likely that there were detailed explanations of the new method of working out the number printed on leaflets or cards and handed out to the citizenry, a method that would be used to communicate with black men and women later in the decade. Everything about the Clearing House numbers had been simple and clear-cut, but under the new regime it was now necessary for the different banks to inform gamblers as to what particular method they were using to work out the number for that day and, if it was the races, which particular race meeting would furnish that number. Printed leaflets seemed the quickest and easiest way to do that.[36] No matter whether they read about it or heard about it, many nickel-and-dime gamblers, even if they managed to avoid being confused by the new system, probably regarded it all with some suspicion, and doubtless many exhibited their barely concealed expectation that someone was trying to con them. Unfortunately, the only turnover figures to which we have access are of the vaguest kind, but it seems very likely that receipts from numbers fell considerably in early 1931 as gamblers warily adjusted to their brave new world. But adjust they did: in the long run, the travails of January 1931 proved to be only a minor blip in the continued exponential expansion of the numbers game.

Relying on mutuel betting at the racetrack as the basis for the daily number led to one important new development. With the Clearing House, the three-digit number was clear as soon as the daily figures were released, but with the new system the three digits came out sequentially at roughly hourly intervals. This allowed banks with heavy bets on particular numbers to lay off some of that money and minimize their exposure to a huge loss. Thus, if a bank had taken a lot of money on, say, 768 and then 7 came up first, they could take a bolita on 68 and single plays on the 6 and 8 with another bank. This would lessen their profit if, say, the much less heavily backed 760 came up, but it also meant that if 768 did hit, at least some of their loss was covered and they were less likely to go bankrupt. The staggered release of the day's number also made the single play, which paid anything up to 8:1, a more interesting bet; and over the ensuing decade, a growing proportion of the money from Harlem that was wagered on numbers would be gambled in this way. Since much of the money wagered on single plays was bet at the last moment, and a runner could cover only about a block in the hour between the third and fifth races or the fifth and seventh races, this development contributed to the employment of more people in the numbers business.

5

Numbers' Lore

To see an arrest **125.**

    —Uriah Konje, *The H.P. Dream Book* (1927)

By 1925, not only was numbers a full-blown craze, obsessing both the waking and dreaming hours of large numbers of Harlem residents, but it was also the case that whites and blacks were pitted in a bitter, occasionally violent struggle over who should control the racket. It had been some time since numbers could be dismissed as something too petty to bother about. Both the police and the city's legal authorities were forced to take cognizance of the new form of gambling known as the Clearing House numbers. Initially, the very novelty of the Clearing House numbers caused the district attorney's office considerable problems. The legislation, specifically Statute 974, was designed to outlaw the old game of policy, or betting on the results of a lottery. In August 1923, Judge Otto A. Rosalsky dismissed wholesale all the numbers cases before him, "on the ground that betting on the Clearing House numbers was not covered by the laws of the State." The following year, in the wake of the *New York Age*'s campaign against numbers, Fred Moore, editor of this crusading newspaper, was invited to a conference with Judge Rosalsky. Following this meeting, "it was announced as the court's future policy that hereafter those convicted on the charge of playing 'numbers,' whether bankers, collectors or players," would be fined a minimum of $25 on their first offense. Moore and Rosalsky may well have made up their minds about the correct way to proceed, but it turned out that "several of the magistrates sitting as a committing court, are said to be utterly out of sympathy with the crusade" and, as the *Age* ruefully noted, "throw the cases out with considerable celerity."[1] As a writer in the *Age* noted, "One hears all sorts of stories in connection with the 'numbers' game, which is officially listed by the police and courts as 'policy playing' since the law takes cognizance only of the game long known as 'policy.'" He explained that "'Numbers' is too new a development to have attained actual legal status, so when arrests are made the charge is made to conform to the legal ban on policy."[2] These difficulties were further exacerbated by the fact that policy cases were felonies, which had to be brought before a jury in the Court of General Sessions, and that juries had little interest in convicting anyone for this offense. Because obtaining convictions was so difficult, the district attorney's policy was to secure an indictment and then recommend to the presiding judge in the Court of General Sessions that a fine be imposed if the defendant would plead guilty. This was a form of plea bargaining. As a result, almost 100 percent of those indicted pleaded guilty, and were fined a mere $25.

As of July 1, 1926, the law changed. The offense of gambling on policy was reclassified from a felony to a misdemeanor, an adjustment that transferred cases to the Court of Special Sessions and neatly sidestepped the problem of recalcitrant juries, as misdemeanors were tried by a judge sitting alone. In an after-dinner address to the Urban League in November 1927, Judge Kernochan, chief justice of the Court of Special Sessions, explained that, after the judges of his court had conferred on the issue, they had decided to divide defendants into three groups. The first was the bankers, "who reaped most of the profits" and were "really responsible for the game." If a banker "was convicted or pleaded guilty our general rule would be to commit him to the penitentiary." The second group was the collectors, the middle men and women, who collected slips for the banker on commission. Here "our rule is a sentence of 90 days, or on a plea of guilty 60 days." Last, there were the players—"the class," Kernochan claimed, that "we are endeavoring to protect." "We decided that on a plea of guilty a sentence of 30 days be imposed, but its operation suspended during the good behavior of the defendant."[3] In practice, classification into the different groups depended on how many numbers slips were found in the possession of the defendant when she or he was arrested. A handful of slips resulted in a suspended sentence, whereas thirty or forty earned the individual the label of "collector," as well as ninety days' hard labor at the Welfare Island workhouse.

The change in legislation may have put some semblance of order into the legal situation with respect to numbers, but that was hardly the end of the matter. Harlem, after all, was part of New York, a city that at least since the halcyon days of Boss Tweed in the 1860s and 1870s had been a byword for urban graft and corruption. There is no doubt that, throughout the 1920s and 1930s, police were being paid off to turn a blind eye to the operations of the Numbers Kings and Queens. Not only was numbers the archetypal "victimless crime," but numbers players typically were arrested after making bets of nickels and dimes—hardly a matter that, after all the paperwork was filled out, was going to make or break police careers. Just to add to the temptation for the police to ignore their duty to enforce the law, collectors and bankers were often caught with large amounts of cash on their persons. It was an open invitation for the police to make money on the side.

A couple of cases, unusual only because they came to light instead of being hushed up, give some indication of what must often have happened. On May 12, 1924, two policemen went to Apartment 30 on the fourth floor of 510 Amsterdam Avenue, looking for a liquor-still supposedly being operated on the premises. There was no still, but police found several slips lying around the apartment, and Bolivar Garcia, a thirty-six-year-old Puerto Rican who had come to New York eighteen months previously, admitted that he was running a policy game. Garcia then said to the two patrolmen, "Here is $200—do not arrest me." In this case the police charged Garcia with bribery, but undoubtedly there were many more instances where the cash was simply pocketed. In another case, at 9:30 A.M. on July 3, 1925, Albert Wolcott was stopped in the hallway of his apartment building at 131 West 133rd Street by two men. One of them, Peter McKay, actually a thirty-one-year-old Cuban, said, "We are policemen and we are going to arrest you for policy." The imposters then searched Wolcott and took $100 in cash from him. Again, on March 19 1928, at a little after eight in the morning, Benjamin Garrick, a dishwasher, was walking up the stairs to his apartment on West 143rd Street when he was accosted by a man who exclaimed, "I am a detective. I heard that you have some numbers on you." Garrick was then informed by the man and his accomplice, who also claimed to be a detective, that unless he "gave them some money they would take him to the stationhouse."[4] The vast majority of cases where numbers runners were robbed did not make it into the legal record. Because they themselves were breaking the law, workers in the numbers business were vulnerable to both police officers and those impersonating officers, and, if they were robbed, they had little or no recourse to the usual authorities.

For the most part, the working assumption of reporters for the black press was that the police were on the take. One writer for the *Age* may have rhetorically asked, "Are the police being paid by the 'numbers' bankers to keep hands off?" but the text of the article made his answer clear. Not only was it all so obvious, as collectors walked "boldly and openly" along the avenues and streets "picking up the slips with the money from the players," but also it was well known that all a collector had to do was flash "a card bearing a certain symbol" to "an interfering cop" and he or she would be allowed to go back to the business of collecting numbers slips. In one instance described in the *Age,* when a numbers runner was stopped by a policeman and a stool pigeon and robbed of $10 in cash, the runner's banker was "quoted as saying" that "while he was perfectly willing to make stated payments for protection at regular intervals he was tired of his men being held up on the streets by officers and stool pigeons and relieved of whatever cash they might be carrying."[5] And as we have seen, Stephanie St. Clair, Harlem's most famous Numbers Queen, publicly and loudly claimed that she paid thousands of dollars in protection money to the police.

Once arrested, numbers players and operatives entered the maw of the New York legal system, an institution whose reputation for corruption and graft almost rivaled that of the Police Department. The usual deal was that bankers paid the legal fees and fines of any of their operatives who were arrested. Any player unfortunate enough to run foul of the law was, of course, left to his or her own devices. Bankers had arrangements with certain bail bond companies and lawyers, and, for set fees, their workers were processed quickly and put back out on the streets to resume accepting bets.

Given that this was New York, and that a huge volume of cases of all sorts went through the legal system, it probably comes as no surprise to learn that all manner of things went on in the city's lower courts.

On January 8, 1926, a certain Edward Turner was caught with numbers slips and arrested on a charge of being a common gambler. Four months later, in early May, Turner was indicted by a grand jury and summoned to attend court on May 14. When he did not appear as requested, his bail was forfeited and a bench warrant was issued for his arrest. At this point, someone—it is not clear who, although probably that person was linked to the Capital City Surety Company, which had written Turner's bond—decided to obtain a substitute who would pretend to be Turner, appear in court, plead guilty, and pay the expected $25 fine. Samuel Johnson, a single man who had moved to Harlem from Adams Run, South Carolina, four years previously, and who worked as a laborer on Pier 28 for fifty cents an hour, was asked if he would like to earn $25 for a couple of hours' work. In order to take home the equivalent of a week's wages, all he had to do was state to the judge that he was Edward Turner, say he was guilty, and pay the fine. Perhaps the organizers of this scam were just carelessly overconfident, but Samuel Johnson was almost comically ill-suited to his role. Somehow they had managed to pick the only person walking the streets of Harlem who had never played numbers. Indeed, as later questioning would show, he had no idea how the game worked. Furthermore, Johnson was not literate. After he'd declared that he was Turner, the judge asked him in "what Court did I have my name signed." As Johnson later explained to the deputy assistant district attorney, "I told him I didn't have my name signed because I can't write. I can write my name but I can't write Edward Turner. The Judge said, 'You are not

Edward Turner' and he sent me to the jail."[6] Perhaps this case merely showed an unusual level of ineptitude on the part of the conspirators, but later the Seabury Investigation of 1930–1931 and the bail bond inquiry of 1935 demonstrated a high level of corruption and incompetence in the way in which the New York court system operated.[7]

Dutch Schultz's lawyer through the 1930s was Richard "Dixie" Davis, who later testified against the gangs and sold his story to *Collier's,* which published his six-part account entitled "Things I Couldn't Tell Till Now" in 1939. Davis had got his start in 1930 as a twenty-five-year-old, with a freshly minted law degree, at the new magistrate's court—"the white limestone trim was spotless, the brass spittoons gleamed"—on West 151st Street. The court may have been "immaculate" but "all the old scurvy gang moved in from the old court, bringing the old, old system with them." As Davis soon discovered, "nearly all the people brought into court were Negroes arrested in connection with the daily lottery called policy, or the numbers game, which had seized Harlem like a form of madness." It was Davis's job "to get a defendant discharged, instead of being held for trial in the bigger court downtown." In this task, Davis excelled, partly because of his courtroom manner. An arrest for policy was hardly a major crime, but the defendants liked "to have it handled with proper style and flourish"; indeed, "when I cross-examined a cop, or flung big words around extolling the virtues of my defendant it was something to make his friends and relatives on the back benches sit up and enjoy themselves." But as was soon revealed to him by "Ike," the bail bondsman with whom he worked, in many cases more was involved than his court performance: the fix was on. This "was made possible by the loose way in which the complaints were drawn, so wide-open that a cop could give any kind of testimony he pleased." For example, if a policeman arrested a man with eighty policy slips in his pocket, the setup for "a perfect case," the clerk would record "eighty slips found in defendant's possession." There was now no reason the policeman could not testify that the slips were found on a counter and the defendant was standing there with several other men. "Then the possession would not be exclusive and the case would go out the window." For collectors, who were liable to a sentence of sixty or ninety days, "we always went after a fix." Davis charged Alexander Pompez, a Numbers King originally from Cuba, $15 or $25 for each case, and somewhere between $200 and $500 for the fix. It was not long, then, before Davis was making thousands of dollars a week and, as he claimed, had "more cash saved up than I ever had at one time before or since."[8]

As with informers the world over, particularly those who publish colorful accounts of their sinful pasts, Davis probably inflated his own importance, as well as exaggerated the efficiency and extent of the corruption in the way numbers offenders were prosecuted. Probably, it was all a bit more hit-and-miss. Nevertheless, payoffs and graft were undoubtedly a part of everyday life in the numbers game, and it is necessary to bear this in mind when the legal record is examined. We went through all the surviving district attorney's case files for Manhattan for 1925 and collected all the records for numbers arrests. If read carefully, these records can help provide a snapshot of the way in which numbers operated in New York in 1925, the last calendar year numbers offenses were dealt with by the Court of General Sessions.[9]

Only a handful of the 553 arrests occurred outside Harlem and San Juan Hill. The distribution of these arrests is a stark reminder that even after Harlem opened up for African Americans, large numbers of them still lived in San Juan Hill and would continue to do so until most were displaced by the postwar building of Lincoln Center, a fact that is seldom considered in accounts of twentieth-century black life in New York. Even when a numbers runner was arrested elsewhere in Manhattan, his employer was often based uptown. When Charles Dyce was arrested on Eleventh Avenue between 14th and 15th streets, at 7:40 A.M. on February 24, 1926, for being in possession of seventeen slips, he promptly told the police, "I'm picking them up for a fellow in Harlem and I get twenty per cent." Similarly, when George Lewis was arrested at 8:45 A.M. on June 1, 1926, in front of 187 Tenth Avenue, he told the policeman "that he got 20% of all plays he collected from a fellow uptown."[10]

The people arrested for numbers in Harlem and San Juan Hill were an ethnic mélange, a collection of mostly recent migrants from Europe, the Caribbean, or the U.S. South trying to get ahead in the big city. They included Cubans, Puerto Ricans, blacks from just about every island in the British West Indies and most states in the South, as well as Italians, Greeks, and Russians, the latter probably mostly Jews. Throughout the year 1925, the struggle between blacks and Hymie Kassell and his associates for control of numbers was at its height, a fact that contributed toward the diversity of those arrested. It is clear from the details of who was being arrested that the black areas of New York City were being exploited by outsiders. If the locations of most arrests for numbers were concentrated in Harlem and San Juan Hill, the home addresses of those arrested were rather more dispersed.

The distribution of the 1925 numbers arrests in Harlem made it very clear that numbers was ubiquitous in the Black Metropolis. Far from being concentrated in any particular area, evidence of numbers was present and obvious on every street and avenue in Harlem. Many arrests occurred in stores. Jacob Goldman, born in

Russia, and Doris Altman, American born, ran a cigar and stationery store at 529 Lenox Avenue. When they were caught with eleven slips, they told the police that they were collectors "for a banker known as 'Sam,'" probably Sam Redd, one of Hymie Kassell's associates. Other arrests, more typically of blacks, took place on the streets. Adolph Isles, originally from the British West Indies, was arrested on Fifth Avenue. A policeman had watched him "accept a slip of paper and some money in coins from an unknown man" on the corner of Fifth and 130th Street and then followed him down to Fifth and 129th Street, where a similar transaction had taken place. He then arrested Isles and found more slips in his possession. For the most part, the police raids netted merely runners and collectors and even a few unlucky gamblers, but very occasionally they managed to catch someone more important. In May 1925, two policemen observed John Diamond "in conversation with a group of unknown men" in front of 231 West 143rd Street from 9:45 A.M. until 10:15 A.M. Diamond was a Numbers King, one of the more prominent black bankers in Harlem. The police followed Diamond into the premises and down into the cellar where they found two men and a woman sitting at a table "separating money from slips of paper containing numbers." Diamond admitted that the slips and money belonged to him and that the others in the cellar were his employees.[11]

One of the most revealing features in the case of the arrest of John Diamond was the observation by the police that Diamond engaged in a half-hour conversation out on the street. Almost inadvertently, the district attorney's records highlighted one of the most important characteristics of numbers: the way in which the business depended on people talking to one another. If this was true of bankers, it was even more the case with numbers runners or collectors, who came in contact with scores of people during the course of a day's work. Talking to them easily and well, establishing some sort of relationship with the clientele, was a crucial part of success in this business. Police reports of arrested numbers collectors often suggest that the suspect's conversing with different people had been what gave the game away in the first place. When the above-mentioned Charles Dyce was arrested, George Treubert detailed in his statement that he had observed "three unknown men approach the defendant at different intervals," and, "entering into conversation" with each of them, Dyce accepted money and slips from them. Shortly after, two more "unknown men" came up, "and apparently entering into conversation with the defendant, the defendant made certain memoranda on a certain pink pad at the same time handing each of the last two unknown men a carbon copy of the said memoranda and respectively accepting sums of money from each of the last two unknown men."[12] Treubert's clumsy and stilted words, his reliance on a policeman's perception of what legal language should sound like, may establish the point about the importance of talk to successful numbers running, but it hardly does justice to the artistry involved in the occupation. For that we need to look elsewhere.

Doubtless there were surly and peremptory collectors, but the ones that stood out and did the best possessed a facile way with the language. In the late 1940s, Ellsworth Johnson, universally known as Bumpy and the most important black banker in New York, gave a nineteen-year-old called Flash a tryout on a numbers route. Decades later, Mayme Johnson, Bumpy's widow, recalled that "Flash was a talker. Ooh, he could talk." The black kid "just had a comment and a compliment about everything; and didn't seem like a phony word was coming out of his mouth." After weeks of importuning Bumpy Johnson, Flash was given his chance. That night, Bumpy Johnson came home and told his wife that Flash was "one of the best numbers runners he'd ever seen." Usually, the route Flash had taken turned over somewhere between $100 and $200, but the young man had brought in $500. A puzzled Johnson muttered to his wife, "I'm going with him tomorrow and see what the hell it is he's doing." The next day, Johnson discovered that "Flash just charmed people into putting more money on a number than they intended." If a woman told him she wanted a dime on 125, he'd say, "125, huh? Oh yeah, that's a good one. Heck, I think I might put a dollar on it myself, I could use the six hundred dollars. Let's see, you say you want a dime on it? That'll get you sixty dollars. Come on, now, Miss Lady. You going to tell me that you can't use more than sixty dollars? Put another nickel on it so you can buy yourself one of them pretty dresses from up on the Avenue and show off that gorgeous shape of yours." Flash always carried several different dream books on him. If someone mentioned having dreamed of a cemetery and, after looking it up in a dream book, was going to play 953, Flash would consult another dream book and say, "Well, you might wanna put a little something on 864 and 851, cause depending on what you was doing in the cemetery it might be one of those numbers. Ain't no harm in hedging your bets."[13]

Even Mayme Johnson's decades-old recollection flattens out Flash's performance. And it *was* a performance. Flash's beguiling words and manner ensnared his clients in their own dreams of easy money, of being able to quit their mundane jobs and live the good life. Drawing on the tradition of the "man of words" that went back to slavery and beyond that to Africa, Flash and a myriad of men and women like him made numbers running an important part of urban black culture. This was part of the reason whites attempting to take over the numbers racket had such a difficult time of it. To be sure, there were whites who were glib-tongued, who were excellent salesmen—but hitting the right cultural notes in tone and manner was, if not impossible, very hard. Black residents in Harlem and San Juan Hill had to put up with all manner of white interlopers such as landlords, policemen, parole officers, and welfare workers regularly intruding into their homes. But when numbers collectors came knocking on the door, they had a choice as to whether to admit them or not. And it should come as little surprise to discover that, for the most part, African New Yorkers preferred to banter and tell lies with black men and women who knew how to talk the talk.

In some of the policy arrest cases, there is more than a hint that Dixie Davis was right and that the fix was on. In early February 1926, acting on "information," the police raided an apartment on West 136th Street. Inside were seven men sitting around a table drinking from a bottle. Two of the men were counting money—some $167, as the police ended up confirming for them—and one John Jackson was "operating an adding machine with 300 to 400 slips of paper in his possession." Several of the black men pleaded guilty and paid fines of $25 or $50. Yet in spite of the fact that it was John Jackson's apartment and that he had been caught at the adding machine, the deputy assistant district attorney claimed that "there is no evidence which would connect, or tend to connect, the defendant Jackson with the possession of these policy slips"—a conclusion with which the district attorney agreed, and the case was dismissed. On the other hand, every now and again the cases contained cheering news for the police as they carried out the thankless task of harassing the operation of numbers. In March 1926,

Charles Dyce was caught again by the police, this time near the front entrance to Pier 57, with twenty-five numbers slips in his right-hand coat pocket. All he had to say was: "I think I'll give up this business. I was arrested last week. I don't like to be arrested too often. I think I'll go to work."[14]

The broader context of the brushes between numbers and the law or the legal authorities, of what was prosecuted and what was not but merely ended up being reported in the black press, reveals much about the way the racket operated. For example, the rapid turnover of personnel in numbers, the meteoric rise and, most especially, fall of the various Kings and Queens, contributed to one of the principal problems that faced African Americans lucky enough to make a hit. Black bankers and agents were notorious for being unable or unwilling to pay what they owed their customers. This problem had bedeviled policy players since the colonial period. It was hard enough to pick the correct "gig," but at times it must have seemed that the odds against a player's being able to collect any significant winnings were correspondingly high. Right from the time the Clearing House numbers established itself in Harlem, bankers began welching on their obligations. As noted in the *Age,* keen to run stories about bankers who reneged, one of the big pitfalls for those who engaged in this form of gambling was "the unreliability of the men with whom they play their money." In May 1924, some of the redcaps at a railway terminal pooled their money and bet $20 on what turned out to be a winning number. Their banker refused to pay, and, as the reporter noted, "not only have they not gotten the $12000, they have lost the original $20, which was their stake, as well." A month or two later, the *Age* published a story about a banker named Bentancourt, who had absconded to Cuba with over $100,000. The reporter had "deduced from the wailings and complaints of his victims" that over a period of time Bentancourt took all the bets he could but paid off as few winners as possible. Then, on a day when a number popular with gamblers appeared in the Clearing House figures, "Bentancourt simply packed his trunk and took ship for Cuba, where he is reported now to be living in luxurious ease."[15]

One "well-informed observer" told the *Age* that it was unnecessary for bankers to skip town when "a player 'hits' a winning combination for a goodly sum." All they had to do was simply not to pay up—"'And what can you do about it, anyhow?' is the attitude the player must confront." In January 1927, a black woman dreamed of three "o's," a circumstance that induced her to place repeated $1 bets on the number; her friend soon followed suit to the tune of fifty cents per day. On February 9, the number **000** hit. By the time their runner arrived, the two women had "already decided in their minds as to how they were going to spend their 'quick money,'" but their hopes were soon dashed. According to the runner, the banker, Wilfred Brunder, was refusing to pay. Eventually, the women were given $120 and $50, respectively (instead of $540 and $270). On another occasion, in 1926, Brunder was looking at a big loss when a popular number hit, but he immediately claimed that a police raid (there had been no raid) made it impossible for him to pay.[16] Sometimes the elation of winning, followed quickly by the evaporation of all their hopes and dreams, was all too much and individuals committed suicide. More commonly, however, upset gamblers directed their violence toward someone else.

In the antebellum years, aggrieved blacks had left matters to the law, and in the 1920s some were willing to continue this tradition. Very occasionally, one of the numbers arrests in the district attorney's files was prompted by information given to police by disgrun-

tled black gamblers who had not been paid their winnings.[17] But by
the 1920s, for most blacks the idea of appealing to the police was
out of the question: angry and frustrated victims of fraud were
much more likely to take matters into their own hands. The court
records and African American newspapers are peppered with stories reflecting the ensuing violence. In August 1929, according to
the *Amsterdam News,* Jeremiah King got into an angry conversation
with Easy Dawkins, a numbers banker, concerning a couple of fif-
teen-cent bets. When they met again later that night, both drew
their guns, but the banker fired first, and King died two hours later
in Harlem hospital. In February 1930, a collector refused to pay off
Willis Robinson, whereupon Robinson abused the collector to such
an extent that he "slew the player in anger." In November 1930, the
felicitously named John Straightlife, rumored to be a former bootlegger and now a man who wrote numbers, was shot dead, supposedly for not paying off on a hit. Nonfatal disputes, involving particularly the ubiquitous knife slashings, were a commonplace.[18]

But such altercations were hardly the limit of violence that numbers engendered. Some of the holdup men who lurked on Harlem
streets were rumored to be plying their trade in order "to secure
funds with which to finance their 'numbers' playing." At times, too,
numbers was at the root of collective violence. In August 1925,
Charles Dancy, "Harlem's most notorious stool pigeon," was seen,
at 135th and Lenox, pointing out to the police the individuals
who, among a group of blacks, were gambling on numbers. Only
police intervention prevented about 100 very angry blacks from
killing him. A few months later, when the police raided a Lenox Avenue cigar store run by a popular West Indian named William
Piper, searching for numbers slips, a crowd in excess of 700 blacks
"stormed the cigar store," roughed up the police officers, tried to

take Officer Coogan's gun, and attempted to rescue Piper.[19] The stakes involved in the numbers game were more than enough to add considerably to the burden of a police department charged with keeping a lid on matters north of 125th Street.

Yet numbers was hardly the only thing that gave rise to such outbursts; violence erupted easily in Harlem. As we have already seen, any arrest or effort by the predominantly white police force to regulate black residents could draw a crowd, quickly stirred to aggression by reports of brutality or injustice. Friends, acquaintances, spouses, and relatives who fell out over slights or sums of money would reach for whatever implements lay close to hand. On Tuesday, August 29, 1917, Hazel Dickson, a twenty-four-year-old domestic, burst into the room of Alice Hooker, a nineteen-year-old-domestic, on the second floor of 68 West 134th Street. In the course of a heated argument between them, Dickson grabbed a flatiron and tried to assault Hooker, who snatched a razor from her dresser and slashed her assailant's left arm several times, inflicting cuts that necessitated a trip to Harlem Hospital. No one thought it worthwhile to record what the two were fighting about, but a bored assistant district attorney created a memorial of sorts to the mundane nature of the violence by doodling on his yellow legal pad, producing several images of both the flatiron and the switchblade razor.[20]

Residents resorted to violence even more readily in Harlem's alcohol-soaked nightlife. In 1926, Edward Atkins, a twenty-seven-year-old stock clerk, and Frank Joyner, a thirty-four-year-old porter, lived nearly opposite each other on 131st Street and had been very good friends for over a decade. Joyner had lent Atkins $6.50, but his friend had not paid him back. On the night of April 24, 1926, they argued about the money while attending the prizefights, at 135th

Street and Madison. Later, as they walked home, they came to blows and Atkins cut Joyner's hand with a knife, prompting Joyner to stab Atkins in the back with a piece of broken glass. Atkins brought charges against Joyner but later declined to pursue the matter. They had both been under the influence of alcohol when the incident occurred and remained good friends.[21] This matter-of-fact acceptance of an occasional flare-up of violence, even between very respectable citizens, while hardly commonplace was not unusual.

For all the uncertainty as to whether a winning hit would be paid off, or whether one might be arrested or caught up in one of the violent eddies that always whirled around Harlem's numbers game, every day tens of thousands of African New Yorkers put their money down and eagerly scanned early editions of the *Sun* or the *World,* hoping to read of the transformation of their own hardscrabble lives. A considerable part of the game's attraction was the way in which numbers managed to embody so many of the hopes and aspirations, as well as the ambivalences and uncertainties, of life in the Black Metropolis. At one and the same time, numbers represented the newness of Harlem, yet still managed to incorporate traditional African American ways of doing things, ways that were familiar both to longtime New Yorkers and to the thousands of migrants from the South. This ambivalence was captured nicely in the way in which the nomenclature for those running numbers alternated between "bankers," suggesting the world to which so many blacks aspired, and the almost archaic "Kings" and "Queens."

In the late 1920s, Wallace Thurman shrewdly noted that the Clearing House numbers was "a modernized and abbreviated version of the ancient game of Policy." But it was not just the game itself that was sleek and streamlined; many of the accoutrements of numbers were also modern. This was obvious from a glance at Lenox or Seventh Avenue, or any important street—places where so much of Harlem life was lived. There was, for example, a certain style to most runners and bankers. Not all of them could match Martin Harris, a Numbers King who at the time of his death had thirty-five suits hanging in his wardrobe, but many became well-known for their ostentatious sartorial display.[22] Most runners are "exceedingly prosperous in appearance," an *Age* reporter noted in 1924, and when, in June 1927, Fred Moore, editor of the *Age,* interviewed a Justice Jacob Panken, Panken complained bitterly that numbers "affords a living to 'bums' and parasites who dress well and corrupt the morals of the young." Not only did the flashy style and the barely concealed money clips of those involved in numbers make them objects of envy for hardworking young men, he continued, but "their lavish display of finery and gifts" often precipitated young women along the "downward path."[23] Fulminate as Panken and Moore might, the figure many bankers and runners cut as they went around town was a walking advertisement for the numbers.

Expensive cars were hardly unknown in Harlem; every night a flotilla of vehicles came uptown carrying slumming whites keen to experience the delights of Small's Paradise or Connie's Inn. For the most part, however, blacks did not own cars. Thus, when, as early as 1925, a writer in the *Age* noted that it was not unusual for numbers runners to do their rounds by picking up slips and money in their own cars, he was slyly hinting at a world of opulence removed from that of most Harlem residents.[24] And then there were the cars of some of Harlem's Kings and Queens. Being chauffeured around in custom-built pieces of gleaming machinery, the epitome of modern style, may have engendered some resentment on the street, but it also enabled the Numbers Kings and Queens to make a regal, albeit none-too-subtle statement about their status in the black city.

Less obviously, the numbers game was one of the important ways in which modern business practices were brought uptown. In the beginning, pencils and ledgers may have been adequate to keep track of bets, but by the mid-1920s the turnover and size of the numbers business compelled bankers to use every new labor-saving device available. Numbers slips and bets were tallied up in some of the more well-appointed, modern offices in Harlem. Almost accidentally, the record of arrests and their prosecutions made the modernizing impulse of numbers abundantly clear. When, in January 1925, the police raided the West 137th Street headquarters of John Diamond, then one of the most prominent of the Numbers Kings, they discovered that the entire premises were "given over to the business of 'playing the numbers.'" The officers made eighteen arrests and carried away two adding machines. Eighteen months later, Diamond's new place on West 142nd Street similarly yielded two adding machines and, among the employees, "four young women who served as clerks for Mr. Diamond."[25] When in mid-1927 an apartment allegedly belonging to Casper Holstein was raided, hundreds of curious onlookers saw police carry out of the building a money-counting machine, an adding machine, and a tabulating machine, as well as more than $3,000 in cash. Few, if any, other Harlem businesses required such a panoply of modern office equipment. A search of Fred "Crackers" Buchanan's Striver's Row apartment, in December 1929, uncovered adding machines, dating stamps, and an ink pad, all of them, Detective Wittenberg claimed, prima facie evidence that the residence was used for numbers.[26]

Numbers bankers also used the telephone, another modern device that was becoming more common in the 1920s. Periodically, the telephone company issued warnings that anyone using a phone to make or accept bets would be denied service—and there were rumors that "listening in" to calls had led to several cautions being handed out to runners, and even some arrests—but there were still many Harlem residents who habitually placed their bets by phone and settled up in person at a later time. In the numbers racket, any new gadget that offered the possibility of gaining an edge over rivals was welcomed with open arms. For a short while in 1926, one enterprising young man had a megaphone installed in the window at 416 Lenox, so he could blare out to anyone walking down the avenue: "We take your numbers!"[27]

6

Of Kings and Queens

"No, the baddest nigga of all time?"
"Who?"
"This nigga from New York, from the olden days, Bumpy something."
"Bumpy?"
"Yo."

—*The Wire*, Season 3, third episode

In February 1927, the *Amsterdam News* printed, in its magazine section, a short fictional piece by Claire M. Halley entitled "Fickle Lady Luck." It described the rise and fall of Sweet Cider, "the cynosure of All Eyes," instantly recognizable as one of the avenue's dandies, sporting his "gray fedora hat, pearl gray suit, suede gloves of a similar hue, gray-topped patent leather shoes, and oh, his cane—the blackest ebony that could be purchased!" Sweet Cider may have started off as "a hallboy or a porter, or something equally as menial," but when he saw the main chance he seized it with both hands. "Oil had made men millionaires over night; the discovery of gold has added many names to an already lengthy list of nouveau riche; men have made fortunes in Wall Street but it took 'The Numbers' to make Sweet Cider the John D. of Seventh

Avenue." Sweet Cider had bet a dollar on 892 and won $540. A week later his wife needed a new hat. "Best in 125th street for five dollars and ninety-five cents. He'll try Five Ninety Five. Two dollars on Five Ninety Five. He's got it! Ten hundred and eighty dollars to the good, and oh, boy, watch 'em grow." Every second or third week Sweet Cider hit the number, and with his winnings accumulated all the accoutrements of success—fine clothes, a string of women, a gray Packard—that were needed to cut a swath through Harlem. "Mayor Walker may be the mayor of this city, but the denizen of Harlem, the ruler of her colored population and the czar of all he surveyed, was Sweet Cider—and everyone in Harlem knew it." But Sweet Cider did not play straight with Lady Luck. Mistrusting banks, the gambler decided to put his money into real estate, and one December morning the gray Packard headed south to Florida. But there, alas, Sweet Cider managed to lose everything, and the story ends with the black man, in a now-shabby gray suit, returning to Harlem, renting a room on Lenox with his last three dollars, and taking a job as an elevator man. "Once lady-luck has left you for another you can't win her back." Sweet Cider is broke, "and all Harlem knows it!"[1]

Halley's story is a fascinating mixture of the closely observed and the preposterous. On the one hand, the verisimilitude of her brief sketch of fast life on the "avenoo" accords well with any number of other accounts. On the other, even though she conveys nicely the way in which, for the aficionado or the addict, everyday life in Harlem continually threw up possible winning numbers ($5.95 for the best hat on 125th Street), and appreciates that numbers was one of the very few ways in which a black man could attain the position of a Seventh Avenue John D. Rockefeller, Halley showed little understanding of the nuts and bolts of the numbers game. This is not entirely surprising. In early 1927, there was still a certain amount of novelty attached to the racket. "Of course you've heard of the Numbers," Halley wrote in her *Amsterdam News* story. "It's a new and fascinating gamble that has sprang up among the inhabitants of Harlem and San Juan Hill." The odds that someone would hit the number twice, in a little over a week, were astronomical; the idea that someone could win at the numbers "every second or third week" was simply ludicrous. Numbers was nickel-and-dime bets, with the occasional plunge of a few dollars. Sometimes a lucky punter won a few hundred dollars, but that was about it. As happens in most forms of gambling, the only people who made large sums of money out of numbers were those who ran the racket. Halley's account of Sweet Cider's swift rise and fall had no real-life counterpart among ordinary gamblers. But what she did depict, inadvertently, or perhaps only half-comprehendingly, was the brief and brilliant trajectory through the Black Metropolis of any number of bankers, of those who became, for a time, the Kings and Queens of Harlem.

Perhaps the most striking feature of the numbers racket, at least in its first decade and a half, was the rapidity with which Kings and Queens came and went. Every few months, it seemed, the police or the press alleged that some new name or other was raking in most of the money. To be sure, the occasional figure, such as Casper Holstein, Alex Pompez, or the idiosyncratic Stephanie St. Clair, remained publicly resplendent for years at a time, but that was unusual. Now and again there was room at the top, but tenure tended to be very brief. Some made enough on which to retire; some were driven out by the law; others quietly decamped to the Caribbean, rather than paying up when a heavily backed number hit. Sweet Cider's path from rags to riches to rags, then, was hardly uncommon.

Marcelino, who had been the first of the Numbers Kings, notorious for doing business from his chauffeur-driven custom-built car and for living in a "veritable palace" on Strivers' Row, was by mid-1926 reported to be "considerably reduced in financial circumstances," or, as one source more bluntly claimed, "broke." On the downward slide, Marcelino had taken to drink, and was, as a writer in the *Pittsburgh Courier* graphically put it, "just another human derelict, a has-been, a man who was shunned." By the late 1930s, Marcelino, who once had had enough funds in his bank account to write a check, that would be honored, for half a million dollars, was a charity patient in a city hospital, dying of pulmonary tuberculosis. John Smith, "one of Harlem's leading 'numbers' bankers" in the mid-1920s, was hauled in front of a court in 1930, unable to raise $37.50 to cover a check that he had written. In the second half of the 1920s, John Diamond was one of the "most prosperous" of Harlem bankers, owning a "fine home" on West 137th Street, a flashy car, and several investment properties, including "the swanky apartment building at 772 St. Nicholas avenue." But several stints in prison, including one of a year and a day for failing to file income tax returns, forced him to retire. Diamond's death at fifty-two, in July 1933, was acknowledged by the *New York Age*'s caption, "Once Wealthy Policy Banker Dies Broke"—an epitaph that would not be his alone.[2]

Strikingly, that pithy description could well have been carved into the tombstone of Casper Holstein, the biggest Numbers King of them all, and a fascinatingly mysterious man. As we saw earlier, Holstein was born in the Danish West Indies in 1876 and emigrated to New York with his mother in 1894. At the time he created the game known as the Clearing House numbers, around about 1920, he was working as a porter on Fifth Avenue. That makes Holstein sound rather more lowly than he was. His rise from rags to riches was certainly spectacular and also very quick, but it seems clear that he had already established himself as a person of some substance in Harlem even before his moment arrived.

Holstein's name first appeared in the *New York Times* as early as 1905, in a supposedly droll story complete with the dialect that the *Times* thought was spoken by African Americans. A black man burst into the West 30th Street police station late one summer night to complain that he'd been robbed while gambling. "I jes' dropped round yere to 500 Sixth Avenue to toy wif de tigah, and I were introduced as a member to de Fair Play Club on de top floor." Apparently, when the lights had suddenly been switched off, someone had grabbed Willis Williams's $150 neatly piled on the table in front of him. The president of the Fair Play Club, one "Caspar Holstein," was held on a charge of maintaining a gambling house.[3]

Throughout the first two decades of the century, Holstein, noted for his facility with figures, was involved in gambling both in some of the city's dives and at the racetrack. Between 1913 and 1922, he was arrested a total of nine times for bookmaking. Yet from very early on, Holstein was looking for acceptance and respectability. He joined the Elks in 1906 when only thirty years old. The Elks were Harlem's largest fraternal order, attracting men with aspirations to respectability; the group promoted educational programs and community service, offered insurance benefits, assisted members in finding jobs and housing, and organized entertainment such as boat rides and parties. Holstein would play a prominent role in that organization throughout the rest of his life, as a member of the Monarch Lodge, based at a hall at 245 West 137th Street that operated as a concert and dance venue and, in the 1930s, housed a bar.[4]

In 1916 the *Chicago Defender* reported that Holstein, "well-known good fellow and club man of New York City," had just spent a fortnight in the Windy City as "the guest of the popular undertaker, Mr. Charles S. Jackson." A banquet and "smoker" had been held in Holstein's honor at Chicago's Appomattox Club, a celebration that prompted the African New Yorker to tell the black newspaper, "Memories of that evening will long live with me." A year later, on another visit to Chicago, Holstein was honored with a ten-course dinner, including three different kinds of wine at the Chateau Garden, an affair attended by notables such as Oscar De Priest, then an alderman but in 1928 to become the first African American elected to Congress in the post-Reconstruction era.[5]

Once the Clearing House numbers began to catch on, in the early 1920s, the money simply poured into Holstein's bank accounts. At the time of the Number King's kidnapping in 1928, the *Chicago Defender* declared that "his wealth is now conservatively placed at more than $500,000." Holstein may have assured an *Amsterdam News* reporter that "all that stuff about my being a millionaire is just bosh," but as far as everyone else living in Harlem was concerned, it looked pretty convincing. Holstein spent money like it was going out of fashion, but very little of it on himself. Unlike most of the other Kings and Queens, he was reserved and reticent, not much interested in flashy cars and a flamboyant lifestyle. According to the *Amsterdam News*, "Holstein was, and is, a 'race man,'" and the way he spent his money demonstrated the aptness of that label. He gave "endlessly" to the Marcus Garvey movement, and, the black newspaper claimed in 1936, "to this present day, the U.S. Shipping Line still owes him $1,000 that he paid on the last Black Star Line ship—the ship that was never delivered." In 1926, when Liberty Hall, a meeting place of the Garvey movement, was auctioned, "it was Holstein, clutching $12,600 in cash in his hand, who bid in at $36,000 to save it for the organization." Holstein spent another fortune on the Elks. In 1929 at their convention in Atlantic City, he ran against J. Finley Wilson for the position of Grand Exalted Ruler. According to the *Defender*, the struggle between this pair "will always be remembered by Elkdom, chiefly because of the fact that money flowed through the various delegates' camps like water." Years later it was reported that Holstein spent over $100,000 in his pursuit of this office. There were allegations of a "double-cross," but in the end Holstein lost the election.[6]

Casper Holstein was indefatigable in his support of his native Virgin Islands, purchased from Denmark by Woodrow Wilson days before the United States entered World War I. By Holstein's lights, and those of many other people, American rule in the islands was a disaster. Holstein wrote articles for the black press, lobbied the government, and most of all donated money. Reportedly, during the heated congressional debate over the fate of the Virgin Islands, Holstein sent $30,000 to be used for lobbying. Later, in the 1930s, Holstein was an aggressive and the most obvious American-based participant in what developed into a mass movement aimed at removing Paul Pearson from the governorship of the Virgin Islands. After the hurricane of 1928, Holstein wrote a disaster-relief check for $20,000—money that was quickly put to use, well before the Red Cross and other agencies managed to organize themselves. In 1922, he bought an estate on St. Croix known as "Jerusalem," and imported purebred cattle from America to improve the island's milk cattle. He also built a dairy which distributed free milk to needy children. In addition, he dispatched "a pedigreed jack to the Virgin Islands in order to introduce a better type of mule among the peasants." With later purchases of the estates called "Hope" and "Blessing," Holstein ended up owning some two thousand acres of farmland, as well as some city real estate. He paid for the education of students from the Virgin Islands who attended Harvard, Columbia, New York University, Howard, and Hampton, many of whom went on to become part of the professional elite of the islands. As early as 1927, Eric Walrond, the Harlem Renaissance writer, noted in an article about Holstein in the *Chicago Defender* that "among the children of the Virgin Islands a legend is beginning to spring up around the magic name of Casper Holstein," and that among the 20,000 natives of the Virgin Islands then living in New York, "he is looked up to as a sort of messiah."[7]

Casper Holstein was *the* black philanthropist in Harlem, probably in America—the only African American with very deep pockets and a willingness to spend money on his fellow citizens. It was Holstein who donated the $1,000 prize money awarded by *Opportunity* magazine in its annual literary contests in the mid to late 1920s, contests that were an important feature of the Harlem Renaissance. According to the *Chicago Defender* in 1928, "hundreds of poor families in Harlem are yearly given food and fuel" thanks to his donations. Moreover, each year Holstein funded a free boat excursion for the "unfortunate children of Harlem" which cost him in excess of $7,000. He also funded a dormitory for girls in Liberia, donated a four-figure sum toward a home for deserted children in Gary, Indiana, handed out some 500 food baskets at Christmas to the Harlem poor every year, and donated thousands of dollars to Fisk University, Howard University, and the local and national Urban League. When plans to build the Vincent Sanitarium and Hospital in Harlem were afoot, "Holstein loaned $20,500 to the enterprise because he saw in it an opportunity for Negro doctors."[8]

Yet for all his liberal contributions to good causes, Holstein did his best to maintain a low profile. As his friend Eric Walrond wrote in the *Chicago Defender,* "Much to his credit, Casper Holstein is the poorest, the rottenest self-advertiser in the world." But this lack of self-promotion was due to more than modesty. Holstein was engaged in an illegal enterprise and assiduously protected his reputation. He was usually described in the newspapers as a "wealthy Harlem sportsman" or some such. When, in August 1927, the *Amsterdam News* printed a story on its front page claiming that "an apartment, said to be owned by Casper Holstein, philanthropist and erstwhile disciple of Marcus Garvey, at No. 507 Lenox Avenue, near 135th Street, was raided Friday afternoon by police sent to round up 'numbers' bankers," Holstein promptly sued the black newspaper for libel. Initially, the protagonists squared off against each other, with Holstein claiming his "credit, reputation, and general standing" had been impugned to the tune of $100,000 worth of damages, and the publishers announcing that they were going to claim truth as a defense. But after a while tensions eased, and the case appears to have been settled out of court.[9]

Everyone in Harlem knew that Holstein made his money from numbers, and many probably also knew that he had been there at the beginning of the new gambling game; but until later in the 1930s, no one was willing to put these facts on paper. What makes this remarkable is the amount of detail about other prominent numbers bankers that can be found in the black press and the legal records. Possibly there was good reason for this silence, given that Holstein's libel suit threatened the *Amsterdam News* with bankruptcy. In our extensive research through New York City's vast legal records for the 1920s, we found two documents that mentioned Holstein's role in numbers. In one numbers arrest on 133rd Street in February 1925, Howard Brown claimed that "I am collecting policy for Casper, my banker"; in another, a few weeks later, Alexander Hansen, found in possession of thirty-two slips on the sidewalk in front of 15 West 136th Street, admitted that "he was collecting for a man named Casper."[10]

There was something similarly elusive about the character of Holstein. Always carefully and conservatively dressed—"quietly, like a dignified broker," Claude McKay thought—and similarly cautious in his habits, Holstein "never paraded his prosperity in the flashy big-shot-of-Harlem way of the 'kings' and 'queens.'" A thinly disguised Casper Holstein appeared in Carl Van Vechten's enormously popular novel *Nigger Heaven* (1926), as Randolph Pettijohn, the Bolito King; and Van Vechten's friend, the Mexican artist Miguel Covarrubias, included a sketch of the Bolito King in his volume *Negro Drawings* (1927). Pettijohn is an awkward character, seemingly never quite in step with the Harlem cabaret world depicted by Van Vechten. Indeed, the novelist's unflattering portrayal can hardly have afforded Holstein much pleasure. For all his money and generosity, Holstein always seemed at some remove from Harlem's elite society. Possibly this was because of his West Indian past; perhaps it was due to the way he made his money, or to his reserved personality. Langston Hughes thought that "Mr. Holstein, no doubt, would have been snubbed in polite Washington society, Negro or white"— not that the black poet thought any the less of him for that. Holstein, though, was highly regarded by the ordinary African Americans living in Harlem. When he was released from his kidnapping ordeal in September 1928, crowds of well-wishers flocked to Holstein's Turf Club to welcome his return, even though it was the early hours of a Monday morning.[11]

Holstein's kidnapping in 1928 seems to have curbed his enthusiasm for being a Numbers King. Slowly he began to ease his way out of the business, a move hastened by the advent of Dutch Schultz in Harlem in 1931. The kidnapping and the consequent front-page stories attracted the attention not only of gangsters but also of the federal authorities. Holstein had several run-ins over his income tax returns, although he avoided the fate of his fellow King, Henry Miro, who went to prison over his tax troubles. Just before Christmas 1935, Holstein was arrested and charged with financing a policy racket. There was a suggestion that his financial strife had caused him to recommence banking numbers, but Holstein and many of his supporters were convinced that he was being persecuted—perhaps because he was a well-known rich Numbers King, perhaps for the way he had embarrassed the government over its ineptitude in the Virgin Islands. Holstein appeared in court in early February 1936, "immaculately dressed" in a "dark brown overcoat with a velvet collar," and watched as his lawyer explained that his client's wealth "had dwindled to nothing during the depression." Holstein was convicted; and the court, obviously unimpressed with the philanthropy detailed in the probation officer's report, sentenced him to the maximum, "an indeterminate term of not more than three years in the penitentiary."[12]

After Holstein served his time, he lived out the rest of his life in what the *New York Times* called obscurity, dying in April 1944 at the age of sixty-seven. Broke and ill after a stroke, he lived his last two years in the home of friends, supported by the $100 a month sent to him by Charles Jackson, the undertaker who had hosted his visit to Chicago a quarter of a century previously. His funeral was a big affair: over 2,000 people jammed into Memorial Baptist Church on 115th Street, and many hundreds more were turned away. Samuel Battle, the first black policeman in New York and now the city's parole commissioner, was there, along with Wilfred Brunder, the former Numbers King, and J. Finley Wilson, grand exalted ruler of the nation's Elks, as well as many officials of Monarch Elks Lodge No. 45. Yet the funeral was strangely flat. As the *Amsterdam News* reporter noted, "Of all the widely publicized sportsmen in Harlem, William (Bub) Hewlitt was the only one to show up." Though friends estimated that Holstein had financed the college education of almost 100 black students, only one of them was known to have sent a message of condolence. In his pomp, Holstein had given away a fortune to innumerable Harlem charities but, as one friend commented, "If he was gambling on whether or not many of these favors were appreciated, he lost because most of his friends let him down when they realized he had no money."[13]

The parallels with the fall of Marcus Garvey, the other great West Indian figure in interwar Harlem, are striking. Garvey's success, too, attracted the attention of both black critics and white authorities, who joined forces to get him convicted of a relatively minor charge: mail fraud. He likewise faded from prominence after his release, at least in Harlem, from which he was effectively exiled upon being deported from the United States. If Holstein gave up running the numbers, Garvey did continue to lead the UNIA—but the organization over which he presided was a fractured and diminished remnant of its former self. On his death in London in 1940, Garvey barely avoided a pauper's funeral, but in Harlem, after a procession from the Garvey Club office on West 133rd Street, some 3,000 people packed St. Mark's Methodist Episcopal Church on St. Nicholas Avenue for a memorial service.[14]

Unlike Marcus Garvey, Casper Holstein is almost totally forgotten in the United States now; but he deserves to be remembered as a similarly towering figure in African American life in the first half of the twentieth century. Not only did he found a multi-million dollar industry that employed thousands of African Americans and that made him wealthy, but he also gave most of his fortune away to a vast array of institutions and charities, at a time when very few were at all interested in funding things that would benefit ordinary black men and women. Only Madam C. J. Walker, the millionaire hair care entrepreneur, achieved comparable stature–in her case, with the largest legitimate black business in the United States–and dispersed similar sums among black institutions and organizations (although she favored the NAACP rather than the UNIA). After her death in 1919, her daughter A'Lelia became a patron of the arts, perhaps the only black who offered more support to Harlem's writers and artists than Holstein did; certainly, he did not seek to match the lavish parties that she staged.[15] In his own way, Holstein was as impressive a figure as any Carnegie or Mellon, and if he'd been white would doubtless still be memorialized all over the place. As things turned out, he was quickly dismissed from the public mind. The four-paragraph story buried on page 34 of the *New York Times* that reported Casper Holstein's death was headed "Former 'Policy King' in Harlem Dies Broke," a caption that relegated him to the ranks of all those other Kings who momentarily flashed across the Harlem sky, remembered only for their expensive cars and sharp suits. Langston Hughes gave Holstein a more fitting summation: he was "a wealthy West Indian numbers banker who did good things with his money." Hughes, a winner of the *Opportunity* poetry prize, then added, "Certainly he was a great help to poor poets."[16]

If Casper Holstein conformed to the pattern of Numbers Kings and Queens, ending up in penury, Stephanie St. Clair was an exception to the rule—but then she was an exception to most rules. Madame Queen was most definitely one of a kind. Born sometime around 1890 in Martinique, St. Clair came to New York in 1912. Setting up as a banker about 1922, she made money, but was one of the lesser numbers luminaries throughout the 1920s, maintaining a low profile. All that changed in 1929, when St. Clair began publishing a series of paid advertisements in the *Amsterdam News* in which she vented her opinion on issues affecting Harlem, particularly police corruption. The advertisements created a sensation, although not all the attention St. Clair gained was welcome. In November 1929, under the usual photograph of an elegantly dressed St. Clair, was the following announcement: "I have received letters and telephone messages from men which have annoyed me very much and I take this occasion to ask them publicly to please not annoy me. I, Mme. St. Clair, am not looking for a husband or a sweetheart. If they do not stop annoying me, I shall publish their names and letters in the newspaper."[17]

One of few women who reached the highest levels of the numbers game, St. Clair carried herself with an imperious style all her own.[18] Her French accent, often conveyed on the printed page with an abundance of *z*'s, and her refusal to back down from anyone, black or white, no matter what their position, marked St. Clair out and made her grist for the mill of the black press. Mind you, she seemed to revel in the attention. Found in possession of some numbers slips, she represented herself in court in March 1930. The *Amsterdam News* reporter present began his story: "Waging a desperate three-hour battle in the courtroom where three busy justices ordinarily dispose of 125 cases in four hours, Mme. Stephanie St. Clair, thirty-one, 409 Edgecombe Avenue, lost her brilliant fight Friday afternoon." He continued, "Mme. St. Clair held the center of the stage in the court drama while spectators and attendants gripped their seats and drank in the proceedings." In September 1932, as she was engaged in a bitter struggle with Dutch Schultz over control of numbers in Harlem, she went to the Washington Heights Court and applied for a warrant for the arrest of Max Rene, alleging that he had tried to induce a woman to lure St. Clair to her apartment where bodily harm would have been done to the Numbers Queen. After hearing the case, Judge Brodsky "expressed his disbelief in the seriousness of the affair." Then, according to the *New York Age* reporter, St. Clair, "with a disdainful gesture, said, 'That's why there is so much crime in these United States,' and walked away from the Bench towards the audience." The judge exploded. "Come back here you," he yelled out. "And don't you walk out on me . . . and never mind all this crime in the United States." St. Clair was then made to listen to a lecture on court decorum, words which undoubtedly were water off a duck's back.[19]

According to a clearly bemused *Age* reporter, St. Clair "seems to possess some indescribable complex and an apparent yen for publicity." He was not wrong. Throughout the decade of the 1930s, St. Clair sought out the black press, clearly viewing it as a key element in her deadly struggle with Schultz. She testified before the Seabury Commission, and a number of times went downtown to see the mayor or Thomas Dewey to describe and complain about what was happening in Harlem; and she was always willing to let reporters know what was on her mind. Yet if she felt she had been wronged, she was as quick as Casper Holstein to serve a writ. On October 8, 1931, the *Interstate Tattler* published a story captioned, "Secret Out! Mme. St. Clair, 'Numbers Queen,' Planned to Frame Cops." St. Clair accused the *Tattler* of "contriving wickedly and maliciously intending to injure" her by publishing material that was "false, scandalous and defamatory." There was also a curious second cause to the action. According to the *Tattler*, St. Clair had made enough money to "afford a special secretary, a lovely little brown-skinned sweetheart, whose father doesn't know yet that she was working for a female digits banker." The term "digit" was a "well understood idiomatic or slang expression," and, according to St. Clair, the *Tattler* "meant and intended to mean that plaintiff had committed the crime of Sodomy." St. Clair claimed that the story had brought her "into public scorn, scandal, infamy, contempt and obloquy" and sought $25,000 in damages.[20]

Stephanie St. Clair appears to have withdrawn from the numbers game not long after Dutch Schultz was shot in 1935. In 1936, she married Sufi Abdul Hamid, one of the instigators of the Harlem boycott movement and often known as the "Black Hitler" because of his anti-Semitic utterances. Instead of undergoing the usual marriage ceremony, the couple signed a "contract" uniting them for ninety-nine years; it contained a clause allowing for a trial year, "during which time the feasibility of the plan could be tested." Without any exaggeration, the *Amsterdam News* labeled them "two of Harlem's most exotic figures." In 1937, the "marriage" obviously and publicly began to fall apart, and early in 1938 St. Clair fired several shots at her husband as he walked in the front door, managing only to graze him. St. Clair's lawyer pleaded for mercy, but the judge told the courtroom: "This woman has been living by her wits all of her life. She has a bad temper and must learn that she can't go around shooting at other people." He sentenced her to two to ten years in state prison. A few months later, Hamid died when his plane crashed. According to Bumpy Johnson's widow, when St. Clair was released she "moved into a mansion in Long Island, never again getting into the numbers business." St. Clair died in December 1969 and, according to Mayme Johnson, was "far from broke."[21]

Holstein and St. Clair were players in the numbers game for a long time. Martin L. Harris's tenure as one of Harlem's Kings was rather more fleeting. In February 1933, the thirty-two-year-old Harris was on top of the world. His rise to power and prominence had been swift. He had started out in the late 1920s as an employee of Casper Holstein, but in 1930 he hit the number **708** for $5, playing against a Broadway syndicate that only accepted large bets, and collected $3,000. Harris bought a "flashy Cadillac" and began writing numbers on his own account, eventually taking over much of Holstein's business as his patron retreated from the fray. He was well known around Harlem: witness after witness at the ensuing trials testified that even though they had never spoken to Harris, they knew who he was—and all said that he cut a striking figure even among the passing finery daily displayed on the "avenoo." As would emerge later, the always sartorially resplendent Numbers King owned thirty-five suits, sixteen pairs of shoes, and nine hats. When August McBean, the carpenter who was fashioning a hiding place for cash under Harris's apartment floorboards, was asked in court where his various conversations with Harris had occurred, he answered, "In the street, naturally." Yet if the Harlem avenues were Harris's milieu, he was also using his newly acquired status as Policy King to establish himself in Harlem society, becoming both a prominent Elk and an usher at the Abyssinian Baptist Church. To be sure, there was talk of an imminent numbers war—Harris was one of the independent black bankers bucking the control of the Dutch Schultz organization—but for all that, Martin Harris was a Harlem success story, a man who had taken the opportunities presented to him by the Black Metropolis and made something of himself.

But on the morning of Tuesday, March 7, 1933, it all turned to dust. Three black gunmen talked their way into apartment 12½ at 101 West 130th street, and when Harris, wearing his pajamas, came out of his bedroom he was shot and killed. It was either a bungled robbery (the gunmen escaped with $5,000) or an assassination made to look like a holdup. The fragility of Harris's success was soon laid bare. His life may have had style, but the substance was lacking: there was less than $600 in the estate, and much of this would probably go to his wife, from whom he was long separated. Myra Macklin, Harris's common-law wife for almost a decade, later testified that life had been good and that numbers had been "a pretty profitable racket." Casper Holstein paid her expenses for a while (he also let it be known that he would pay a reward for securing Harris's killer), but within months of Harris's murder she was working as a domestic for a white family in Brooklyn. And—a final indignity—the Abyssinian Baptist Church washed its hands of its former usher: last rites for Martin Harris had to be performed in a funeral parlor.[22]

Martin Harris was one of the last Harlem blacks to assume the title of King. With the advent of Schultz, and later the Mafia, that title no longer seemed appropriate; it was all a rather different world. The most important figure in Harlem's underworld in the ensuing decades was Ellsworth Raymond Johnson, universally known as Bumpy. He had acquired his nickname when he was a child because of a small lump or knot about the size of a marble on the back of his head.[23] Bumpy Johnson started out in the times of the Kings and Queens, but brokered the transition to an industry run by whites even if operated by African Americans. It was more than just the absence of the title that separated Johnson from the Kings and Queens who preceded him. Bumpy Johnson, unlike Holstein, St. Clair, or any of the other Kings and Queens, was a career criminal, and that difference reflected an important change in the nature of Harlem life.

According to his widow, Mayme Johnson, Bumpy Johnson was born in Charleston, South Carolina, on October 31, 1905, and that is the generally accepted date. Interestingly, in a detailed question-naire about her son, filled out in 1925 when Johnson had just been admitted to the Elmira Reformatory and which no one has read in some eighty years, his mother penciled in quite carefully that he was born October 31, 1908. Johnson was the youngest of seven chil-dren, his mother, a domestic, being thirty-nine at the time of his birth, and his father, a fisherman, fifty-one. Johnson attended a school in Calhoun Street, Charleston, leaving in 1921 when he was in the eighth grade. According to his teacher, a Miss E. E. Sanders, he struggled with Mathematics, did best in Reading, and had a par-ticularly marked interest in History. She summed up her former pupil for the Elmira authorities as being of "fair" ability and as "mischievous and easily led." Margaret Johnson informed them that her son had always had ambitions "to be a lawyer or an eye doctor." From the age of eleven, Johnson worked as a paperboy, sell-ing copies of the *Charleston American*. His mother, keen to illustrate how her son could "resist temptation," sent along with the ques-tionnaire to the authorities at Elmira a painstakingly handwritten letter in which she detailed that in all his years as a paperboy he "has handled their money, never being one cent short." She went on to explain that "after Bussness became dull in Charleston, he ask my consent 'to go north to work and help himself to finish up school.'" With his mother's agreement, Johnson "saved his money and bought his ticket."[24]

As with so many other young Charleston blacks in the postwar years, Johnson headed to New York, probably in late 1921 or early 1922, and like many others fresh off the boat or train, initially stayed with a relative—in his case, a sister named Mabel, living in a railroad flat on 150th Street and Seventh Avenue. In spite of Johnson's promise to his mother, school did not feature prominently in his new life. He was employed as a house painter for six months at $24 a week, as a counterman on a Hudson River day boat at $50 a month, and, for another six-month period, as a porter in a store on Lenox Avenue at $18 a week. But regular employment at a laboring wage held little appeal for the ambitious teenager, and he was quickly absorbed into the life of Harlem's streets. Although Johnson was only in his mid-teens, and hardly physically prepossessing, he rapidly developed a fearsome reputation working for William "Bub" Hewlett in the protection racket, particularly as a bodyguard for numbers bankers. One evening in February 1924, Johnson and another young black were escorting a Cuban man named Alex Pompez, one of the early Numbers Kings, back from a night on the town in Spanish Harlem, when a man carrying a gun stepped out from an alleyway and demanded that Pompez hand over his wallet. Bumpy Johnson promptly slashed the mugger across the cheek with his knife, causing him to drop the gun. He shoved Pompez into his car, and then cut the assailant twice more. At this point, as a policeman came running toward the scuffle, Johnson dropped his knife in the gutter and the other bodyguard kicked it into the open sewer. Asked by the policeman what was going on, Johnson, in his widow's retelling of the story, "said he didn't know, he'd only just arrived on the scene himself and found the man on the sidewalk trying to put his guts back in his stomach." When the policeman tried to question Pompez, Johnson blocked his path, telling him that Pompez did not speak English. He then turned to the other bodyguard and told him to get in the car and drive Pompez out of there. The policeman attempted to push Johnson out of the way, but the young black man punched him, and the two began to fight. Several police officers eventually managed to subdue Johnson, by which time Pompez was miles away. Convicted of disorderly conduct, Johnson, only fifteen years old, was placed on probation for a year. Not surprisingly, the incident gave Johnson's street credibility an enormous boost, and within a short time he was working for Stephanie St. Clair.[25]

In early 1925, Bumpy Johnson and Theodore Stewart, a young black man originally from Charleston who was apparently Johnson's roommate, were both arrested, convicted of breaking into an apartment on West 133rd Street and stealing six suits and $300 worth of jewelry, and sent to Elmira Reformatory in upstate New York. The admission records provide a snapshot of the young Bumpy Johnson at sixteen and a half years of age (though officials listed him as eighteen). Johnson was five feet eight inches tall, weighed 135 pounds, and neither drank nor smoked. All Elmira inmates underwent what was called a "psychogram," a series of simple tests designed to determine mental ability. Reading the records of such examinations—and we have read hundreds of them—is more than enough to puncture early twentieth-century pretensions to scientific objectivity. What these files reveal is a mix of prejudice, opinion, superficial observation, intuition, and, occasionally, genuine insight. Theodore Stewart, for example, was diagnosed as "subnormal" and classified as a "moron"; officials described him as having "a poorly developed mind and is lacking in general intelligence—reads only cheap love stories—does not make much of his opportunities," as being "lazy and satisfied to take life as easily as possible," and as having "a rather clownish appearance and personality." Bumpy Johnson was diagnosed as "dull normal," classified as "psychopathic," and described as possessing "fair native ability with fair formal educational advantages" and "fair industrial capacity as a waiter or hotel worker." But what is most striking about his records is the extent to which Johnson clearly disrupted the rather low expectations set up by a science that was simply racist. According to a J. R. Harding, M.D., Johnson "is intelligent—rather unusual for a colored inmate—is apparently bright and fairly informed." He was also "rather *egotistic*—is in the habit of *telling lies* when convenient—shows some latent psychopathic traits." In addition, "his sense of right and wrong is rather poor and consequently, he is *criminally inclined*—is rather suggestible—has a tendency to boast of his accomplishments—is also suggestible and *easily led* although apparently able to resist ordinary temptation when he tries." Notations about the way Johnson had solved various puzzles included "good perception of form and object relationship," "good planning ability," "good visual memory," and "logical account of details and sequence." The state-employed doctor summed up by stating that Johnson was "somewhat suggestible and inclined to be a braggart," and then, very unusually, concluded with: "is quite above the average for his race."[26]

Johnson was paroled after two years in Elmira, but hardly came out reformed: "two hours after I was on the street I was on a heist." Not surprisingly, he was soon convicted of assault and sent back to

Elmira for another two years, then sentenced to two years and six months in Sing Sing for grand larceny.[27] When he was released from prison in the second half of 1932, he was, as we shall see, immediately drawn into Stephanie St. Clair's struggle with Dutch Schultz over control of numbers. For just over three decades following Schultz's death in 1935, Johnson, even though he spent more time in prison than out, was the key figure in the Harlem underworld, due mostly to his links with the Mafia. He died of a heart attack in 1968 at the age of fifty-nine (although obituaries said sixty-two), while out on $50,000 bail and fighting charges of importing a very large quantity of cocaine. Ironically, his name is probably known best today for a brief cameo appearance, played by Clarence Williams III, near the beginning of the film *American Gangster* (2007)—a portrayal that his widow hotly disputes.[28]

For all the dismissive comments by the officials in Elmira, Bumpy Johnson was a fascinating and complex man. In the summer of 1935, he began an affair with Helen Lawrenson, an editor at *Vanity Fair*. They were introduced at the Alhambra on Seventh Avenue and 126th Street. Only a few weeks later, in another strange link between the city's financial district and numbers in Harlem, Lawrenson met and began an affair with Bernard Baruch, millionaire titan of Wall Street and advisor to several presidents. Johnson knew about Lawrenson's relations with Baruch, but she did not tell the South Carolina–born stockbroker of her trips to Harlem to see the black gangster. In Lawrenson's telling, Johnson was always impeccably polite, opening doors for women, lighting their cigarettes, and so forth. He also dressed immaculately, albeit very conservatively, eschewing the sharper and flashier style displayed by many a Harlem numbers man. At Lawrenson's suggestion, he started patronizing Sulka's, the exclusive haberdasher famous for its hand-sewn shirts, to buy his shirts and ties. Others began to imitate him, and, as Lawrenson wryly noted, "I wondered what the salesmen in Sulka's thought about this sudden influx of black customers."[29]

For Lawrenson, part of the attraction of Johnson was that he was "vulnerably sentimental in some ways." Johnson was "a push-over for a hard-luck touch" and "kept a framed picture of Shirley Temple, aged six, on his bureau." Occasionally, Lawrenson was perhaps too revealing of her lover's foibles: "Frankly, Bumpy was no great justification for the Southern white man's manic sex fear of the black male." After meeting Canada Lee, then a boxer but later an African American film star, at a party, Lawrenson told Johnson that Lee had thought her beautiful. Johnson retorted, "He's a fighter. I'm a fucker." To which, Lawrenson replied, "Well, I certainly hope for his sake that he can fight better than you can fuck." Johnson laughed and commented: "I guess it's all that saltpeter they give you in prison."[30]

An autodidact, Bumpy Johnson read extensively throughout his life, particularly when he had the most free time—in prison. Back in 1924 he had told St. Clair that Joseph T. Wilson's volume *The Black Phalanx* (1887), an account of the deeds of African American soldiers in the American Revolution, the War of 1812, and the Civil War, was one of his favorite books, and that he had read it about ten times since first encountering it in school. Mostly he read history, particularly American history, and philosophy. When Johnson was incarcerated yet again in the late 1930s, he asked Lawrenson to send him Thomas Paine's book *The Rights of Man* (1791) and a life of Robespierre, which she duly did. Johnson wrote poetry about love and friendship and, later in life, had three of his poems published in *Freedomways,* one of the key journals of the freedom movement. He wrote an unpublished and unperformed three-act play, *Not Un-*

appeased, whose title was taken from a Homer couplet. It tells the story of a young black man named Joe who had sought a better life in the North, but returned to the South in order to avenge his sister's rape and murder. Joe kills the four people he had determined were responsible for the unpunished crime, and manages to remain undetected and free. Bumpy Johnson was no believer in nonviolence.[31]

At the time of Johnson's death in 1968, a "police official" was quoted in the *New York Times* as saying that "Johnson had the reputation of being a 'staunch race man.'" And that was a fair enough description of him. Johnson detested places such as the Savoy and Clinton Moore's, where white "slummers" would come to see Harlem. "We ain't in no zoo," Johnson explained to Lawrenson very soon after they had met. "How would you like it if we was to go downtown to your clubs and restaurants to stare at you people?" Clearly, self-interest was the overwhelming factor in Johnson's involvement in the struggle to retain control of numbers; but in the case of both Johnson and St. Clair, their strident advocacy on behalf of black business in Harlem was more than just hollow rhetoric. Johnson was proud to be black, and proud of and interested in the history of the race. He was not willing to yield to any man, particularly a white. At his eulogy in 1968, John H. Johnson, rector of St. Martin's Church (and no relation to Bumpy Johnson), claimed that "he would never allow the Caucasian majority to run roughshod over him or the community he lived in. He was a man that, strangely, I respected." And yet for decades he was the Mafia's man in Harlem, the enforcer of directives from downtown. It must have taken considerable ingenuity to negotiate the problems of that position and keep his reputation intact. Perhaps he was helped by his famed skill at chess—according to one of his regular opponents,

John H. Johnson, Bumpy Johnson's "killer instinct" was almost immediately apparent in the first game they had ever played. Even the *New York Times,* at Johnson's death, conceded that "his exploits became a legend" and that he was widely admired in Harlem "because of his strong sense of personal independence." And Mayme Johnson's recently published memoir of her husband's life, *Harlem Godfather* (2008), is a paean to the man who was "the man" in Harlem, in thrall to nobody.[32]

For all his charm and charisma, though, Bumpy Johnson was in a rather different category from the Black Kings and Queens who had preceded him. John H. Johnson related a story of one of Bumpy Johnson's numerous court appearances. Asked what he did for a living, Johnson replied: "Your Honor, I am a professional gambler. I have been a gambler all my life. I don't know how to do a thing but gamble. I make my living gambling." In the rector's telling, the judge dismissed the charge, ruefully commenting, "At least the man told the truth."[33] But the judge was wrong. While "making a living from gambling" was, to a greater or lesser extent, a fair enough description of Harlem's Kings and Queens, it was a totally inadequate way of viewing Bumpy Johnson. The Kings and Queens had their brushes with the law, and many were imprisoned for a few months here and there on gambling charges or for not paying their income tax; but Johnson spent some twenty-five years, or well over half of his adult life, in prison, in lengthy stints for violent crimes. Bumpy Johnson was a hardened violent criminal, a pimp, and a dealer in hard drugs, as well as a numbers banker. Perhaps, indeed probably, only such a man could survive at the top of the Harlem underworld once the white gangsters and the Mafia became involved in numbers.

Bumpy Johnson's friend John Johnson wrote that his namesake

"had too much of an ego, and was a violent man with a terrible temper." He added: "Perverted and wrong as his acts in the underworld were, Bumpy Johnson had a code of honor and he lived by it scrupulously. He paid his debts. His word was his bond." Above all, he "was never a squealer, never a rat." During the time Lawrenson spent with Johnson in the second half of the 1930s, she witnessed several violent incidents that filled her with "fear and revulsion," yet in her memoirs she softens her account of these events. Having just pulverized a man and gouged his eyes in the Alhambra, Johnson quietly asked Lawrenson, "Is my tie straight?" After a gun duel on a Harlem street, Johnson returned to Lawrenson in a restaurant and calmly ordered a banana split for dessert.[34] Those on the other side of the law were rather less inclined to romanticize him. Calvin Boxley, a police lieutenant attached to the Sixth Division, attended Johnson's funeral, and spoke to a *New York Times* reporter: "Don't make him an idol. He was a hoodlum—a stone hoodlum." A Harlem reporter for another newspaper told the *Times* man that Johnson handled all the "disciplinary action" in the rackets in Harlem; he was "vicious, unabashedly wicked."[35]

Yet for all the contrasts between the lives led by Bumpy Johnson and his Numbers King and Queen predecessors, there was one constant in Harlem life from the 1920s until World War II and beyond. Things may well have been better in New York than in the South or the West Indies, places where so many Harlem residents had been born, but opportunities for advancement in the northern city were still severely limited. As Claire Halley had recognized in her story published in the *Amsterdam News* in 1927, numbers was one of the very few ways in which a black man could ever attain the position of a Seventh Avenue Rockefeller. Helen Lawrenson once told Bumpy Johnson that "any dumb gorilla can beat up people." "What would you have me do?" Johnson replied. "Go down to Grand Central Station and carry bags for dimes?" He pointed out that "I ain't no Paul Robeson and I ain't no Angelo Herndon," the latter being an African American Communist Party organizer who had been jailed in Atlanta in 1933 because of his political activities, and whose case was a cause célèbre in the 1930s. "I'm just an awful lot of black," Johnson concluded. "White people ain't left us nothin' but the underworld. They made hoods and thieves outta every nigger that's got any guts." No doubt this was self-serving and about as close to the maudlin as Bumpy Johnson was ever likely to get, but there was still a considerable element of truth in what he said. Life on the "avenoo," running numbers and aspiring to be a King or Queen, was one of the few readily apparent ways to get ahead in Harlem in the 1920s and 1930s, and many of the best and brightest young blacks would be drawn into the racket. Those who succeeded and rose to the top, people such as Holstein, St. Clair, and Johnson, were remarkable men and women and, in different and fairer circumstances, may well have turned out to be more legitimate spokespersons for their race. In the very early 1930s, Lewis Lawes, Sing Sing's most famous warden, told Johnson: "Ellsworth Johnson, you could have been a great leader of your people." Maybe. But the pleasures of the life were addictive, and they always included more than just the money. After a short, sharp, violent incident, Lawrenson asked Bumpy Johnson if he knew the meaning of the word "fear." "Lissen," Johnson said, "when something like this happens, it's like a cool breeze blowin' through me. Man, it's beautiful."[36]

7

The Dutchman Cometh

They were the only people I ever knew who had the nerve to stand up and fight the Dutchman.

—Dixie Davis, *Collier's,* July 29, 1939

For the Black Kings and Queens of Harlem, the late 1920s was a fabulous time. Even the onset of the Great Depression seemed of little moment, barely making an impact on the Kings' and Queens' rapidly growing businesses—businesses that were turning over tens of millions of dollars. From the perspective of the late 1930s, one writer in the usually measured *New York Times* went so far as to label numbers in those years before 1931 "a brilliant Harlem success story."[1] There was, of course, a price for this success. Numbers was no longer a secret outside Harlem and San Juan Hill. Starting with the Seabury Investigation of 1931, the decade would be marked by similar inquiries and headline-grabbing trials as the authorities—in particular the indefatigable Thomas Dewey, who held several different positions during the decade—did their best to rid the city of Tammany Hall's seemingly endemic corruption, a condition increasingly linked to the growth of numbers. More important, the brilliant success story of numbers attracted renewed attention from the city's criminal element. Dewey's investigative incursions into the running of numbers were an inconvenience, but the Black Kings and Queens could live with them, indeed take advantage of them at times. Living with the white gangsters now coming to the fore in New York City in the 1930s would, however, prove to be a rather more difficult matter.

The one discordant note to the good times of the late 1920s was the widely held knowledge that white gangsters were hovering around Harlem waiting for the right time to make their move. Casper Holstein's kidnapping in 1928 had changed the tenor of Harlem life: it was as though the Black Metropolis had lost its innocence. To be sure, the Black Kings and Queens were hardly choirboys or choirgirls, were perfectly capable of being ruthless and on occasion brutal, and were most certainly not to be crossed; but compared with what was about to descend on Harlem, they were as innocent as children. Holstein resisted all blandishments to say anything about who had spirited him away, but it was a common belief in Harlem that one of the men involved was Vincent "Mad Dog" Coll, at the time in the pay of the volatile gangster known as the Dutchman.[2]

Dutch Schultz had been born Arthur Flegenheimer in the Bronx in 1902. Although a hard childhood had forced him to leave school in the sixth grade to help support his family, he was an avid reader of books and newspapers throughout his short life. He explained to one reporter that he had changed his name to Dutch Schultz because "it was short enough to fit the headlines. If I kept the name of Flegenheimer, nobody would have heard of me."[3] Schultz formed a gang in the Bronx based around East 149th Street and rode to prominence and power in the years of Prohibition, eventually becoming the "Beer Baron of the Bronx." A diminutive man, Schultz, according to some of his female contemporaries, "looked like Bing

Crosby with his nose bashed in." He wore expensive ties and hand-kerchiefs—gifts from sycophants—but bought his own suits off the rack and cheap. The gun that Schultz habitually kept tucked into his waistband made his clothes look even more ill-fitting. As a result, there was always something incongruous about his appearance, though no one would ever comment on this to his face. The Dutchman was erratic and violent, almost a caricature of a gangster as played by James Cagney, but he was also shrewd and employed a couple of very clever men as well as the expected retinue of thugs. Unusually, Schultz ruminated about his place in history and was fond of brooding about the parallels between his career and that of Napoleon. On one occasion, when the Dutchman was in hiding and was reading a book about the Russian Revolution, he lectured Dixie Davis about the Bolsheviks. "Those guys are just like me. They're just a mob. If I'd been there with my mob I could have taken over, just like they did." Then he added wistfully, "But over here the time isn't ripe yet."[4]

It was probably inevitable that the determined Dutch Schultz would seize the prize of Harlem numbers, but it was also the case that African Americans were complicit in their own decline, almost inviting him into the Black Metropolis. In 1931, in the glare of publicity surrounding the Seabury Investigation, Wilfred Brunder and Henry Miro relinquished control of their operations to Joe Ison. Ison, who had migrated from the West Indies nearly a decade and a half previously, and had initially worked as an elevator operator, was nicknamed Spasm, according to the *Amsterdam News,* "because he nearly had one when he holds the wrong cards in poker." He succeeded handsomely and soon attracted the attention of toughs, who tried to shake him down.[5] His lawyer, Dixie Davis, told him: "Joe, I've been thinking something like this might happen. Policy has been making lots of money, and so far it has not been bothered, but some mob is likely to move in." What Ison needed, according to Davis, was protection; and for that reason Davis introduced him to Bo Weinberg, Schultz's chief lieutenant, and worked out an arrangement between the pair.[6] For $500 a week, Ison was to receive protection from the Schultz gang. This was the thin end of the wedge. When Miro wanted to return to numbers banking, it was Schultz who brokered the deal between Miro and Ison. At a meeting in Davis's West End Avenue apartment, Miro tried to argue percentages, but Schultz took Miro into the bathroom and, as Davis found out two years later from Miro, told the Numbers King, "Henry, you do what I say or I will kill you." On returning to the living room, Miro cheerfully said, "Okay, Joe. When do we start?" A few weeks later, Schultz raised the cost of Ison's protection to $1,000 a week.[7]

Ironically, it was an element of black culture that, for all their pomp, laid bare the fragility of the position of the Black Kings and Queens. Many African Americans believed that, around Thanksgiving, any combination of the numbers 2, 5, and 7 would prove to be lucky.[8] On the day before Thanksgiving in 1931, **527** hit and broke every bank in Harlem. Even the usual fallback when a banker had a liquidity crisis—namely, borrowing from a colleague—was closed off, as everyone was short of cash. Alex Pompez lost more than $70,000; and after Joe Ison scraped together all of his ready cash, he was still $12,000 short of what he owed.[9] It was the perfect storm. A hit on a popular number, leveraged by the remorseless mathematics that flowed from offering odds of 600:1 (after all, it was the wagering of only some $115 that had caused Pompez's devastating loss), wreaked its havoc just as the specter of the Dutchman loomed over Harlem. Gamblers who managed to get paid off may have celebrated, but for the Black Kings and Queens the day was quickly labeled Black Wednesday. Even in their moment of disaster, they strove to identify with the financial establishment, by linking their travails with Black Thursday, the first day of the catastrophic stock market crash in October 1929 almost exactly two years previously.

Schultz acted quickly and decisively. He paid off the hits of various bankers, not for the usual extortionate interest rates that gangsters charged, but for a share of the business. Joe Ison's $12,000 was covered and Schultz took over two-thirds of his operation. Other bankers made similar deals, either because they had a cash shortage or because coercion had been used. Alex Pompez held out for a while, but an involuntary visit to Dixie Davis's apartment—where the Dutchman "took me in a small room and placed a gun on the table"—induced him to throw in his lot with Schultz's organization.[10] The only beneficial feature of this new regime was that players who hit could now be much more confident that they would be paid (black bankers had been notorious for welching). Other than that, the new system simply meant that every day carloads of money left Harlem for the Bronx. In August 1932, Wilfred Brunder, the Black King whom Thomas Dewey had pursued for income tax evasion, was released from federal prison after serving a little more than seven months of his nine-month sentence. As Brunder testified later, on his return to Harlem, Joe Ison told him "that in his absence the impossible had happened and that one man had assumed control of the entire policy racket." Schultz was now the "policy king."[11] As the *Age* reported in the same month, Harlem's numbers business was currently in "the hands of a white king after the valiant effort of the Negro bankers to keep the money in Harlem."[12]

What was remarkable about this takeover was that no blood had been spilled. As Dixie Davis commented: "There was no violence. None was needed."[13] White gangsters, mostly first- and second-generation immigrants keen to demonstrate their Americanization by sporting ludicrous nicknames, had introduced a whole new way of doing business in Harlem, and the mere threat of action brought most of the Kings into line. When pressure was being placed on Wilfred Brunder to join Schultz's combination, Abe "Misfit" Landau sidled up to the Numbers King on the street one day, admired his new car, and simply "asked to know if Brunder wished to keep on living so he could keep on riding in it." Brunder was so terrified that he immediately left town and spent a few weeks in the West Indies.[14] The thoroughly deserved reputation of these gangsters for savage violence would prove to be a problem not only for the Black Kings and Queens, but for the legal authorities as well. In 1937, Thomas Dewey, then a special prosecutor, told the press that he had been pursuing "the gangster element which took control [of numbers] about 1931." Dewey "expressed amazement at the spirit of fear that people have of gangsters." No one was willing to testify voluntarily, and prosecutors had to "get the evidence, accuse the victims, and wring their stories from them." One witness told Dewey that he would rather serve three years in prison and live than take the stand "against the mob."[15] Dewey may have been surprised at the unwillingness of most to stand up to the villainous Dutch Schultz, but no one else was.

In the waning days of Prohibition, white gangsters in New York diversified and began to make the word "racket" synonymous with the way things were done in a myriad of different service industries. To a remarkable extent, this criminal element had a one-size-fits-all business plan that they proceeded to put into operation. This plan was firmly rooted in the 1920s, the decade in which the business of

America had become business. It was a combination of a belief in the virtues of monopolies, derived from the American corporate world, and a reliance on violence, the utility of which had been clearly demonstrated to gangsters at least by the struggles over who would supply the city with alcohol. The model was the way in which Charles Luciano, known as "Lucky" after surviving an attempted throat-cutting when he was kidnapped in 1929, reorganized prostitution in New York City. Concentrating on the bookers, who sent prostitutes for week-long sojourns to different brothels in what Dewey called "a sort of Orpheum circuit in the business of women," gangsters introduced a system of payments and bonds from madams, designed to rationalize prostitution and hence extract more money from the business. As Luciano was quoted as saying, his intention was to create an organization that was "the same as the A&P stores are, a large syndicate."[16]

In the 1920s, the Black Kings and Queens may have used every modern labor-saving device possible, but their organizations were run like feudal fiefdoms. Schultz set out to bring the industry into the twentieth century, the century of American corporate business. Wherever possible, he wanted to pay his employees salaries, rather than letting them share in the profits by earning a percentage of the turnover. Black Kings, who were now "partners" with Schultz, were reduced to earning a weekly salary of $100 or $200. It was true that, at the end of the year, the banker was entitled to half of any profits once Schultz had deducted "expenses," but that was hardly a reassuring prospect. Bankers also had to suffer the presence of one of Schultz's employees as a "shadow," working side by side with them and continually checking the business's receipts and disbursements. If, after the figures were tallied up, the black bankers were not meeting their expected targets, they were fined.

Schultz, following in the footsteps of Hymie Kassall and his colleagues six or seven years previously, also attempted to shift the balance of numbers away from runners and collectors, usually black, and paid a commission to stationery stores, tobacconists, and the like, where the owner was usually white and paid a weekly stipend.[17] These changes turned the numbers business upside down and had a dramatic impact on a Harlem already struggling to cope with the onset of the Great Depression. The once proud Black Kings were reduced to salaried lackeys of the volatile and capricious Dutch Schultz. What was even more important, an increasing number of the people employed in the business were white, and most of the profits from numbers were now leaving Harlem. On both counts, numbers now conformed with the other businesses operating in the Black Metropolis.

A criminal combination of the size that Schultz was putting together required political protection, and that too was part of the Dutchman's plan for numbers. Harlem bankers had been paying off members of the police force and judiciary throughout the 1920s, but there is no evidence of any close links between those running numbers and politicians from that time. Schultz, though, had a more grandiose vision of what numbers could be than did the Black Kings and Queens, and knew that running an operation of the size of his numbers combination made political connections an imperative. The gangster knew exactly whom to approach. James J. Hines, born in 1877, was a former blacksmith, partial to telling audiences that he had shod some 40,000 horses. In 1912 he became the Democratic leader of the Eleventh Assembly District (on the Upper West Side and including part of Harlem), a position he would hold for a quarter of a century, and by the 1930s he was the most powerful politician in New York City. Genial, always dapperly dressed, and with a reputation as a fixer, Hines, thanks to his support of Franklin Roosevelt rather than Al Smith in 1932, became the principal dispenser of New Deal patronage in Manhattan during the 1930s.[18] As with most Tammany Hall fixers, Hines viewed cash payments as simply part of normal business practice.

At a meeting in Schultz's Upper East Side apartment that occurred just as the gangster was taking over the numbers, he explained to Hines that "I can arm [force] these different bankers in but I can't protect them in the courts, or protect them from the police making raids." George Weinberg, Bo's brother, then told Hines: "We did not mind the small arrests, but if we got any large arrests we would want them dismissed in the Magistrate's Court to show the people in Harlem that are working for us that we had the right kind of protection up there, and that we could protect them from going to jail." Weinberg then added that they needed "to stop the police from making any drives against our numbers stores which were operating wide open." According to Weinberg, Hines replied that he did not control the police, but "he still would be able to do quite a lot." The price was $1,000 a week.[19] And it was worth every penny because Hines delivered. The Tammany Hall boss arranged to have policemen transferred if they interfered with the smooth running of numbers, to have magistrates dismiss cases against controllers made by honest policemen, and to support the election of a district attorney who, in the words of Dixie Davis, "didn't bother us much."[20] The district attorney in question was William Dodge, whom Hines memorably characterized as "stupid, respectable and my man."[21] The corrupt politician was simply indispensable to Schultz: "When it got around that Schultz and Hines were behind the numbers," Davis informed his readers, "the game boomed."[22] Thomas Dewey concurred, explaining at Hines's trial in 1938 that the Tammany Hall boss was "the man who made this huge lottery enterprise possible, by providing protection."[23] And of course what flowed from Hines's connection with Schultz were contributions from numbers to Democratic Party politicians. Alex Pompez and Joe Ison discovered after the fact that they had respectively contributed $10,000 and $5,000 to William Dodge's campaign for election to district attorney in 1933. Schultz, or one of his minions, had simply ordered that the money be taken from the accounts of his "partners."[24]

Once again, however, the obituaries for the black bankers were premature. Despite all his plans, Schultz faced a real problem with his new business. With Prohibition at an end, he had to find another source of income to pay the expenses involved in maintaining his gang. Throughout 1932 and 1933, the former "Beer Baron of the Bronx" attempted to rationalize Harlem's numbers business in order to maximize profits. Unfortunately for Schultz, however, while modern business practices might have worked well for organizing the sale of artichokes or the like, numbers in Harlem proved to be rather more intransigent.[25] Not only did the black bankers, both those in "partnership" with Schultz and the few remaining independents, bristle as the gangster applied the squeeze, even eventually banding together to form a union, but ordinary residents were also unenthusiastic about Schultz's move into Harlem, many preferring to bet with independent black bankers or not to bet at all. A "social restlessness" and intensifying grassroots political activity in response to the Depression pushed Harlem's reaction beyond that produced by the earlier white efforts to take over numbers. There was a new mood in Harlem, and public demonstrations were now a commonplace. Street meetings and rallies protested unemployment, police brutality, lynchings, evictions, and inadequate relief.

Huge crowds turned out in support of the Scottsboro Boys, nine young black men accused in Alabama of raping two women. Pickets trod the pavements in front of government offices to protest cuts in personnel and pay rates, and demonstrated outside department stores on 125th Street, demanding the hiring of black staff. Crowds paraded the streets in protest, boycotts were mounted, petitions circulated. The full spectrum of black organizations participated, and collaborated, in this activity: Communist Party members rallied alongside congregants from the Abyssinian Baptist Church; supporters of the NAACP and the Urban League joined with Elks and other lodge members. The frustrations of young blacks and Hispanics would continue to intensify, eventually leading in 1935 to a further expression of anger and collaboration: a riot, in which crowds, enraged by reports that police had killed a sixteen-year-old shoplifter, ranged down 125th Street and up Seventh and Lenox avenues, smashing windows.[26] Efforts to reorganize numbers did not lead to rioting, but blacks did employ the other forms of collective action that were in the air of 1930s Harlem. And possibly for the first time in his career, Dutch Schultz found himself in a situation where there were distinct limits to what could be achieved by his usual means—which is to say, by violence.

The principal thorn in Schultz's side was Stephanie St. Clair, "Harlem's fearless policy 'Queen,'" as the *Amsterdam News* called her. A very early opponent of Schultz, she made several forays into small white-run stores and smashed plate-glass cases, ripped up policy slips, and warned the proprietors to "get out of Harlem." On another occasion, she ordered her chauffeur to drive her limousine to the corner of 125th Street and Seventh Avenue, stepped out of the car, and harangued the crowd who had gathered to listen to the soapbox orators, assailing them for backing numbers with bankers who were part of Schultz's organization. She swore that she was going to drive the white racketeer out of Harlem, even if she personally had to place a picket at every one of the Dutchman's numbers stores, from 125th Street to 155th Street. Several times, killers in the employ of Schultz almost succeeded in doing their job. St. Clair recalled one attempt where several gangsters were hunting her: "I had to hide in a cellar while the super, a friend of mine, covered me with coal." It was she who was the catalyst behind the banding together of the black bankers, and she made no secret of the fact that she was responsible for furnishing information that led the Children's Society to pursue whites who sold policy slips to minors, and for the indictment of Dutch Schultz on charges of tax evasion. Decades later, recalling her war with Dutch Schultz from 1931 to 1935, St. Clair stated simply: "It cost me a total of 820 days in jail and three-quarters of a million dollars."[27]

Things rapidly came to a head. In an eerie coincidence, the crisis in Harlem numbers banks kept apace with the even larger crisis in the nation's banks. The waning days of the Hoover administration, in February 1933, saw a rash of bank closures and enforced bank holidays. On February 24, after a run on Baltimore banks, Governor Ritchie of Maryland announced a three-day bank holiday. That evening, two jam-packed meetings, with the overflow in both cases spilling out onto the sidewalk, were held in Harlem. The first was at Schultz's headquarters at 351 Lenox and was presided over by henchmen armed with machine guns and shotguns. Here it was explained to workers in the numbers industry that the position of "numbers collector" or "runner" was to be abolished, that plays would be accepted only in stores, and that controllers were to have their percentages cut. Some intrepid collectors protested at the abolition of their livelihoods; they threatened to strike and to prevent plays from being made in the stores—a challenge that was met by the promise that anyone so foolish as to do that would be "taken for a ride." A little more than a mile away, at a Seventh Avenue ballroom, the other meeting resolved to strike against Schultz and to allow plays to be placed only with one or more of the twenty independent black bankers. As the *New York Age* noted, "The teapot is boiling and at any minute the lid may be expected to blow off."[28]

The strike began on Monday, February 27, 1933, right in the middle of the nation's banking crisis and what historian William Leuchtenburg described as "the most harrowing four months of the depression," and when there was already an acute shortage of cash in Harlem, indeed in the nation as a whole. There were doubts, therefore, as to whether any banker would be able to pay off a hit. Numbers, it seemed, was effectively crippled. Then, on Tuesday, March 7, 1933, Martin L. Harris, an independent black banker, was shot to death in his apartment, a development that caused the *Age* to predict that "Harlem will be the scene of a long drawn out gang war waged on the one side by white racketeers who are determined to continue their domination of the rich takings of the game and on the other side by the Negro bankers who are working hard to exist and to win back for themselves the game which they once controlled."[29] There would be more than enough drive-by shootings, killings, and beatings over the ensuing months to justify that prediction. The nation's banking crisis may have been stabilized in the first weeks of Roosevelt's administration, in March 1933, but the problems in Harlem numbers banks would drag on for years.

Dutch Schultz may have taken over numbers in what was effectively a bloodless coup following Thanksgiving 1931, but as the resistance to the gangster's move into Harlem coalesced around Madame Queen in the ensuing years, violence became more of a factor in the struggle for control of numbers. Chief organizer and recruiter for Schultz in Harlem was William "Bub" Hewlett, a former bondsman and "strong-arm" man, according to the *Amsterdam News*. It was Hewlett who had visited all of the black bankers and urged them to join with Schultz, making them an offer that most felt unable to refuse, although Stephanie St. Clair gave him very short shrift. Early in 1933, St. Clair made public a letter she had written to Hewlett in which "she bitterly berated Hewlett for working against the interests of Negroes in the community" and stated that she was going to run him out of Harlem too. Arrayed against Schultz were Ellsworth "Bumpy" Johnson and his friends. Johnson had been released from prison in the latter part of 1932, and at the instigation of St. Clair he started hiring thugs to stop the depredations of Schultz and his hired gun Hewlett (who a decade previously had given Bumpy Johnson his start in Harlem's protection racket). It was all more than obvious enough to make the black newspapers. In March 1933, the *Amsterdam News* reported that "the Negro operators are girding for open and violent warfare against the representatives of the white syndicate." Not only were the independent black bankers making a determined effort to lure black runners, employees, and their clients away from the "white barons," but they were also about to initiate "a policy of violence and possibly bloodshed" against the backbone of the Schultz syndicate," and the black newspaper named Hewlett as constituting a goodly part of that backbone. It is difficult now to assess how much violence did occur. Helen Lawrenson, Johnson's occasional white lover in the mid-1930s and an editor at *Vanity Fair*, wrote of Johnson in overwrought prose: "With fabulous personal courage, he shot it out in dark alleys, in the sinister dimness of streets off Lenox Avenue, against great odds, when the battle cry of the opposition was 'Get

Bumpy!'" The account by Mayme Johnson, Bumpy's widow, was, for once, slightly less breathless, but she still included some lines about the way the *New York Age* had commented "with awe" on the number of white bodies found dumped in Mount Morris Park at this time.[30] Perhaps. Bloodshed was undoubtedly a feature of this struggle, although it probably was not as decisive as either the black newspapers or Bumpy Johnson's lovers suggested. Violence, as was so often the case in Harlem, formed part of the backdrop to what was occurring; it was other factors, other tactics pursued by the various protagonists, that were going to resolve the dispute over the control of numbers in the Black Metropolis.

Schultz's heavy-handed attempt to squeeze every last cent out of Harlem had stirred up a hornet's nest. Each side in the battle over numbers furiously informed to the authorities about the doings of the other, and the furor in Harlem was such that eventually the police had to intercede. On March 15, 1933, the police, acting "on a tip believed to have been furnished by Negro rivals" (St. Clair several years later told the *Amsterdam News* that she had leaked the address to the authorities), staged a spectacular raid on the Schultz headquarters at 550 West 146th Street, an operation that netted $2,164 in cash, more than ten million blank policy slips, and fourteen arrests. The apartment, "luxuriously furnished with desks, chairs and adding machines," according to the *Amsterdam News*'s reporter, was "said to be the clearing house for all policy rings operated by the gangster in Brooklyn, Queens, the Bronx and Harlem." As the *New York Age* commented, "The fact that the white race now enjoys quite a monopoly on the game was easily seen in this instance as all of the fourteen persons, all men, arrested at the time were white."[31]

The struggle over numbers in Harlem was an all-out war, with every possible means that could give one or the other side the edge being brought into play. In late March 1933, according to the *Amsterdam News,* the "white racketeers who control the game" held "a downtown conference from which all Negro operators were barred." As a result, it was announced on Saturday, April 1, 1933, that the daily number would no longer be worked out from race-track results, but instead would be based on the Cincinnati Clearing House figures. The switch, the *News* reported, "was advertised on printed cards distributed throughout Harlem over the week-end." Simultaneously, the Cincinnati Clearing House figures, "here-tofore unknown," began appearing on the front page and financial section of two daily newspapers.

Black bankers were immediately suspicious, and most persisted in using racetrack results. To many African Americans, it was clear enough what was going on: somehow the white gangsters were able to influence the Cincinnati numbers and planned to use this to their advantage. The *Amsterdam News*'s informant claimed that once the black bankers were "inveigled" into using the new method, "they will be methodically broken by their white competitors, who will scatter heavy bets among them on 'fixed' numbers." Once the black bankers were eliminated, the racketeers "will then prey upon the playing public, taking all bets and allowing only lightly played numbers to appear." For the *Amsterdam News,* it was "the most gi-gantic swindle ever planned in the policy racket." Interestingly, this story in the *News* was one of very few in the New York papers that linked developments in Harlem with what was occurring elsewhere in the country. According to the reporter, "A similar change in the paying-off system in Washington recently forced all Negro bankers out of the game in the capital," where numbers was now controlled "by a small group of white racketeers." Similarly, he claimed to have evidence of "an attempt on the part of white racketeers to control the policy game in Winston-Salem, N.C., where 'hits' are paid on the butter and egg totals in the Chicago market."[32]

For all the mayhem and violence, or even the attempt to hijack and rig the game, the deciding factor in determining the outcome of the struggle was always going to be black public opinion. One of the more noticeable features of the writing on gangsters and organized crime—be it in contemporary newspapers, memoirs, and autobiographies, or in subsequent histories (histories, it should be added, that are often described as "popular" or "informal")—is the way the story is told in an old-fashioned, top-down manner. The criminal world is rendered as a pyramid, and while those at the peak have ideas, ambitions, and volition, those who occupy the broad base, whether soldiers or customers of the enterprise, are seen as passive ciphers simply doing what they are told to do. Disputes between rival leaders are portrayed as clashes of wills that are usually resolved by violence. To be sure, there is often much merit in this approach: the struggles of twentieth-century gangsters may, perhaps, be the closest modern parallel to the doings of kings, queens, and feudal lords that used to be the stuff of history. Prisoners of our sources, we have certainly at times relied on this mode of history in our telling of the story of numbers in Harlem. Yet, palpably, the explanatory power of such a narrative is insufficient to explain what was going on in Harlem in 1933. It was the ordinary men and women of the Black Metropolis who made numbers so lucrative, and both sides in the struggle for control needed to court and mobilize this group in order to ensure the success of their businesses. For just about the first time in the history of New York City, the opinion of ordinary African Americans mattered— and to a quite remarkable extent, both sides tried to make their play through the black newspapers.

Stephanie St. Clair certainly recognized the centrality of the black newspapers to the struggle. Some five years later, in 1938, she told an *Amsterdam News* reporter about her concern that "she was not able to get as much propaganda in the papers as she had hoped." Energetic as ever, the Numbers Queen apparently began negotiations to publish a paper of her own, but nothing came of her plans.[33] St. Clair's expectations of the black press must have been inordinately high; quite clearly, the sympathies of most reporters working for black newspapers lay with the independent black bankers. Even Fred Moore's *New York Age*, which in the 1920s had excoriated anyone and everyone associated with the industry, conceded that Black Kings and Queens were preferable to white gangsters. As this black newspaper pointed out, money from numbers had been kept in Harlem, with bankers playing a prominent and charitable role in the black community. This was little short of nostalgia, a view of black bankers that must have seemed scarcely credible to anyone who had read the *Age* through the 1920s.[34]

Not surprisingly, however, the independent black bankers took every opportunity to get their story across. The "Big Shot" of the Harlem bankers gave the *Amsterdam News* what its reporter thought was "perhaps the first newspaper interview ever granted a reporter in the history of the game here." According to this unnamed insider, the Harlem union, after an eight-week underground recruiting campaign, now included all the major black bankers and most of the smaller operators as well, who, between them, employed roughly 1,100 people. It was expected that the union would establish a central fund to pay off all the bets of bankers who were "hit" too heavily and to create a "central bureau" which would make "announcements on the change of race tracks on which all bets are paid." The union had already "established a propaganda office from which it will conduct a program of 'education' in its efforts to get community support in its drive against the stores which take policy bets." It anticipated the Harlem-wide distribution of 75,000 copies of a pamphlet explaining the union's case. "You know this is a Negro game in a Negro neighborhood," the banker declared, "and it has been carried on by Negroes for twelve years without outside groups." The black banker made it absolutely clear that the union was going to appeal to blacks not to play policy in the stores, and if storekeepers carried on writing numbers their businesses would be boycotted.[35]

For white bankers who were trying to persuade ordinary Harlemites to entrust them with their hard-earned dimes and quarters, this press campaign was a public relations disaster. As early as August 1932, there were rumors around Harlem that a reporter for a black newspaper had been paid $500 for not writing any more stories about the numbers.[36] By early 1933, the situation had gone well beyond the point at which attempts to stanch the flow of information would have any effect. In an extraordinary move, white bankers responded to the press interview with the black banker and "issued a statement taking issue with contentions advanced by the leader of the colored operators in a recently published interview." According to the white bankers, they had been "unfairly attacked by the new Harlem policy union." Not only had whites "often come to the aid of distressed Negro bankers," but, unlike the black bankers, they always paid off on big hits. Moreover, their statement claimed, they employed "thirty-five Negro girls working regularly, all of them making an excellent wage," as well as "a large number of Negro men and women, all of whom we pay regularly and well." The "downtown syndicate refused to concede the Negro union's contention that the policy game is a 'Negro game,'" and concluded with a rhetorical flourish and a barely veiled threat: it suggested that violence was hardly the best way to sort out the industry, but warned that "if it is warfare that is wanted, then we are prepared to protect the interest of the vast army of people who play numbers."[37] This must be one of the very few occasions in U.S. history when a bunch of white gangsters felt compelled not just to issue a press release, but to issue a press release to an African American newspaper.

What made things much more difficult for Dutch Schultz was that, since January 1933, he had been in hiding in order to avoid tax evasion charges that the persistent Dewey wanted to pursue in court. Indeed, Schultz's absence led the *New York Age* to speculate in June 1933 that there was "a new leader who has gathered the fast waning forces of the former beer czar." It did not name this new figure, but the *Age* report was in fact referring to Dixie Davis. The black newspaper was on firmer footing when it detailed other developments in numbers. According to the *Age,* the "racketeers" had reorganized the business, bringing all the banks together into the syndicate, or "combination"—a consolidation that "cut down overhead." "Colored girls" who had been working in numbers establishments for about $50 a week "were replaced by white girls who are working for less than half that amount," a salary reduction justified by the reduction in the chances of arrest, due to political protection.[38]

The intention of the syndicate was "to make the policy game as popular through New York State as it is in Harlem." After the spectacular raid on Schultz's headquarters in Harlem, the center of his operations had moved "to a point just outside the city limits," about twenty miles from Harlem; there, "they are safely ensconced in a large garage," with six banks operating on the second floor. Every day, cars "carrying hundreds of thousands of policy slips and the money they represent" made their way to this building, "to the unconcern of the rural cop whose troubles are limited to speeding motorists and occasional smash-ups."[39]

All through the second half of 1933, Harlem was in turmoil as the war over the control of numbers continued. In early July, a "conference of colored numbers bankers and collectors" aimed at diverting "thousands of dollars in Harlem numbers profits from the pockets of white downtown numbers bankers" was to have been held in the banquet hall of the Imperial Elks' Lodge on 129th Street—but the arrival of police, apparently tipped off by a phone call from "white stool pigeons," put an end to the meeting before it could start. In August a meeting was held at the Dunbar Palace on 139th Street and Seventh Avenue. A very light-colored man chaired the meeting and began by deploring "the fact that Negroes were spending their money with the Jews—every cent of which he said went to the Bronx afterwards." All agreed that the press was "the best 'weapon' possible to be used in defense of the Negro collectors." According to the *Age* reporter, "a local contemporary and a Communistic publication were repeatedly cited as the organs which could be used in the effort, for a small fee." He summed up the mood of the meeting: "Are we going to stand by and be licked—or are we going to get up and fight?"[40]

By January 1934, Schultz had spent a year hiding from the authorities, mostly in New York City, and he was still struggling to bring the numbers business into line. At a mass meeting of controllers held that month in the combination's Harlem headquarters at 351 Lenox Avenue, Schultz explained to a mostly black audience the way things were going to be. As one African American controller later testified, "He told the controllers that the combination would get their own men if we did not accept a cut in our take from 10 per cent to 5 per cent." As the *New York Times* reported nearly a year later, "The Negro controllers who supervised collections rebelled against Schultz's cutting their split," and promptly called a strike. The numbers business dwindled to a trickle. Collectors out on bail did not show up in court, and their bonds, paid for by the combination, were forfeited. It took only a week before Schultz and the racketeers were forced to yield, and abandoned their plan to cut the controllers' percentage of the take. A genuinely impressed Dixie Davis later commented, "They were the only people I ever knew who had the nerve to stand up and fight the Dutchman."[41]

Even though Dutch Schultz was rebuffed, and still (as some of colleagues were wont to describe it) "on the lam," a predicament making elaborate subterfuge a daily necessity, he still persisted in trying to extract more money from Harlem. The final element in his business plan for numbers was to eliminate, wherever possible, any element of chance for the banker as a factor in the daily number. Rigging the system and controlling which particular number won would enable the gangsters to extract even more money out of their already lucrative enterprise. They needed to devise something rather more subtle than the scheme of April 1933, when there had been a sudden switch to the Cincinnati Clearing House as the source of the daily number.

Otto Berman, universally known as Abadaba, was an official handicapper with access to the computation rooms at some racetracks, and he was also, in Thomas Dewey's somewhat grudging words, "a mathematical wizard." Berman devised for Dutch Schultz a way of controlling the last digit in the daily number. George Weinberg would collect from all the banks details of every bet of fifty cents or more. Then, to cite an example that Dewey used in

court, if the first two numbers on a given day were 1 and 7, Weinberg would calculate which numbers in the 170s would damage
them the most. If there was a lot of money on 175 and 178—and,
as it happened, 177, a number of some religious significance, was
always popular and heavily played—then Weinberg would phone
Berman and say: "No five, seven or eight." Berman would take the
totals from the first six races, compute what was needed to make
the seventh-race odds give a last digit that was anything but 5, 7, or
8, and then make a series of last-minute bets at the track on the seventh race to get the desired result. Berman's system was complicated, did not always come off, and could be used only for slightly
less than half of the year, but it made a lot of money for the combination. Some indication of how highly the gangsters valued these
manipulations was that, at the height of the Depression, the nor-
mally parsimonious Schultz was paying Abadaba Berman $10,000
a week.[42]

Members of the combination did their best to keep this system a
secret, involving as few people as possible in the collecting of information on the bets that had been made on any given day; but, inevitably, rumors swirled all over Harlem. In January 1935, the *New York
Age* conducted its own "secret investigation" and printed a front-
page story about the "vicious number-fixing system" that was "responsible for the series of 'funny' numbers which have been appearing daily in Harlem during the past few weeks." The paper detailed
the manipulations occurring at the track, and claimed that the
gangsters "were then able to not only control the final number so
that the racketeers would not be hit too heavy on any number, but
were also able to place bets, through their agents, with unsuspect-
ing Negro banks taking back figure plays." As a result, "the Negro

independent policy bankers were being heavily hit for the third figure." The following week the *Age* reported that the racketeers "have been actively engaged in attempting to counteract the report."[43]

As became clear from Dewey's investigations a few years later, the black newspaper essentially was right in what it had printed. The situation was a replay of what had happened in the nineteenth century: when white criminals controlled the game, sooner or later they managed to rig the system, and do so mostly at the expense of ordinary African Americans. But perhaps the most revealing element in the *Age* story was what the paper regarded as corroborative of its argument. According to the paper, the "regular numbers player" was feeling the effects of the fixing. Indeed, "numerous players who, heretofore, were fairly consistently lucky in 'hitting' have suddenly found it almost impossible to guess right and certain combinations which are generally regarded as 'regulars' have failed to show, in most cases the last figure being the one to 'spoil the play.'"[44] Absurd as this sentence is in terms of logic and probability, it accurately represented the way most Harlem residents thought numbers worked. Even the *Age,* as staunch and persistent an opponent as numbers ever had, simply accepted this way of viewing the world.

By the second half of 1934, with Schultz still in hiding, Stephanie St. Clair openly taunting him, and the black controllers having successfully struck against him, the Dutchman's combination was in considerable disarray. Keen to imbue events with a larger meaning, the *Amsterdam News* claimed later, in March 1935, that Schultz's combination had broken up when he "tried to draw a color line," and there is considerable truth to this claim. As was well known, Schultz was contemptuous of his black "partners." Several had never even met him; others were frisked none too gently and relieved of all weaponry, when summoned to the Dutchman's "penthouse hideaway." Such behavior was symptomatic of the disdain with which the gangster treated all his black employees, whom he replaced with whites at every opportunity. Little wonder, then, that as soon as they could, "influential colored bankers and controllers" wriggled free from the racketeer's grasp.[45] Dutch Schultz made a fortune out of numbers and changed forever the way the gambling game was run in Harlem—but, in the end, it was also Harlem, and the bitter refusal of so many of its inhabitants to acknowledge his dominion over them, that would lead to his bloody demise.

8

OF BANKS AND BANKERS

Oh, you won't be in the swim unless you get in the game.
—Numbers runner overheard in a hardware store
on Lenox Avenue, *New York Age,* July 3, 1926

For all the modernity of the way in which the numbers business was conducted, there was a brittleness at its core. It was as though blacks in Harlem were striving too hard, too eager to show that they were part of twentieth-century America. Indeed, perhaps the most intriguing aspect of numbers was the way in which, right from the start, organizers of the game deliberately attached it to the coattails of the city's financial system. This was apparent not only in the method of calculating each day's number from Clearing House and (later, in the 1930s) New York Stock Exchange figures, but also in the very *language* of numbers—the quick adoption of the term "Black Wednesday" to label that calamitous day in November 1931, and especially the use of the term "banker" to describe the people running the game. Even sworn opponents of what many regarded as the scam—such as the *New York Age*—spoke of "bankers," and of players who "invested" their money on a number, thus avoiding the more pejorative term "gambled." The denizens of Wall Street and members of the boards of the city's great financial institutions were probably as indifferent to such borrowings and imitations as they were careless of the concerns and good will of their African American customers. But whether this was so or not, the aligning of numbers with such august establishments as banks, no matter how tenuous the links, struck a chord with the tens of thousands of migrants from the South and the West Indies who were striving to remake their lives.

The designation "banker" may well have predated the invention of numbers in the early 1920s, but the term still had a special resonance for Harlem's residents. Throughout the 1920s and 1930s, New York City had no banks owned or managed by African Americans. In 1922, Banking Commissioner McLaughlin had encouraged a group of African American businessmen to apply for a bank charter, which he was keen to grant, but nothing transpired. Yet despite the absence of black-run institutions, thousands of ordinary residents of Harlem opened and used savings accounts in existing banks, quietly ignoring the fact that these institutions were staffed entirely by whites. By 1927, the Harlem Post Office's Savings Unit (in those days, the U.S. Postal Service offered interest-bearing savings accounts to its customers) had more than $1 million on deposit in some 11,000 accounts belonging to blacks. At the same time, it was estimated that Harlem blacks had another $16 million deposited in savings accounts in banks all over Manhattan. On a Saturday night in early 1927, Harry Pace, president of the Northeastern Life Insurance Company, visited the bank at the corner of 135th Street and Seventh Avenue. The line of eighty-six black male and female customers, which had begun forming half an hour before the 8:30 P.M. opening, now doubled back on itself and snaked around the corner into 135th Street. A few days later, Pace visited the College Station Post Office, which served Harlem. The recently enlarged lobby "was a seething mass of colored folk who waited patiently in line to reach the Postal Savings window." In both cases, the clients were all black, but invariably the teller who served them was white.[1]

Many blacks who needed bank services had to trek considerable distances to institutions on the margins of Harlem, down on 125th Street, or even further afield. Indeed, one of the surprising incidental things we uncovered as we trawled through tens of thousands of Manhattan court cases from the 1920s was the number of Harlemites who had accounts, often containing hundreds or even thousands of dollars, in banks located at Columbus Circle (59th Street) or even as far south as 34th Street.[2] Despite the indifferent service provided by white-run banks, many Harlem blacks yearned to be part of modern America and to have their own accounts.

More often than not, depositing money in a bank or in a savings account at the Post Office proved to be a daunting procedure for Harlem residents; borrowing money to open or expand a business, or indeed for any purpose, was almost an impossibility for African Americans. In order to understand the obstacles in the way of ambitious blacks, one must shuck off contemporary understandings of banking shaped by the recent decades of easy credit, when seemingly anyone capable of signing her or his name could obtain a bank loan. Between the wars, banks were for the most part conservative and cautious, and bankers were respectable and staid members of society—hence the shock of the Great Depression, when banks collapsed all across the nation. In those days, what we would now label "racial profiling" was normal business practice. As the *Amsterdam News* editorialized in 1931, banks did not "readily extend credit to Negro depositors," even those who met "every requirement demanded, except that of a white skin."[3]

This inability to borrow money was a matter of some importance. When Ulysses S. Poston, writing in 1927, called for a commercial bank to be established in Harlem, he noted that almost all businesses in that part of the city were owned, controlled, and run by
whites, and attributed this fact to the absence of a financial institution run by African Americans. According to Poston, "The real
cause of the death of Negro business and commerce is due to the
lack of financial institutions owned and controlled by Negroes, and
primarily interested in the development of Negro business." Undoubtedly Poston overstated his case, but it was undeniable that
the difficulty of obtaining credit inhibited the growth of black
business. On the eve of America's entry into World War II, almost
fifteen years later, Walter Chivers, a black columnist writing for the
Atlanta Daily World, commented: "I remember hearing one of the
soundest Negro business men tell of the hardships encountered by
qualified and ambitious Negroes in getting business credit."[4]

Something of the way in which banking worked in Harlem was
revealed in September 1928, when the Dunbar National Bank
opened. The bank was devised by John D. Rockefeller Jr.; its elegant
premises were located at Eighth Avenue and 150th Street, on the
ground floor of the Dunbar Apartments, Rockefeller's experiment
in housing for respectable African Americans; and it was an institution designed to cater "particularly for the residents of Harlem."
One of the advertised claims of the new bank was that the staff
would treat customers "with all the courtesy that is accorded to the
most influential depositors at downtown banks," an aim based on
the assumption that dealing with other banks was at best a trial for
blacks. Not, of course, that Harlem's residents needed any convincing of what, for them, was one of the simple facts of life. A spokes-
man for the bank went on to detail a particular facet of the dis-

crimination confronted by blacks. Apparently, the normal practice in Harlem was that individuals "finding it necessary to raise mortgages on property for some reason or other are frequently compelled to pay exorbitant bonuses, sometimes amounting to 25 per cent." Once the Dunbar's mortgage department was established, the bank "will be prepared to mortgage up to fifty per cent of the value of the property without bonuses of any sort." Loans would be for five years, but they could be renewed.[5] Other banks were slow, exceedingly slow, to follow the Dunbar National Bank's example in employing African Americans, let alone in treating their African American customers any better.

There was always a certain tentativeness to the way in which blacks embraced the twentieth-century world of modern banking, an ambivalence due to more than simply the inferior treatment meted out by the white-owned banks they patronized. Sweet Cider, protagonist of Claire M. Halley's story printed in the *Amsterdam News* in 1927, was hardly the only Harlem resident who mistrusted banks. Rumors circulated widely in Harlem that white-owned banks would not allow African Americans to open accounts, or that if blacks did deposit money in a white-owned bank, a sum would be routinely deducted from their account each month. As ever, black confidence men, predators who lurked around the edges of Harlem's African American dream, were attuned to the fault lines in black society and ruthlessly exploited such beliefs. At the heart of every scam practiced by black con men was the act of convincing the mark to make the journey to her or his bank for the purpose of withdrawing funds.

Early on a Saturday evening in November 1930, John Richardson, twenty-two and unemployed, was strolling along Eighth Avenue between 127th and 128th streets, when he was accosted by George

Webb. Webb claimed to be from Mississippi and sought Richardson's assistance in finding his uncle. While they were talking, Henry Geter walked by and Webb called him over supposedly in order to enlist his help. Apparently Webb's father had died and left $1,700 to Webb's uncle, a fact that Webb demonstrated by flashing a roll of notes that he had in his pocket. Geter quickly warned Webb, his fellow conspirator, "You should not show money like that because some one might knock you over the head and take it away and it is a good thing you met this gentleman and I." Webb then explained why he was carrying the money with him: "My white folks in Mississippi told me not to deposit my money in the bank in New York," because "the white folks will take some money out of it every month." Geter objected that this was not so, that, in fact, the bank would "add interest to your money every three months."[6]

Six weeks later, when the assistant district attorney questioned Richardson, he asked the victim whether he had contributed anything to the conversation at all. Richardson replied that he "just stood there and listened for a while." Apparently, Webb and Geter kept up a nonstop patter. Webb refused to believe that whites would pay interest on a black's money in a bank account, arguing that "colored folks in Harlem haven't got no money or no place to stay," and that "they live in basements and holes and have not got any clothes to wear." Geter countered this assertion by pointing out that he had on good clothes, and pulled a dollar bill out of his pocket to demonstrate that he was not a bum. He then turned to the mark and said, "Perhaps Mr. Richardson has some money too to show that he is not a bum either." Richardson had only fifty cents in his pocket, but he blurted out, "I have got money otherwise." It turned out that the money was in two bank accounts, but of course Webb, the supposedly artless Mississippian, claimed he'd never seen a bank book, which he kept referring to as a "money tablet." Indeed, Webb offered to pay twenty-five dollars to anyone who would show him a bank book. Here Geter took Richardson aside and muttered, "Mr. Richardson you might show him the bank book and let him give you twenty-five dollars because he is so dumb he will give it to anybody if you do not accept it." Once Richardson had, as he thought, made some easy money, he was keen to make more and agreed to meet the pair of con men on the following Monday morning on a Harlem street corner in order to help Webb deposit his money in a bank account.[7]

As they traveled to the bank about thirty-six hours later, Webb kept on voicing his skepticism: they were trying "to April fool him," for "colored folks have no money in white folks' bank," and Richardson's bank books were only grocery bill books. Webb then stated that he would pay $100 if someone could "prove to me they can draw money out of the white folks money house without being locked up." Richardson then proceeded to take $70 out of his account at the North River Savings Bank on 34th Street and $79 out of his account at the Greenwich Savings Bank at 36th Street and Broadway. Now apparently satisfied, Webb turned to the mark and said "Mr. Richardson you take my money to the bank and make the deposit." But first, for safety's sake, Webb insisted that Richardson put his money with Webb's money inside a handkerchief. Once all the money was secure in the handkerchief, Webb placed the handkerchief underneath Richardson's shirt and told him to go and make the deposit, after which they would all meet up again at the subway station at 135th Street and Lenox Avenue. Of course, as soon as Richardson opened up the handkerchief in the bank he discovered nothing but newspaper. Although the pair of con men were caught and pleaded to petit larceny, Richardson never saw a cent of his $149 again.[8]

In Harlem, such cons were a commonplace. Roland Wilson accosted Franklin Mathews, a porter, on the street in September 1929, claiming to be a recent migrant, to have an inheritance of $900, and to have been told that "he couldn't put his money in any white bank and get it out when he felt like and he was afraid he'd get kicked out if he entered a white man's bank." Matthews withdrew $200 from the Union Dime Savings Bank at 40th Street and Sixth Avenue to show Wilson that it was easy enough and, of course, lost it all to the black con artist. A few months later, James Hurtt, claiming to be from Oklahoma and supposedly fearing "that it was dangerous to trust a white man with money in New York," convinced David Diaz to take $460.48 out of his account at the same Union Dime Bank, money that the unsuspecting victim never saw again.[9] What was telling in all these cases was both how ready black people were, back in the 1920s and 1930s, to mistrust, even fear, white banks, and how eagerly the marks, usually only a year or two out of Mississippi or South Carolina themselves, tried to demonstrate to the "green" migrants their skill in dealing with banks and, by implication, modern city life.

Contrasting with the usual image of Harlem is the fact that a surprising number of residents of the Black Metropolis invested in stocks and bonds. As is well known, Marcus Garvey raised scores of thousands of dollars by selling stock in the Black Star Line to ordinary African Americans in the United States and the Caribbean, but the situation went well beyond this. Reading through the documentary record of Harlem between the wars, one continually comes across stray references to blacks owning shares. In March 1930, a Harlem man on probation and his wife were interviewed by a probation officer. The man was hopelessly in debt, owing money to stores all over Harlem, and was always on the look out for the quick fix to his problems. He had managed to obtain five days' work in the previous week, but to the horror of his probation officer, had bought three shares in the *Amsterdam News* at $5 a share. Moreover, he was contemplating further purchases in the stock of the black newspaper, and was also thinking about investing in the Harlem Broadcasting Company. The probation officer firmly reminded his charge "that a man in his financial situation ought to put any available cash he might have in a savings bank where it would be safe and not with a company which might depreciate and cause him to lose the few dollars he had accumulated."[10] Yet of course all the black man wanted was to participate in the American Dream, to make money, and, incidentally, to do so in a distinctly black way. After all, how many denizens of Wall Street were likely to invest in such uptown enterprises as the *News* or the Harlem Broadcasting Company?

As was always the case in Harlem, black con men were hovering, quick to take advantage of the gullible who had little understanding of the brave new world of stocks and bonds. Kemel Baxter chased ambulances in the Black Metropolis on commission for a downtown lawyer; he was a minister who preached at Liberty Hall, the United Negro Improvement Association (UNIA) building on 138th Street between Lenox and Seventh avenues, and was also a member of the association, but the ethics of some of his money-making activities were, at best, questionable. In the latter part of 1925, he solicited Harlemites to invest in Liberty Hall Apartments, a cooperative apartment house that was supposedly to be built on the site of Liberty Hall. Carthila Johnson, a seamstress, made cash payments to Baxter totaling $479, and also gave him jewelry, cut glass, and tapestries valued at some $332. Baxter claimed that he was working on commission for William Sherill, then vice president of the UNIA, that he'd paid him the money, and that he was now simply waiting for Sherill to deliver the bond that Johnson had purchased. When the deputy assistant district attorney finally managed to contact Sherill while he was in New York and arranged for him to make a statement in 1932, some three years after Johnson had instituted legal proceedings, Sherill testified that the UNIA had no such project and was not selling bonds. The then former UNIA official could only conclude that "I guess he must have just concocted that story." Needless to say, Carthila Johnson never recovered any of her money.

The words "Wall Street" acted as a talisman that carried considerable weight in Harlem. Arthur Millwood, one of the Black Metropolis's most notorious con men, was certainly aware of their power. In August 1924, Millwood started chatting to Louis Blenman, a laborer originally from Barbados, as they were walking back from the Carpentier-Tunney fight at the Polo Grounds, along with a friend of Millwood's. After a general conversation about the fight, Millwood and his confederate confided to Blenman that they had made a great deal of money by following the advice of Professor Balenger, a native African, who possessed "supernatural powers and was their financial adviser." Balenger had been brought to America by "some prominent men of Wall Street," who took up most of his time; but as Blenman was their newfound friend, they agreed to introduce him to the professor. Difficult as it may be now to understand, this subterfuge succeeded time and time again. Blenman's interest was sufficiently piqued by Millwood's spiel for him to go to his bank at 116th and Madison and withdraw his and his wife's life savings of $675. Six years later, Millwood was still playing variations on the same theme. In May 1930, he convinced Herbert Reid, an expressman, "that he knew a certain African who was making white men rich," and he relieved his mark of some $1,695.[11]

As we saw in Chapter 3, Millwood trod a broad path through interwar Harlem, defrauding a string of black men out of tens of thousands of dollars. Many blacks regarded any association with Wall Street, no matter how tenuous, with a considerable amount of awe, knowing that the world was rigged, yet, perhaps naïvely, believing that, for once, they too could be in the know, able to take advantage of inside information, in the same fashion as had the gray-suited white men of finance from downtown.

Inevitably, the thousands of black migrants from the U.S. South and the West Indies—often fleeing the most impoverished of lives, jamming into northern cities in the years after World War I, looking to get ahead economically but still attached to the cultural baggage they had brought with them—created strains that would fissure and, in time, transform urban black life. Nowhere was this more so than in Black Manhattan. Harlem in the 1920s and 1930s was a constantly surprising mixture of sophistication and naïveté, an astonishing place that at one and the same time could produce the hit musical *Shuffle Along* ("a honey of a show," according to Langston Hughes) and where Moms Mabley could try out her folksy stage persona; a place where a black man could make a living as a tropical-fish salesman catering to a black clientele and where Lillian Harris or Pig Foot Mary amassed a small fortune selling pig's feet, chitterlings, corn, and hogmaw at the corner of 135th Street and Lenox Avenue; a place where one could hear the cries of a street vendor and the strains of Duke Ellington playing his "Black and Tan Fantasy" at the Cotton Club. It was the landscape in which numbers had been created and where the gambling game had flourished so vigorously that many of its most prominent residents were linked to what was an illegal business. In order to succeed, bankers, many of whom had started off as penniless migrants, needed to be not only attuned to the New World a-coming but also firmly rooted in the culture of ordinary African American men and women who invested their nickels and dimes searching for the realization of their dreams.

Writing in his column in the *Atlanta Daily World* in 1941, Walter Chivers pointed out that setting up as a banker was "an avenue of large income for the more intelligent, adventurous, and astute, of the Negro masses." Indeed, "this type of banking is an even more lucrative business than legitimate banking because it is free from legalistic controls." As a result, those "with real business ability and acumen accumulate big money hurriedly." In the world of mirrors and distortions that constituted Jim Crow America, numbers banking was one of the very few avenues open to talented young blacks who wanted to get ahead; and as Chivers noted of the bankers themselves, "because of their wealth they soon develop prestige equivalent among Negroes to that of licensed stock brokers among white people."[12]

Yet black numbers "bankers," whose workplace, after all, was the passageways of apartment buildings and the streets of Harlem, were rather less forbidding figures than their better-known namesakes. Indeed, sociability was one of the key features of the numbers in Harlem. Blacks may have placed their own individual bets, but the amount of discussion and talk about which number to back, or who had won yesterday, or entirely peripheral matters, at times made the whole business seem like a collective enterprise. In sharp contrast to the austere figure of the downtown white banker, one of the marks of a successful Harlem banker was his or her approachability.

Almost inevitably, in a context in which sources of credit for African Americans were virtually nonexistent, black bankers, particularly the Kings and Queens—among the very few Harlem residents with ready access to large amounts of cash—made small loans, often for gambling on numbers but also for other purposes as well.[13] Basil Paterson, a Democratic Party politician in Harlem in the 1950s and 1960s, a New York State senator, and an unsuccessful candidate for lieutenant-governor in 1970, is probably best known nowadays for being the father of David Paterson, the current governor of the State of New York. In 1971, in an interview with a reporter from the *New York Times,* the elder Paterson stated that "the numbers man is often the one to whom people go for loans—and get them with no interest, or little interest." The wily politician, who certainly knew how things worked above 125th Street, then added: "It would be interesting to find out how many businesses in Harlem survived because some numbers man loaned the money, knowing the fellow who borrowed was reliable and that he would get it back."[14] And of course Paterson was right. The problem for the historian is that transactions based on a handshake and a banker's peeling off of a few notes from his wad of "walking-around" money were designed not to leave a paper trail and are difficult to recover. But there is evidence that suggests something of the importance of this role of black bankers.

As in so many things, Casper Holstein was the archetypal banker in this regard. The Bolito King was celebrated in Harlem for having "helped hundreds of enterprises, even against good judgment, because he wanted to see Negroes prosper in business and lift the next generation upward economically." According to the *Amsterdam News* in 1936, Holstein contributed to the financing of "everything from hot dog stands to night clubs to steamship lines, and when these ventures went on the rocks he was no Shylock, demanding his pound of flesh, according to the testimony of many Harlemites." To a lesser extent, this was true of the other Harlem bankers as well. Almost to a man or woman, Harlem bankers were what was then known as "race men," champions of black enterprise and fervent believers in the importance of the black community in northern cities. They also had deep pockets. That is why the white takeover of numbers in Harlem during some of the worst years of the Depression was such a disaster for the Black Metropolis. When Dutch Schultz put many bankers, now referred to as his "partners," on a salary, rather than allowing them simply to continue pocketing the profits, even the *New York Age* was forced to admit that Harlem was considerably worse off as a result. Under the new regime, if a banker wanted to distribute "handouts," that money came not out of the operating expenses of the numbers bank, as it used to, but from a very ungenerous salary. The *Age* reporter readily conceded that before the advent of Schultz, black bankers used their profits "to invest money and liberally spend their funds in charity work." And, he added, "it must be said that they were all charitable."[15]

Part of the problem for the black bankers who were successful, the ones who became Kings and Queens, was that when times were good, they simply made too much money. The difficulties of laundering money, of legitimizing wealth derived from criminal enterprise, are familiar enough to us today from *The Godfather* (1972), *The Godfather Part II* (1974), and, more recently, *The Wire* (2002–2008), but they were rather more novel for African Americans in the 1920s and 1930s. Never before had so many blacks—and it should be remembered that this was occurring to a greater or lesser extent in every city in the country—made their fortunes so quickly. Many had little education, were hardly well-equipped to take advantage of their newfound wealth, and had to learn very quickly and on their feet how to avoid some of the traps. After the federal prosecutions of Wilfred Brunder, Henry Miro, and others for income tax evasion, any sensible Harlem banker promptly cleaned up his or her accounting practices. As one former banker told Walter Chivers in 1941, he always "kept his income taxes paid, thereby eliminating any interference from the federal government."[16] Ironically, in Depression America those who made their money from criminal enterprises were probably more assiduous about paying taxes than many businessmen with more legitimate sources of income.

To be sure, black bankers managed to differentiate themselves sharply from their white counterparts. This they did by lavishing money on ostentatious lifestyles, thus opening up a path that would be trod by drug dealers in the second half of the twentieth century. According to a reporter for the *Chicago Defender*, Henry Miro, just like Wilfred Brunder, "cut a wide swath in the Harlem community with outward evidences of ready money, such as flashy clothes, fine cars, obvious jewelry, palatial living quarters and generally sporty surroundings." Apparently, Miro "purchased several expensive automobiles" and at least thirty fine suits a year. Similarly, Marcelino, one of the first of the Black Kings to make a fortune, was not shy about displaying "his expensive tastes," and was well-known for "the numerous ten dollar bills which he handed out as tips to cabaret entertainers who caught his fancy, and . . . the thousands of dollars which he distributed to friends and beggars."[17] But consumption on this scale was inconsequential in comparison to the income pouring in from numbers.

Money from numbers was invested in a myriad of different enterprises. Holstein bought apartment buildings; Miro at the time of one of his court appearances had some $55,000 invested in mortgages; another banker opened a grocery store. As one reporter writing about Harlem for the *Pittsburgh Courier* claimed, "It was a way of pooling the wealth of the race for the benefit of the masses, because any number of Negroes found employment in these enterprises—employment that they could not get from the whites." Another way of putting it was that black bankers partially filled the vacuum left by the failure of banks to service Harlem's credit needs.

Yet banking in this more traditional sense was not necessarily the *métier* of the numbers bankers. What was interesting here was the way in which black bankers, extremely astute at making money from numbers, often came unstuck in their investments. Marcelino bought a share of a gold mine in the Cuban hinterland; but when he visited his native island in order to see how his money was being used, he discovered that the enterprise did not exist. This and other instances led a *Courier* reporter to suggest that Marcelino's bankruptcy was due "in a big way" to "his commercial and industrial ventures, real and imaginary."[18] One must also remember that Harlem was a poor area suffering greatly from the Depression, and this fact made it inevitable—even if we set to one side deliberate fraud—that investing in anything in the Black Metropolis was a high-risk enterprise. As we have seen, Casper Holstein was a driven man, struggling with demons of his own that made him almost disdainful of the bottom line on a balance sheet; through a combination of philanthropy and his form of "banking," he managed to reduce one of the largest fortunes ever amassed by an African American to nothing in a very short time.

For all its glaring inefficiencies and shortcomings as a way of financing black business, the activities of the numbers bankers performed an essential capital-raising role in the effectively, if not legally, segregated world of northern cities. They did something that no one else had the slightest interest in doing. According to a historian of black business, "Access to black policy dollars provided black communities with a privately funded, informal cash subsidy, which was used as venture capital in the promotion and support of black business." Indeed, "without these funds the picture of black business in the first half of the twentieth century would be even more dismal than the historical record shows."[19]

Perhaps the clearest example of the importance of numbers money in the black economy was in the world of commercialized leisure. Not only were many of the clubs and speakeasies in the black sections of town at least partially funded by bankers, but the very root of any new development in these areas was money derived from the gambling game. In the mid-twentieth century, Joe Louis was arguably the dominant figure in African American sports and one of the most significant in African American life. Yet the Brown Bomber got his start through numbers. John Roxborough, one of the most important numbers bankers in Detroit and an ardent "race man," used his money to encourage black kids in his city to get involved in sport. Recognizing that the young Joe Louis had enormous ability, Roxborough took him into his home, fed and clothed him while he trained, and, in historian Lewis Erenberg's words, "unofficially adopted him." According to the Numbers King, "Joe became a kind of son to me." Roxborough showed Louis a new way of living, one that the impressionable future champion took careful note of: "I never saw black people living that way, and I was envious and watched everything he did." Under Roxborough's tutelage, he carved out an amateur record of forty-nine wins, two losses, and two draws. When the time came for Louis to turn professional, Roxborough brought in Julian Black, a policy banker who was a player in the Chicago syndicate run by Al Capone. As Erenberg has commented, "Together, their criminal backgrounds and business skill gave him and Roxborough the confidence that they could navigate through the murky world of shark-like promoters and greedy gangsters who traditionally had treated black fighters as mere cannon fodder for promising young white boxers."[20]

Promoting boxers and bouts was, of course, relatively cheap compared with involvement in baseball. The profits from numbers gambling were simply indispensable to the existence of the fledgling Negro National League (NNL) in the 1920s and 1930s. Gus Greenlee, owner of the Pittsburgh Crawfords, Alex Pompez, owner of the New York Cubans, Abe Manley, owner of the Newark Eagles, and James Semler, owner of the New York Black Yankees, all financed their baseball operations with income derived from numbers. Neil Lanctot, historian of black baseball, concluded that numbers money "played a vital role in black baseball during the Depression, filling a void by providing much of the necessary cash to sustain a struggling organization." Yet of course this was a double-edged sword. On the one hand, who else in black America but a Numbers King could afford to invest in black baseball. On the other hand, there was an inevitable taint to numbers money, and this did not help as the league tried to establish itself as a legitimate enterprise. Quips, such as when the *Baltimore Afro American* labeled the NNL the "Bankers' League," suggest something of the tarnished image of the sport. The respected sportswriter Sam Lacy cautioned that organized baseball had to be "more discriminating" in its "membership requirements," a sentiment with which many no doubt agreed.[21]

The principal link between numbers in Harlem and black base-ball was Alejandro, or Alex, Pompez. Pompez claimed to have been born in Key West, Florida, but may actually have got his start in life in Havana. Pompez considered himself to be one of the "people of the darker races," but his links to both Latinos and African Americans positioned him well for negotiating the increasingly complex landscape of race in Harlem. He started the Cuban Stars, a team of mostly black Cubans who, beginning around 1916, barnstormed the United States during baseball season and then returned to winter in Cuba. Pompez involved himself in numbers very near the beginning, in the early 1920s, and by the time of the coming of Dutch Schultz was one of the most important bankers in Harlem. The advent of Schultz caused Pompez to drop out of numbers for a while, but by the mid 1930s he was again one of the prominent players. According to a report in the *Amsterdam News* in 1937, Pompez had "a daily 'take' of $40,000 from the racket and a $15,000,000 bank."[22]

Yet for all his success in the world of numbers, baseball remained his passion; he was renowned for being a particularly good judge of young talent and specialized in scouting Caribbean and Central American players. Indeed, it was his passion for baseball that eventually tripped him up. In early 1937, Pompez fled to Mexico to avoid an indictment as Thomas Dewey hotly pursued the Democratic Party fixer Jimmy Hines. It was only what the *Amsterdam News* labeled as his "fatal desire to communicate with Roy Sparrow secretary of the New York Cubans Baseball Club" that undid him. Federal agents had tapped the phone at the Cubans' home ground, Dyckman Oval, and as a result the Mexican authorities were able eventually to detain the Numbers King. Pompez fought extradition for months, but eventually brokered a deal whereby he would testify against Hines in return for a sentence of only two years' probation. The headlines about Pompez hardly improved the image of black baseball, but Cum Posey, formerly one of the game's most illustrious players and by the 1930s the widely respected owner of the Homestead Grays, somewhat surprisingly came out and publicly supported him. According to Posey, Pompez "had been a bigger benefactor in the life of Harlem than he has been a nuisance," and furthermore Posey argued that "lotteries of any kind should not be put in the same illegal category as burglary and other major crimes." Pompez continued his association with the NNL until its demise in the early 1950s, and then went on to a successful career as a scout for the Giants. He died in 1974 and was elected to the Baseball Hall of Fame in 2006.[23]

Numbers gambling was the most successful enterprise in Harlem between the wars. Not only did it employ thousands of black men and women, but money from the illegal game found its way into every crack and crevice of the Black Metropolis. Some scholars have seen fit to relegate numbers to what they call the "informal economy" or the "underground economy." While such terms do highlight the illegal nature of numbers, they slight the game's importance to the economic life of cities in Jim Crow America. Indeed, for a half-century, from its invention around 1920 to its demise in the 1970s, numbers was not some subsidiary part of the economy of the black areas of cities; it was, to a remarkable extent, *the* economy. Measuring exactly how important numbers was in the interwar years is, of course, fraught with all sorts of difficulties. When, in 1971, a *New York Times* reporter suggested to Francis A. J. Ianni, a sociologist then researching organized crime, "that some 60 per cent of Harlem's economy depends on the numbers," the academic initially demurred: "That seems a bit high." After some time for reflection, though, Ianni changed his mind: "I was shocked at first when you mentioned it, but I guess, when you think about it, that estimate sounds fairly sensible."[24] Although there is little doubt that this figure is too high for the 1920s and 1930s, it does suggest something of the dimensions of numbers' role in Harlem. Numbers may have been illegal but, far from being "underground" or "informal," it was obviously a mainstream and significant part of the everyday bustle of Harlem's economic life.

And it contributed more than just money. When John Roxborough and Julian Black combined to launch Joe Louis's career as a professional boxer, the fact that they were well-heeled was hardly insignificant, but equally important was their business acumen, their ability to deal confidently with a world not at all inclined to grant concessions to beginners. Numbers was the source of this pair's money and experience. In James Weldon Johnson's *Autobiography of an Ex–Coloured Man* (1912), the protagonist twice experiences New York City. When he first arrives, identifying himself as a black man, the narrator plunges into an underground world of gambling in the Tenderloin district, a world in which gamblers passively accept the fact that fate, something beyond their control, would determine the outcome of their endeavors. On his return, now as a white, the ex–colored man jumps with even more enthusiasm into the marketplace, opens a savings account, invests in real estate, and carefully calculates the increase in his fortunes. No longer acquiescent, but now actively shaping his own destiny, he delights in his new entrepreneurial guise, exclaiming, "What an interesting and absorbing game is money making!" In Johnson's telling, the allegedly value-free marketplace was marked by racial and cultural barriers, obstacles that prevented his protagonist from becoming a bourgeois economic man until he had shucked off his black skin.[25]

Writing in the early years of the twentieth century, Johnson used fiction to make his point, but that point still had much merit. In the 1920s, the obstacles to blacks entering the business world were beginning to crumble, albeit at a glacial pace, under the pressure of the aspirations of thousands who were desperate to get ahead and to transform Harlem into their Promised Land. We have written this book to suggest that numbers played a part in this process, that it was a bridge between the separate worlds that Johnson described in his novel.

In February 1927, a columnist for the *New York Age* spoke to a black businessman involved in insurance and briefly printed his views, thus providing, as the newspaperman freely admitted, a very rare dissenting voice from the publication's usual line on numbers. The businessman gave "the numbers" credit for both the "business confidence which Negroes are developing among themselves in Harlem" and the "progress of members of our race in commerce," arguing that "we are acquiring confidence in each other's business integrity in New York through the 'number' game." Although the businessman conceded that not all numbers bankers were honest, he declared that "the majority of them have [been], and are so now." "This paying to players hundreds of dollars with no idea of welching when they are hit," the insurance man pointed out, "has stimulated a confidence in Negroes by Negroes that all other mediums of race persuasion have failed to accomplish."[26]

A dozen years later, Claude McKay made a related point. After Dutch Schultz took over much of the numbers business in the early 1930s, many of the little stores that were fronts for numbers and that were run by blacks (these small establishments were not all white-owned) faced ruin. According to McKay, quite a few of these stores increased their inventories of cigars, candy, soft drinks, and the like. Often, wives and children ran the store while the men tried to find jobs elsewhere. New clients began to patronize these shops, and "the owners were surprised to discover that they could successfully compete with whites who formerly monopolized such small businesses in Harlem." In 1940, McKay observed, there were "hundreds of such places, which do not need the numbers game to exist."[27] Whether or not those African Americans who entered the world of the market with at least a modicum of success also lost their creative souls, as did the protagonist of Johnson's *Autobiography of an Ex–Coloured Man,* was of course another matter entirely.

If workers in the numbers industry, ranging from bankers to collectors and runners, fully embraced the newness and modernity of the way in which they made their living, the individual decisions about gambling that many of their clients made often revealed a more traditional set of beliefs about the way in which the world worked. Of course, any attempt to discern the motives and attitudes of tens of thousands of people, distant from us in time, is difficult, but there is enough evidence concerning those motives and attitudes to allow us to make some tentative observations. For example, something of the routine, everyday nature of gambling on numbers is conveyed by the following scrap of information. In June 1930, the soon-to-be-released Edward Colon, or "Spannie the Terror," as he signed his letters, wrote to his friend James Cooper, or "Herc," who lived on West 135th Street, telling him how he was faring in prison in the last months of his captivity. He penciled, in a postscript, "Herc play my number with Flossie 672 with a dime. Don't forget you big Bum."[28] For some, that kind of everyday regularity became merely an addiction. In January 1925, after a series of arrests of bankers, one Harlem resident told the *New York Age,* "I am suh glad to see dat de 'Number Kings' am losen out. Dey has hit me hard, but I jest cudden stop." And of course, particularly given the Depression's savage impact on Harlem life, everyone who gambled envisaged the prospect of plenty. As the *Age* primly noted in December 1932, numbers was "a game which is now looked forward to by hundreds of Harlemites as a means of surcease from their financial ills."[29]

What is most difficult to convey to modern readers is a sense of the way in which playing the numbers was not considered "gambling," and was not viewed by blacks as being dependent on luck. For many, the term "investing" on the numbers was meant literally and, in an environment where dealing with banks was often difficult, putting down, say, a dime every day was seen as a form of savings. Something of this attitude is conveyed in the following story from the *New York Age*. In March 1927, a reporter spoke to a young married woman who made some extra money on the side by acting as a numbers collector, soliciting business from her friends and residents in her apartment block. With the commission she made, she backed her own plays, which were always on **555.** Although she had had no success over quite a period of time, the woman was "still confident that some fine day the Clearing House balances will bring her '555,' and then she will be repaid for the long and patient daily putting up of her hard earned (?) coin."[30] For all the reporter's smugness and appropriation of the woman's story into the one he wanted to tell, it remains clear that this woman viewed things rather differently from her questioner.

The principal question, of course, is: Why did ordinary African American men and women choose to "invest" their money in numbers rather than in a savings account? This was particularly so when, in the long run, numbers gamblers would get a return of just slightly more than one dollar for every two dollars wagered on a number. Part of the reason for their choice lies in the abovementioned widespread distrust of banks, a distrust that was hardly allayed by all the bank failures of 1932 and 1933. Banks and savings accounts were also associated with the hectoring of the white professional and middle class, always keen to discipline what they saw as the unruly behavior of most residents of Harlem. Probation officers, for example, were constantly battling with their charges, urging them to open bank accounts and institute a regular program of planned savings. One of the headings in probation reports was "Thrift," in which the probationer's attitude toward this issue was detailed. To be sure, some upwardly striving blacks associated bank accounts with progress and were keen to embrace them, but many more reacted about as enthusiastically to this interference in their lives as most people do in similar situations. And there was the added dimension of race: Why support an institution that might take their money disdainfully, but was never going to offer them a loan?

For probably the majority of blacks, though, savings accounts did not fit into the texture of their lives. Saving requires certainty, regularity, and sureness, conditions that favored long-term planning and a conception of the future that encompassed more than just next week.[31] But Harlem between the wars was a constant whirl of movement as African Americans shifted in and out and around the Black Metropolis; few held steady jobs for long periods of time, particularly in the years of the Great Depression. Employment was typically intermittent and this generated its own economic rhythm in individual lives, one of debt and credit. Investing on the numbers fitted more easily into this pattern than did queuing up in the lobby to make a deposit in some forbidding white-owned bank. One must remember that winning at numbers was nothing like winning millions of dollars in the lottery today. Hitting the number usually resulted in a payoff of a few score dollars, at most a few hundred. This made an enormous difference to a person's life for the next few weeks, but it did not mean that the individual never had to work again. In this context, regularly investing spare nickels and dimes on a number, and every few months receiving a windfall that allowed debts to be paid off, made sense. Gambling on the numbers played an important role in the economic lives of ordinary African American men and women.

More insight into the minds of individual gamblers can be gained from a remarkable source. In the 1930s many African Americans wrote to the New York Stock Exchange about numbers. The letters were duly filed away, and many were included in an appendix to Gustav Carlson's brilliant ethnographic study of numbers in Detroit. Typical of most of these letters was one written from a beauty shop on Orlean Street in Baltimore, Maryland. The writer wanted someone at the Exchange to phone through the day's stock sales as soon as "you close out you total," as there "is a number Racket here and only way you can win is to get a tip." In return, she was willing to pay: "Please write me and let me no. and if we can we take it slow and for a long time 3 hundred dollars a week." The writer had been betting "for 2 year [and] haven hit yet," and this proposal would allow a more equitable redistribution of money. After all, "they have this number racket here and the Banker have mad[e] Billions of dollar they can stand to loose a little now."

Many of the letters were from desperately poor people savaged by the Great Depression. One from Columbus, Ohio, began: "I am a little girl 11 year old and please let the main man read my letter." She was "a little girl my dady out of work and mothr is Sick and we don't have verry mutch to live on and god Just told me to write to you." On October 30th "I will have 10 ct and I will give it to Mother and tell her to play it on this number 225 please put this nomber out on this day I wont tell know one I wrote this My Mothr and dady don't know I am writing." She concluded with "God bless you is my prays." Another, from Clarksville, Pennsylvania, simply stated: "Pleas send me a number that will hit I have a large family and nothing to go on I play and play I cant never hit."

Occasionally the letter writer, baffled that his or her investment had not paid off, was more interested in raising the issue of the propriety of the way the Stock Exchange was conducting its business. One letter from Pittsburgh began by referring to the "Stock number you publish daily in the Pittsburgh Post Gazette" and then asked, "We would like to know if these numbers are correct or are being tampered with." He then pointed out, "There's talk around here saying the numbers are crooked. Can it be possible a man employed in your firm be tampering with the Stock numbers." Others simply assumed that numbers was a part of the Stock Exchange's normal operations: "I would like a book of your clearing house number I would like to play some of your numbers please send me a book and instructions how to do as I never play befor." This last letter was written in 1934, several years after the Clearing House had ceased publishing its daily totals, but the phrase "clearing house" was still being used to refer to numbers. Whether august financial institutions such as the Clearing House and the Stock Exchange liked it or not, for many African Americans they were still intimately involved in the numbers game.

In January 1931, after the New York Clearing House had ceased publishing its daily figures which had been the basis for numbers, the New York Stock Exchange announced that it would withhold the release of some figures in what proved to be a futile attempt to stop the organizers of numbers from latching on to the NYSE as a replacement. The decisions of both the Clearing House and the Stock Exchange were of import not just in New York City but all across urban America. One disgruntled citizen from Pittsburgh wrote a letter to the manager of the Stock Exchange. After reading in the newspaper of the Stock Exchange's decision, designed "to discourage 'Numbers' gambling," this person gently reprimanded the manager: "The thought came to me that if you would compare the stock gambling with the other you would find that considering it from every angle you would be better off not to make a statement of that kind." He then pointed out that "my savings of a life time are all tied up in the stock market at an appalling loss. . . . Yet I am not a hard loser, but have resorted to the 'Number' game to try and retrieve at least a part of my losses." The "only unfair" part of numbers was when racketeers rigged or changed winning numbers, a circumstance that made it all the more important that the Stock Exchange should "still continue to publish the figures" and thus "help it to be strictly on the square."[32]

There was no recorded response from the manager of the Stock Exchange, but doubtless he was horrified at the easy equation of numbers gambling and buying stocks and bonds. Yet the early 1930s was hardly the best vantage point from which to make an argument about either the sanctity of the Stock Exchange or the purity of the market. Casper Holstein was scathing on this point, telling the *Amsterdam News* in 1936 that "people in Harlem have paid out thousands upon thousands of dollars buying stock in oil wells, gold mines, and so forth, which often did not even exist on paper." Not only did they lose "all their earnings," but residents of the

Black Metropolis "did not even know where to find the man who brought around the picture of the pretty Indian princess who had grown rich overnight by finding oil."[33]

Most African Americans simply refused to accept that there was a distinction between numbers and the Stock Exchange. While conducting the research in the 1930s for his study of numbers in Detroit, Gustav Carlson elicited a number of responses from the people he interviewed. According to one African American he questioned, "I plays numbers because it is a speculation and an investment of money just as the stock market is." In both forms of investment, the aim was "to gain big money off of [a] small amount of money." Another claimed: "Number gambling is really not gambling 'cause you've got a good chance of winning and if you do win you're sure to get your money. That's more than you white folk can say about your gambling." Increasingly, the weight of scholarly opinion offers rather more support to the views of ordinary African Americans than it does to the officials of the Stock Exchange. Reuven Brenner and his colleagues have argued that although financial markets try to separate themselves from gambling, the two activities have more in common than is usually acknowledged. Indeed, the way in which the residents of Harlem and other black cities created their own way of doing things based on numbers gambling—in the absence of sophisticated financial institutions willing to deal with people of color—does nothing so much as hark back to the role gambling and lotteries played in the birth of modern entrepreneurial capitalism in Europe in the seventeenth and eighteenth centuries.[34]

For most Harlem residents, the difference between the mainstream economy and the "informal economy" was a distinction without meaning. The complex empire of numbers, founded on

Casper Holstein's brilliant invention, neatly encapsulated both the aspirations of Harlemites to be part of twentieth century and modernity, and the reality of life lived in a discriminatory Jim Crow America. Every now and then, in the financial turmoil of the Depression, the world of the numbers bankers and that of the modern financial institution converged in reality, as well as in the minds of Harlem residents. Very early in the 1930s, the Numbers King Henry Miro was almost wiped out by the failure of the Bank of the United States. Apparently, Miro had a considerable amount of money deposited in ten separate accounts under fictitious names at the bank's branch at 116th Street and Lexington. But sweetest of all, in July 1932 the *Amsterdam News* reported gleefully on an incident that had recently occurred in Washington. When a run had started on the Prudential Bank, an alleged Numbers King quickly slipped off home, returned to the premises, and made a very public deposit of $5,000, in an attempt to restore confidence in the beleaguered institution.[35]

9

ALL OVER TOWN

There can be no denying that the number racket was born and nurtured in Harlem where its popularity today is greater than ever; but for the sake of the record and the truth, the game has spread to other Manhattan districts, the Bronx and Brooklyn, and is no longer known as an exclusive sport of the colored folks.

—*New York Age,* March 9, 1935

After almost two years "on the lam," hiding in and around New York City to avoid being arrested by Thomas Dewey, being indeed unable to go anywhere without the most elaborate planning, Dutch Schultz was going a little stir crazy, and undoubtedly did not realize how isolated he and his gang had become. In these years, Lucky Luciano was melding the Unione Siciliana into what we know as the Mafia, and Dutch Schultz and his operation were the last big independent power left in the metropolitan area. Even then, Schultz was not all that independent: the Unione Siciliana, through Ciro Terranova, the Artichoke King, and (after he was removed) "Trigger" Mike Coppola, owned a 25 percent stake in Schultz's business. To an extent, Schultz was also protected because his lieutenant, Bo Weinberg, had very good relations with Luciano and could often smooth problems out, but things were unlikely to continue as they were for very long. As Dixie Davis pith-ily pointed out, "the world was moving fast," and Schultz's gang was "a sort of Balkan state surrounded by hungry axis powers."[1]

The end unfolded as quickly and surely as any Greek tragedy. In November 1934 Schultz, sick and tired of being in hiding, had turned himself in to the authorities, and throughout the first half of 1935, Dewey spent a good deal of his time prosecuting Schultz for income tax evasion. The first trial, in Syracuse, New York, re-sulted in a hung jury; the second, in Malone, New York (even far-ther upstate), led to an acquittal, a verdict that defied comprehen-sion and induced the judge to deliver a verbal flaying of the jury as he dismissed them. In the aftermath, Dewey made it abundantly clear that "I had decided to go after Schultz in connection with his domination of the numbers racket." Schultz concluded that the only quick way out of his troubles was to have Dewey assassinated, but Lucky Luciano refused to allow an act that would bring down the wrath of the legal authorities on organized crime and disrupt business. Schultz disregarded Luciano's warning and boasted to as-sociates that Dewey would be shot within forty-eight hours. For a long time, Luciano and other mob leaders had barely tolerated Schultz, a loose cannon that was now completely out of control. He was a dead man walking.[2]

At about 10:30 P.M. on Wednesday October 23, 1935, the only cus-tomers in the Palace Chop House on East Park Street in downtown Newark, New Jersey, were Bernard "Lulu" Rosenkrantz, Abe "Mis-fit" Landau, Abadaba Berman, and Dutch Schultz. On their table were sheaves of figures and an adding-machine slip, which bore the total $827,253. Charley "The Bug" Workman, armed with a pistol, and Mendy Weiss, carrying a sawed-off shotgun, walked in and fired a fusillade of shots, which the barman later said reminded him of nothing so much as his experiences in the trenches during World War I. Rosenkrantz was shot twelve times, Landau just once, and Abadaba Berman, the financial wizard, was, as the *New York Times* somewhat gruesomely reported, "riddled with bullets in the abdomen, chest and face." All three died in the hospital early the next day. Dutch Schultz, who was in the lavatory at the back of restaurant, was shot once in the stomach by Workman. After the gunmen had fled, the wounded gangster walked to the bar and said, "Gimme two nickels. I want to make a call." The barman did what he was told and Schultz then went to the wall phone, rang the police, and gasped: "This is Dutch Schultz. Send an ambulance. I'm dying." Schultz was taken to Newark City Hospital, where some hours later he developed a fever of 106 degrees and began to ramble incoherently. Hoping to learn something about the identities of the killers, the police had a stenographer record his words. The transcript, which included numerous sentences such as, "Oh, oh dog biscuits and when he is happy he doesn't get snappy—please, please to do this," and "Mother is the best bet and don't let Satan draw you too fast," has long been available and is now easily accessible on the Web. Dixie Davis wryly noted that "the newspapers said it read like Hemingway." The stream-of-consciousness character of what amounts to pages of meandering thoughts and aphorisms would later prompt William Burroughs to write an experimental book and film script entitled *The Last Words of Dutch Schultz* (1969).[3]

The killing of Dutch Schultz in Newark had a curious, if now almost totally forgotten, place in Harlem folklore. As Schultz lay dying in Newark Hospital, he received a telegram from Harlem: "Don't be yellow. As ye sow, so shall ye reap." It was signed "Madame St. Clair, Policy Queen." According to the *New York Times*, the Newark police were mystified "and were unable to learn its meaning."[4] A quick phone call to colleagues in Manhattan would have enlightened them. Word of the telegram penetrated every corner of Harlem within hours, further burnishing the legend of Madame Queen. Much later that Thursday, toward nightfall, African Americans all over the Black Metropolis opened the evening papers at the sports pages to check on the day's number. The three-race, five-race, and seven-race pari-mutuel totals at Narragansett Park in Rhode Island produced **000,** a number that had not turned up in four years. A *Time* reporter in Harlem recorded the reaction of blacks: "Triple-zero! 'At's Dutch's number. 'At's good-bye Dutch. It's all over with 'at boy." That evening, at 8:35 P.M., the Dutchman "drew life's blank." On Friday morning, blacks by the hundred put all the money they could scrape together on the number they knew would win that day—**835.**[5] There was, however, to be no poetic ending—the day's number was **214** and bankers made a killing, a parting gift from the Dutchman.

Schultz left a mixed legacy. By 1935, his much-feared "combination" was in a state of disarray and had been for some time. On the other hand, the amount of money gambled on numbers had increased at a phenomenal rate during some of the worst years of the Great Depression. Testifying before a bail bond inquiry in March 1935, Dixie Davis, counsel for Schultz, claimed that numbers was far more prevalent than it ever had been: "Policy used to be played only by the colored people in Harlem," Davis declared. "Now it is played all over town by all kinds and colors of people." Reportedly, Davis, because of this comment, was quickly hustled off the witness stand, but he was quite happy to elaborate on his testimony to the waiting newsmen outside. According to Davis, in 1931, when numbers was confined almost entirely to Harlem, the daily gross was $300,000—that is, roughly $80 million a year; but in 1935, after the game had spread to all five boroughs, he estimated that the daily gross was $1.5 million and that New Yorkers were spending between $300 million and $500 million a year on numbers.[6] Doubtless some of these figures were exaggerated. In his autobiography, Dewey claimed that Davis's "wild estimate poured more fuel on the fire," but he seemed prepared to accept that the numbers racket was taking in some $100 million a year.[7] What was agreed upon by all was that numbers was an extraordinarily lucrative business.

Schultz and his associates had taken a game that offered the hope, however chimerical, of winning a considerable sum of money for a small wager, and sold it to whites, most of whom were suffering through the worst Depression the country had ever seen. To be sure, there had been some whites gambling on numbers in the 1920s. An indignant editorial writer in the *New York Age* pointed out that "back in 1927, 1928 and 1929, hundreds of white people were playing the numbers by securing the assistance of colored acquaintances to place their bets in Harlem." Every day, "colored elevator operators working in apartment houses on Riverside Drive" and elsewhere in Manhattan were "entrusted with the money of white bettors." Furthermore, whereas most blacks bet only between a dime and a quarter, "a large number of white people" wagered "from $1 to $5 daily." But for all the protestations of the *Age,* it was in the early 1930s that the game spread all over the city: gangsters gave the white working class the opportunity to make the numbers a part of their everyday life, just as blacks had done a decade previously. According to Davis, in 1935 there were "one hundred bankers in Harlem, forty to fifty in lower Manhattan, one hundred in Brooklyn and from fifty to sixty in the Bronx—a total of some three hundred and fifty in the entire city."[8] As a *Time* reporter noted,

"The game has spread far beyond the borders of Harlem under the high-pressure promotion of the numbers hawkers, who have enlisted a salesman in nearly every second-rate cigar and drug store, [and] widened their distribution to include porters, office boys, taxi drivers, elevator operators."[9]

One sign of the new expanded market for numbers was obvious in the city's newspapers, complicit as ever in the gambling game. In the 1920s, the *Mirror* and the *News,* the two morning tabloids, sold surprisingly well in Harlem. Beneath the cartoons on the sports pages, both newspapers used to print, inconspicuously, a series of digits. White readers were usually puzzled by the figures, but blacks were well aware that they were random suggestions that could be backed in the numbers game. By the second half of the 1930s, it was all rather more blatant. The *Mirror* collected on one page the racing results, including the mutuel payout totals, the Curb Exchange total bond sales and stock sales, the Stock Exchange bond and stock sales, the Cincinnati bank clearing figures, and the U.S. Treasury totals. Every possible set of figures that could be used to generate the daily number was included. For aficionados of Italian policy, the *Mirror* even printed on the same page the tax disbursements of the eight Italian provinces. For the statistically minded, the *Mirror* also ran a column entitled "Numberology," which tabulated "the most significant numbers of the past 30 days." Doubtless for legal reasons, the newspaper avoided using the words "winning number" in this section. The table also listed "the number of times a certain number played straight has *appeared*" in the previous five years. As if all this was not enough, a one-panel cartoon entitled initially "Pete," later "Policy Pete," appeared on this page. Pete and his offsiders say nothing about the numbers, but, for no apparent purpose, there were always two three-digit numbers somewhere in the cartoon. Readers so inclined could take them as possible suggestions for backing later that day.[10]

Dutch Schultz and his colleagues at the Palace Chop House in Newark had not been the only gangsters killed on October 23, 1935. Earlier in the day, Louis "Pretty" Amberg was "hacked to death" and "left in a burning automobile near the navy yard in Brooklyn." At precisely midnight, Martin Krompier, Schultz's lieutenant, was shot four times in a barbershop underneath Times Square. Moreover, it was only during the previous fortnight or so that Bo Weinberg had disappeared; his body was widely rumored to be at the bottom of the river. For Police Commissioner Lewis J. Valentine, this all added up to a gang struggle between the Italians and the Jews, looking "like a racial war of extermination, because there isn't an Italian victim, and a fight over spoils."[11] This was an unlikely explanation, but clearly something was afoot in New York's underworld. In the very early 1930s, there had been a violent generational change in the leadership of the Mafia in every major city in the country. The so-called Moustache Petes, who refused to deal with anyone who was not Italian—indeed, were skeptical of anyone who was not Sicilian—were eliminated and replaced by the Young Turks. Bo Weinberg later told Dixie Davis that on the same day that he, Weinberg, had shot Salvatore Maranzano in New York in 1931, "there was about ninety guineas knocked off all over the country. That was the time we Americanized the mobs."[12] Perhaps Weinberg exaggerated the numbers, but he was correct about the process. Maranzano's replacement, Lucky Luciano, a prime example of the new generation, adhered to one creed only: business. During the next couple of years, Luciano, in the words of Davis, transformed the Unione Siciliana "from a loose federation of Italians into a close-knit national organization, affiliated with the mobs of other national origin."[13] Luciano had no problem dealing with Jews. He had known Bugsy Siegel and Meyer Lansky since they were school-kids on the Lower East Side, and they remained friends and business associates throughout the 1930s and 1940s.[14] What happened on October 23, 1935, was neither the beginning nor the end of a racial war, but it was a flexing of muscles on the part of the newly invigorated Mafia.

Even before the killing of Dutch Schultz, Luciano had been negotiating with some of the principals involved in numbers in Harlem. Supposedly, Bo Weinberg, who had been in charge of Schultz's operations while Schultz was in court in Upstate New York defending himself against Dewey, was talking to Luciano and, as a consequence, according to the rumors, it was the Dutchman who arranged for Bo Weinberg to be executed. Far from being killed by the Italians, as the city's police commissioner had surmised, he was almost certainly killed for talking to the Italians. By Dixie Davis's lights, Weinberg was a more interesting man than many gangsters, but nowadays he is known only for the method of his demise: Weinberg was taken out on a boat, each foot placed in a bucket full of wet concrete and then he was made to wait while it set before being dumped in the East River. His gruesome death was memorialized in a sort of way by the term "concrete shoes" (or "concrete overshoes"), which entered gangster argot and later popular culture, and much later by E. L. Doctorow's *Billy Bathgate* (1989) and the 1991 film based on the novel. According to Bumpy Johnson's widow, Johnson met Luciano in late 1934, but Luciano made it clear that, while interested in the numbers, he was not yet prepared to make a move against Schultz. A week after Schultz's death, Luciano summoned Johnson to another meeting. They worked out a deal whereby Luciano would leave alone any bankers who had been arrayed against Dutch Schultz; Johnson would be his man in Harlem, but any new bank that started up would be under Luciano's control.

Luciano and Johnson were an unlikely pair, but seemingly they respected each other. They played chess regularly, Luciano on occasion even having a game with Bumpy Johnson at his favorite spot, in front of the YMCA on 135th Street. Their relationship would grow closer when, in 1937, Johnson was sent to prison at Dannemora, where Luciano was already serving thirty to fifty years, and, according to his widow, Johnson on one occasion saved the gangster from being shanked (stabbed) in the prison yard. Hardly surprisingly, there were teething problems as the details of the new order were worked out. Sometime in 1936, Italian gangsters started to move in on a black banker whom they were supposed to leave alone. According to Mayme Johnson, Bumpy Johnson called a meeting of bankers, controllers, and runners at the 369th Armory at Fifth Avenue and 143rd Street that lasted some two hours. The following day, half of the runners working for the Italian-controlled bank were sick and stayed at home; those who did turn up worked only in an extraordinarily lethargic way. Receipts plummeted, and within a day Luciano summoned Johnson to his suite at the Waldorf Astoria. Apparently the banker owed the gangsters money, which, by their rules, meant that they owned the banker and were entitled to do what they wanted to him. Johnson, however, insisted that in Harlem Luciano and his acolytes had to negotiate such matters with him. After some haggling, the pair came to an agreement: Luciano and his men would leave the banker alone, on condition that Johnson guaranteed he would pay back his debt, and at an even more extortionate rate of interest than usual.[15]

Mayme Johnson told this story to demonstrate the independence of Bumpy Johnson, to show her readers that he was in thrall to no man. The reality, however, was that from the killing of Dutch Schultz in 1935 down to World War II, numbers in Harlem was primarily controlled by mobbed-up white bankers. Yet that control could never be taken for granted. What rings most true about the story related by Mayme Johnson was Johnson's clever use of passive resistance, given that the white gangsters relied on blacks to keep numbers running. They had learned from Dutch Schultz's mistakes, and most low-level and salaried employees in numbers in Harlem were black. It was also still the case that there remained a few black bankers managing to make a living. And of course things were never static. In 1937 and 1938, as the terrier-like Thomas Dewey pursued organized crime, culminating in the two headline-grabbing trials of the Tammany Hall boss James J. Hines and his eventual conviction for providing political and police protection to numbers racketeers, white gangsters tried to fade into the background. According to Henry Lee Moon, writing for the *New York Times* in July 1937, "With the power of the syndicates curbed, men of smaller means and less violent practices have re-entered the game." A year later, another *Times* reporter commented that Dewey's prosecutions were beginning to break down the monopoly and were "returning policy to the small, independent bankers."[16]

Yet despite the temporary rise in fortunes of black bankers at this time, the overall pattern was clear enough. By the second half of the 1930s, what had begun as a small-scale African American enterprise had expanded exponentially into a racket worth hundreds of millions of dollars a year. The business was no longer confined merely to Harlem, or to colored gamblers, because in the early 1930s white gangsters had ensured the game's spread into all five boroughs. But Harlem remained the jewel in the crown of New York City numbers, being by far the most profitable neighborhood in which to run a numbers bank, even though the simple fact was that most of the profits now left the Black Metropolis.

Perhaps the clearest sign that the days of black control of numbers were gone forever was the mood increasingly pervading Harlem, a nostalgic longing for the days of the Black Kings and Queens. In the 1920s, those involved in the gambling game had hardly been held in much regard by the black establishment; but just as it all slipped out of black hands, opinion began to shift. Confronted by the specter of Dutch Schultz and yet another business in Harlem run by and for the profit of whites, all manner of people began to discover some virtue in the way things had once been. As we have already seen, the *Age,* having relentlessly pursued the numbers game throughout the second half of the 1920s, suddenly began to support the black bankers, simply on the grounds that they were far preferable to white gangsters. This new pragmatic mood was captured by Assistant Commissioner of Correction Fishman in a May 1932 memo to Walter White, leader of the NAACP, in which he argued that "the numbers racket was always a bad thing for this poor section but it was at least carried on by colored people," and this "resulted in a certain amount of this money staying in Harlem." With the advent of Dutch Schultz, "the collection of numbers is being put in the hands of . . . white people and in some instances, aliens, who are not even voters." Consequently, "the absolute total of money derived from the numbers racket goes into the hands of white people."[17]

Ironically, it was the relentless Thomas Dewey, always interested in "turning" those he had caught (getting them to take a plea and testify against more important wrongdoers) as he doggedly pursued organized crime, who helped publicize the story of the take-over of numbers. Although many in Harlem in the early 1930s knew what had been going on, and regular readers of the *New York Age* and the *Amsterdam News* certainly picked up at least the broad out-lines of developments in the business, testimony in the investiga-tions and trials in the second half of the 1930s nevertheless filled in the fine detail, so that the story of numbers could be packaged as one of black innocence followed by a white-induced fall. When Wilfred Brunder was a Black King in the 1920s, he had tried to maintain a low profile and keep his name out of the newspapers, but he became something of a celebrity in the following decade, tes-tifying at the bail bond investigation in 1935 and Hines's trials in 1938. The story of numbers was news not just for the black press, but for the *New York Times* as well; indeed, in 1938 the *Times* devoted an entire page to printing digests of the testimony of Brunder and other lesser numbers operatives in the Hines trial. The contrast be-tween, on the one hand, the urbane and always beautifully dressed Wilfred Brunder, or the elegantly attired Alex Pompez, or indeed any of the other important black figures in numbers, and, on the other, the white gangsters, seemingly behaving as if Harlem were a Hollywood set for a James Cagney film, could hardly have been greater, and further fueled the nostalgic longing for past glories.

Following the Hines trial, various of the protagonists were will-ing to reveal even more, for a price. Dixie Davis, the white lawyer for Schultz, sold his story to *Collier's,* which ran a six-part exposé in 1939. The following year, "The Insider" spoke extensively to a re-porter from the *Chicago Defender* (a black newspaper read widely outside Chicago), which printed a series entitled "How Dutch Schultz Took Over Harlem." Some names were thinly disguised—Dixie Davis became "Yankee Mavis"—but for four weeks, reader were treated to the sensational story of how Jimmy Hines had "protected rackets and gangsters at the expense of black people" and "how Dutch Schultz 'muscled in' through gangland threats, backed up by guns and a murder record, to rule a Black Kingdom built on the numbers game," told in overblown language and illustrated by racy pencil sketches of key moments in the white takeover.[18] With the Depression still crippling Harlem, and with newspapers constantly reminding residents that now whites were in control of "their business," it was hardly surprising that many looked back to the 1920s with so much fondness.

And of course the biggest celebrity of them all, the inimitable Stephanie St. Clair, continued to make her periodic forays onto the front pages of the African American press. In January 1935, while Dutch Schultz was free on bail after being charged with income tax evasion, she told reporters, "I will kill Schultz if he sets foot in Harlem," adding somewhat unnecessarily, "He is a rat." Madame Queen claimed that "the policy game is my game," and that the white gangster "took it away from me and is swindling the colored people." She had always run the policy game "on the level," unlike the current regime, who constantly manipulated the results. "They're betting their relief money up there and without a chance to win." Two and a half years later, in November 1937, as her "marriage" to Sufi Abdul Hamid was publicly disintegrating, St. Clair told an *Amsterdam News* reporter that she was merely a "citizen interested in the welfare of the community game," albeit one uniquely qualified "to see the evils brought about since the entry of the late Dutch Schultz into Harlem." She wanted "to drive the white racketeers out of Harlem and return the policy game to its inventors." Her plan was "to make the daily newspapers print clearing house returns" and to "base the entire system on those figures, as it was several years ago."[19] Within two months St. Clair would be preoccupied with yet another legal battle—this time for taking several shots at Hamid with a pistol—but regardless of her troubles, there was never any chance of a revival of the golden age in which blacks ran numbers.

Yet that was not quite true. There was still one place in late-1930s Harlem where residents could return to a time in which white interlopers did not exist, and in which blacks were in control—and that was at the movies. The so-called "race film" had reached its height in the early 1920s, had slumped during the early years of the Depression, when expensive sound technology became a requirement, and then risen again in the late 1930s. Although blacks could attend movie theaters downtown if they wished, for the most part they preferred to patronize venues in Harlem. Occasionally these theaters may have been dilapidated, the equipment not the best, but it was here that black audiences felt most comfortable. It was also readily apparent that what paying customers in Harlem, Chicago's South Side, and the black areas of other Northern cities desired more than anything else was to see images of modern black sophistication projected onto the big screen. This demand was at least partially met by a steady flow of films with all-black casts, even if they were often produced by white companies.[20]

The most important and successful of these films was a gangster picture entitled *Dark Manhattan* (1937), which, according to one of many breathless press releases, was "the first all-colored cast motion picture with modern story, setting, and costumes." Produced by the black actor Ralph Cooper and some white associates, and starring Cooper, it was the story of "underworld activity in happy, hearty Harlem." And yet it is a better and much more interesting film than the press release might suggest. *Dark Manhattan,* as film scholar Paula Massood has argued, managed to conjoin "the urban and the urbane" by using "contemporary fashions (not work clothes), urban slang (not rural dialect), and the performance of contemporary music (not spirituals)."[21] This was most definitely not a film set in the South, but one identifiably about contemporary Harlem (even if filmed near Hollywood), and residents of the Black Metropolis flocked to see it. The film broke all attendance records at the Apollo Theater; indeed, the crush to see it was such that overflow crowds were ushered to the Harlem Opera House less than a block away. Frank Schiffman, white owner of the Apollo, had only one print of *Dark Manhattan*, which meant that each reel had to be rewound quickly after it had been shown and then couriered to the other venue for the next session.[22] As the film wended its way around America's circuit of black venues, the black press gave *Dark Manhattan* extensive coverage in terms that demonstrated considerable pride in this black achievement.[23]

Dark Manhattan was a black gangster film with a storyline that would have been familiar enough to anyone who had viewed white gangster movies. The producers even ran into the same problems with censorship that Warner Brothers and other major studios constantly battled against. In February 1937, the examiner in the Motion Picture Division of the Education Department of the State of New York instructed Cooper and his associates to "eliminate all views of men deliberately destroying man's store, following demand for money," in every print of the film to be shown in New York, on the grounds that this scene would "tend to incite to crime."[24] As with so many gangster movies, *Dark Manhattan* traced the rise to prominence and eventual demise of a hoodlum—only this time the hoodlum was black. Curly Thorpe, a young up-and-comer, was plucked from a pool hall on 63rd Street in San Juan Hill by Larry B. Lee, the biggest numbers banker in Harlem, and became his protégé. Almost from their first meeting, a generational struggle is set up between the pair over business ethics: when Lee explained that success was based on hard work and "underhand methods are never used," Thorpe initially demurred, claiming, "All is fair in love and war," and then let the issue slide with, "I think I understand." When Lee's health forced him to take a lengthy convalescence, Thorpe stepped in and started running the business his way, ruthlessly expanding it in such a heavy-handed fashion that he attracted the attention of the district attorney and a black gang, who, discovering how much money was involved, tried to take over numbers in Harlem. In the dénouement to the film, there is the inevitable shootout and Curly Thorpe and several of his rivals die.[25]

By virtue of its setting in Harlem, *Dark Manhattan* was always more than just another gangster movie, merely one more remake of *Scarface* (1932). Clearly, the official charged with censoring films for the benefit of the citizens of New York State did not understand this difference, and had little idea of the way numbers worked; the scene he had objected to was in fact not about a "demand for money" but about standover tactics being used to force a storekeeper to switch allegiances and run numbers for Curly Thorpe instead of his current banker. The white censor may well have been confused by what was occurring in the script, but the film was made with a more knowing audience in mind. Up in Harlem, and doubtless in most other northern black centers, *Dark Manhattan* was first and foremost a numbers film.

Dark Manhattan was not simply a fictionalized account of what had occurred in the Black Metropolis over the previous decade. It was in fact a pastiche, drawing freely from elements of the way in which the gambling racket functioned, reworking incidents and moments from the recent past into a new story, although anyone who knew Harlem, in particular anyone who knew numbers, would instantly have recognized its origins. At 8:00 on Curly Thorpe's first morning at his new job, Larry Lee asked him, "Well, Curly, how do you like the setup?" Lee's office—ostensibly he was a "Real Estate Expert"—was the epitome of modernity, with several male controllers, bookkeepers, and cashiers, and five or six young women sitting at desks using telephones, dictographs, typewriters, and adding machines to process numbers slips. There was also an intercom between the outer office and Lee's inner sanctum. Thorpe answered, "Oh, it's swell, Mr. Lee—Must take a lot of business to keep it going." While the business looked modern enough, with all the accoutrements of an up-to-date office, it was in fact Curly Thorpe who very quickly transformed the old and inefficient practices of Larry Lee. Thorpe introduced duplicate paperwork, and as one disgruntled employee noted, "All he does is sit there and study the reports from the different districts." Al Jackson, the controller for the Sugar Hill district, is peremptorily summoned to the office and harangued by Thorpe: "Listen, Al, there's no excuse you can offer to make me see a $300 a day falling off in your business up there. Now get this straight, we don't have any controllers working for this bank that lose business like that." Once Lee began his convalescence and Thorpe assumed total control of the bank, he turned not just the business but all of Harlem upside down. A spokesman for the other banks opened a meeting of the Bankers Association by announcing that "for the last ten days a reign of terror has been carried on in Harlem. Control men have been forced to leave the bank they work with—stores have been wrecked. Runners have been beaten for writing in certain districts." As Thorpe's combination became all-powerful, he told the other bankers that he was going to place one of his men inside each of their operations in Harlem, in return for 20 percent of the gross receipts.

All of this, of course, echoed aspects of what had occurred in Harlem as numbers was taken over by Dutch Schultz and as he introduced "shadows" to keep tabs on a bank's business as part of normal practice. Even some of the headlines projected onto the screen—"District Attorney's Probe Rocks Harlem: 'Number' Racket Doomed, He Tells Gamblers," for example—could have been purloined straight from the *New York Age* or the *Amsterdam News*. Supposedly, in Harlem, it was the kidnapping of Casper Holstein and the demand for a $50,000 ransom that alerted outsiders to the fact that the "nickel and dime" game brought in very large sums of money. In *Dark Manhattan,* the outsider was not Dutch Schultz but Butch Williams (the similarity of their first names was hardly accidental), and it was Curly Thorpe's spending of more than a thousand dollars an evening, night after night, in Klub Kongo (an alliterative echo of the Cotton Club) as he pursued singer Flo Gray (a name similar to that of the adored Florence Mills, who had died a decade earlier), that made it clear to the rival gang that numbers was lucrative. As Butch Williams, who owned the Klub Kongo (just as Owney Madden, a white gangster, owned the Cotton Club and as Dutch Schultz was rumored to be a silent partner in Connie's Inn, another Harlem club), muttered to an offsider, "Anytime a guy has a nickel and dime game and spends dough like that, I want to know more about the game." It was Williams's bald-faced attempt to move in to the numbers and replace Curly Thorpe that led to the climactic gun battle.

But for all its echoes of contemporary Harlem, *Dark Manhattan* differed from real life in one crucial aspect: everyone in the film was black. *Variety*'s reviewer wrote that the film was "framed around the

Harlem numbers racket operation" and opined that *Dark Manhattan* "will get by in Negro houses chiefly because of the novelty it embodies for such audiences in that no white person is lensed in the footage." Thomas Cripps, the historian of black films, has sharply criticized "race movies" for creating "a world in which black characters acceded to the white ideal of segregation, and unreal black cops, crooks, judges, and juries interacted in such a way as to blame black victims for their social plight." Although conceding that "'race movies' could have deep meanings for blacks," Cripps still concluded that "like all black hopes, they were threadbare."[26] Perhaps. But for all the dismissive comments of film critics, the totally black world of the 1930s race movies existed as a kind of utopia, a place where there were no whites, and where blacks could easily assume any and every social position. It certainly made for thought-provoking viewing, raising endless possibilities for ironic comparison with life in Depression America. In *Dark Manhattan*, though, the utopia was set not in some possible future, but in a past that, leaving aside the all-black police force, had already existed. It was this rich associational history that gave the film much of its resonance with Harlem audiences. Yet critics of the race movies certainly have a point. The absence of whites, more specifically the absence of Dutch Schultz and those of his ilk, is a disconcerting feature of *Dark Manhattan*. It makes watching the movie for anyone, then and now, who knows anything about numbers an almost surreal experience. In the end, then, *Dark Manhattan* fed into the powerful current of nostalgic longing for a world that Harlem blacks had let slip from their grasp.

In the 1920s, numbers had been the largest black business and largest employer in Harlem, and the Black Kings and Queens had cut a broad swath through the Black Metropolis. By the second half of the 1930s, all that had changed. Ordinary blacks by the thousands continued to gamble on the numbers, and would do so for decades more; but their nickels and dimes, which added up to scores of millions of dollars a year, flowed out of Harlem. The makers of *Dark Manhattan* and its audience could simply imagine away white control of the numbers and pretend that the gangsters did not exist, but in real life that was not possible. Gangsters and the mob moved into Harlem in the early 1930s, and there they would stay until numbers was eventually made redundant by the state-run lotteries in the 1970s.

EPILOGUE

I'm gonna play 529 tomorrow.

—*Amsterdam News,* February 6, 1937

The reign of Harlem's Black Kings and Queens was relatively short, their glory days lasting less than fifteen years. By the late 1930s, the terms "King" and "Queen" had fallen into disuse, to be replaced by the seemingly more appropriate "numbers banker" or "racketeer."[1] Dutch Schultz and others of his ilk had tainted the numbers game, and it would never quite regain its former splendor. In the 1920s, there had been very occasional rumors of leaked Clearing House numbers or fixed results; but by the mid-1930s, when the basis on which the winning number was worked out had been changed, it was common knowledge that numbers results were often rigged. This was particularly the case any time the day's number was computed from races "at the Fair Grounds track in Louisiana, the State of King Fish Huey Long," but it was also true of other venues as well.[2] Not only were mobbed-up white bankers raking in the usual profits from numbers, but it increasingly seemed that when they wanted to, they could rig the system even more heavily in their favor. As Claude McKay almost wistfully concluded in 1940, "The invisible white syndicate now held the power and the secret of the gaudy 'kings' and 'queens.'"[3]

Yet as African Americans knew from hundreds of years of their history, white control over them was never total. For all the thuggish takeover of the numbers game by white racketeers, there were still cracks in the system and a certain amount of space in which entrepreneurial blacks could carve out a living for themselves. In February 1937, almost exactly nine years after Lester Walton wrote his piece for the *World*, another black reporter, this time working for the *Amsterdam News*, ventured out onto the streets of Harlem looking for a story, and found himself "at Harlem's famed numbers mart at 143d street and Seventh avenue." There he came across Susie, who, as the newspaper's headline declared, was a "Big Time Harlem Banker."

"What's leading, Susie?"

"Eight, 'Big Boy.'"

"Just missed the first 'digit' by 1. And I dreamed 'bout a pig last night, too. A pig's 8, but I didn't play it, like a fool! Here, Susie, put this two-bits on 66. Doubles have been coming out in the back for the last two weeks and I got a feeling that it's gonna be 66 today."

The banker and Big Boy were part of a crowd of a couple of hundred that gathered every afternoon, except on Sundays, at "New York's most peculiar market." Virtually all of the participants lived "between Lenox and Seventh avenues and 142d and 143d streets, which is one of the most thickly populated blocks in the United States." The first number came out at 4:15 P.M. and the second and third at hourly intervals. Six bankers operated there, accepting bets at odds on one number of 8:1, on two, 20:1, and on three, 600:1.

At 5:15 P.M. a young banker crossed the street to a phone, returned, and announced that the second number was "five." At least half of the players were women, and one of them was now "brimming with excitement." "I got half a 'buck' on 853," she said to another woman who walked up. "Gawd, if that number comes out, I'll be the happiest person in Harlem. I ain't hit for over a year." By 6:00 there were still 150 blacks waiting for "it" to come out. "It," the reporter explained, "is always the number." At 6:15 the young man traipsed back across the road, and on his return yelled out that the third number was "nine." As the black observer noted, "The figure 9 was very unpopular. No one in the crowd had a hit." The woman who had plunged on 853 "moved away slowly with bended head." Susie retired into Daniel's saloon for a shot of rye, and within ten minutes the crowd had melted away. As one of the last of the players "wended his way east towards Lenox avenue," he declared: "I'm gonna play 529 tomorrow."[4] If Scarlett O'Hara's declaration on the last page of the almost contemporaneous *Gone with the Wind* (1936)—"After all, tomorrow is another day"—underlined the novel's reaffirmation of traditional American values in a time of Depression, who knows but that, on the lower frequencies, this almost-invisible man's "I'm gonna play 529 tomorrow" spoke to many Harlem blacks of their position within that culture.[5] Regardless of whether it was Black Kings and Queens or white racketeers who made all the money from numbers, the optimism of ordinary African Americans—no matter how baseless this confidence—the sense that justice would be done and that they would hit the number, was one of the distinctive factors animating black culture. For perhaps the vast majority of black residents living in Harlem in the 1920s and 1930s, "I'm gonna play 529 tomorrow" was as good a summation of their credo as one was likely to find.

NOTES

ACKNOWLEDGMENTS

INDEX

Notes

PROLOGUE

1. Quotations in this prologue are from Henry Lee Moon, "Policy Queen," Writers Program New York City: Negroes of New York, The Schomburg Center Collections, Microfilm Roll no. 1. Also from *Amsterdam News,* March 8, 1933, p. 1; March 15, 1933, pp. 1, 7; and March 22, 1933, pp. 1-2. On Henry Moon, see Thomas J. Sugrue, *Sweet Land of Liberty: The Forgotten Struggle for Civil Rights in the North* (New York: Random House, 2008), 87-90.

INTRODUCTION

1. Black Draught and 666 were two laxatives popular in the South.
2. *New York World,* March 25, 1928, p. 17. We would like to thank Clare Corbould for this reference. On Lester Walton, see Susan Curtis, *Colored Memories: A Biographer's Quest for the Elusive Lester A. Walton* (Columbia: University of Missouri Press, 2008); on Hubert Harrison, see Jeffrey B. Perry, *Hubert Harrison: The Voice of Harlem Radicalism, 1883–1918* (New York: Columbia University Press, 2009).
3. Kenneth T. Jackson, ed., *The Encyclopedia of New York City* (New Haven: Yale University Press, 1995). There is a brief entry on "numbers" that covers the nineteenth and twentieth centuries. The piece claims that "penny ante numbers," a game for the poorest neighborhoods, was invented by Meyer Lansky. It is difficult to reconcile

that claim with the contents of this book. Clearing House numbers are not mentioned. There is an entry for the Clearing House, but it does not mention numbers at all. And there are no entries for such Harlem luminaries of numbers as Stephanie St. Clair or Casper Holstein.

4. Many of the histories of Harlem now seem dated. See James Weldon Johnson, *Black Manhattan* (1930; repr. New York: Atheneum, 1968); Seth Scheiner, *Negro Mecca: A History of the Negro in New York City, 1865–1920* (New York: New York University Press, 1965); Gilbert Osofsky, *Harlem: The Making of a Ghetto* (New York: Harper Torchbooks, 1971); and the more popular Jervis Anderson, *This Was Harlem, 1900–1950* (New York: Farrar, Straus and Giroux, 1982). The writing about black writers and the Harlem Renaissance has been extensive. See, for example, Nathan Huggins, *Harlem Renaissance* (New York: Oxford University Press, 1971); David Levering Lewis, *When Harlem Was in Vogue* (New York: Alfred A. Knopf, 1984); James De Jongh, *Vicious Modernism: Black Harlem and the Literary Imagination* (New York: Cambridge University Press, 1990); Ann Douglas, *Terrible Honesty: Mongrel Manhattan in the 1920s* (New York: Farrar, Straus and Giroux, 1995); George Hutchinson, *The Harlem Renaissance in Black and White* (Cambridge, Mass.: Harvard University Press, 1995); Brent Hayes Edwards, *The Practice of Diaspora: Literature, Translation, and the Rise of Black Internationalism* (Cambridge, Mass.: Harvard University Press, 2003); Martha Jane Nadell, *Enter the New Negroes: Images of Race in American Culture* (Cambridge, Mass.: Harvard University Press, 2004); Jeffrey B. Ferguson, *The Sage of Sugar Hill: George S. Schuyler and the Harlem Renaissance* (New Haven: Yale University Press, 2005). See also Marcy S. Sacks, *Before Harlem: The Black Experience in New York City Before World War I* (Philadelphia: University of Pennsylvania Press, 2006); and Clare Corbould, *Becoming African Americans: Black Public Life in Harlem, 1919–1939* (Cambridge, Mass.: Harvard University Press, 2009). On Harlem nightlife, see Kevin J. Mumford, *Interzones: Black/White Sex*

Districts in Chicago and New York in the Early Twentieth Century (New York: Columbia University Press, 1997); Shane Vogel, *The Scene of Harlem Cabaret: Race, Sexuality, Performance* (Chicago: University of Chicago Press, 2009); and Chad Heap, *Slumming: Sexual and Racial Encounters in American Nightlife, 1885–1940* (Chicago: University of Chicago Press, 2009). For previous treatments of numbers, see Rufus Schatzberg and Robert J. Kelly, *African American Organized Crime: A Social History* (New Brunswick: Rutgers University Press, 1997); Irma Watkins-Owens, *Blood Relations: Caribbean Immigrants and the Harlem Community, 1900–1930* (Bloomington: Indiana University Press, 1996), 136–148; Ron Chepesiuk, *Gangsters of Harlem: The Gritty Underworld of New York's Most Famous Neighborhood* (Fort Lee, N.J.: Barricade Books, 2007), 21–103. By far the best studies of this form of gambling, though, are centered on Detroit, not Harlem. See Victoria W. Wolcott, "The Culture of the Informal Economy: Numbers Runners in Inter-War Detroit," *Radical History Review* 69 (1997), 46–75; and, more generally, Victoria W. Wolcott, *Remaking Respectability: African American Women in Interwar Detroit* (Chapel Hill: University of North Carolina Press, 2001); and the truly remarkable work Gustav G. Carlson, "Number Gambling: A Study of a Culture Complex" (Ph.D. diss., University of Michigan, 1940).

5. Wallace Thurman, "Few Know Real Harlem, the City of Surprises: Quarter Million Negroes Form a Moving, Colorful Pageant of Life," in *The Collected Writings of Wallace Thurman: A Harlem Renaissance Reader,* ed. Amritjit Singh and Daniel M. Scott III (New Brunswick, N.J.: Rutgers University Press, 2003), 69.

6. *New York Age,* December 27, 1930, pp. 1–2; *New York Age,* October 18, 1924, p. 4. Ease of access, through newspapers, to numbers results was important in the expansion of the game: "The numbers game owes much to the newspapers, especially the dailies, which have published the clearing house balances." *New York Age,* January 3, 1931, p. 4.

7. *The Autobiography of Malcolm X,* with the assistance of Alex Haley (1965; repr. Harmondsworth, U.K.: Penguin, 1987), 171.

8. Johnson, *Black Manhattan,* 165.

9. Thurman, "Few Know Real Harlem."

10. Arthur P. Davis, "Growing Up in the New Negro Renaissance: 1920-1935," *Negro American Literature Forum* 2 (Autumn 1968), 54.

11. Throughout this book, we are following James Gregory in using the term "Black Metropolis" in order to redirect attention to what was present in black neighborhoods, rather than what they lacked. See James Gregory, *The Southern Diaspora: How the Great Migrations of Black and White Southerners Transformed America* (Chapel Hill: University of North Carolina Press, 2005), 114-116.

12. Anderson, *This Was Harlem,* 8.

13. Details of the way numbers worked are embedded in numerous issues of the *New York Age.* For a convenient summary see Claude McKay, *Harlem: Negro Metropolis* (New York: Dutton, 1940), 109-110.

14. *New York Age,* December 27, 1930, p. 1. Saunders Redding suggested that several "well-known insurance companies" got together to pressure the Clearing House. See J. Saunders Redding, "Playing the Numbers," *North American Review* 238 (December 1934), 537.

15. See *Amsterdam News,* December 24, 1930, pp. 1-2.

16. *Interstate Tattler,* September 2, 1927, p. 1.

17. On policy in Chicago, see St. Clair Drake and Horace R. Cayton, *Black Metropolis: A Study of Negro Life in a Northern City,* 2 vols. (1945; repr. New York: Harcourt, Brace, and World, 1970), 2:470-494. The Will Rogers number is on p. 475. See also Davarian L. Baldwin, *Chicago's New Negroes: Modernity, the Great Migration, and Black Urban Life* (Chapel Hill: University of North Carolina Press, 2007), 45-51; Nathan Thompson, *Kings: The True Story of Chicago's Policy Kings and Numbers Racketeers: An Informal History* (Chicago: Bronzeville Press, 2006), 19-39.

18. *Collier's,* July 29, 1939, p. 37.

19. *Amsterdam News,* June 21, 1933, pp. 1-2.

20. Claude McKay, *A Long Way from Home* (1937), quoted in Colin Grant, *Negro with a Hat: The Rise and Fall of Marcus Garvey and His Dream of Mother Africa* (London: Jonathan Cape, 2008), 186.

21. On Prohibition in Harlem, see Michael A. Lerner, *Dry Manhattan: Prohibition in New York City* (Cambridge, Mass.: Harvard University Press, 2007), 199–226.

22. On Detroit, see Carlson, "Number Gambling," 54–55.

23. Cheryl Lynn Greenberg, *"Or Does It Explode?" Black Harlem in the Great Depression* (New York: Oxford University Press, 1991), 114–139.

24. See Eric Lott, *Love and Theft: Blackface Minstrelsy and the American Working Class* (New York: Oxford University Press, 1993).

25. Christopher John Farley, "Elvis Rocks. But He's Not the First," *Time* magazine, July 6, 2004.

26. Irma Watkins-Owens has emphasized, in particular, the role of migrants from the Caribbean in the game of numbers. See Watkins-Owens, *Blood Relations,* 136–148.

27. Thomas M. Kavanagh, *Dice, Cards, Wheels: A Different History of French Culture* (Philadelphia: University of Pennsylvania Press, 2005), 3.

28. There is a larger historiographic point to be made here, with which it was unnecessary to burden the text. More than a quarter of a century ago now, in a review of David Levering Lewis's *When Harlem Was in Vogue* published in the *American Historical Review* in 1982, Lawrence Levine proposed that Lewis's book should have had as the subtitle *High Culture in Black Harlem, 1919–1935;* see Lawrence W. Levine, "Review of David Levering Lewis, *When Harlem Was in Vogue,*" *American Historical Review* 87 (1982), 552. For Levine, Lewis "seems" to be aware that "there were other Harlems besides the one he concentrates upon," but he "subjects none of it to close scrutiny." It was a devastating review and aroused some controversy. The matter is of some importance because Lewis's work, in so many ways, is the foundational book in modern writing about Harlem between the wars. And we would suggest that, to a remark-

able extent, the modern historiography of Harlem in the 1920s and 1930s exhibits the same flaws that Levine pointed to in Lewis's volume.

Partly, the problem is one of sources. Historians have been rather more interested in exploiting the wonderful James Weldon Johnson Collection at Yale University's Beinecke Library than in ferreting out other possible ways into the Harlem life of the interwar years. In our view, black newspapers are a rich and underutilized source for the writing of the social and cultural history of African Americans in the twentieth century. We are more familiar with other historiographies, particularly those of nineteenth-century America, and as we came to this project, we were surprised to see how historians have scanted these newspapers as a source. This is beginning to change—a number of recently completed and almost-finished dissertations make extensive use of the newspapers—and will continue to change as historians work out how to exploit imaginatively the availability of so many American newspapers online in searchable formats.

Taking our cue from Levine, our intention in this book is to recover a different Harlem from the one that is routinely presented in other historical accounts of the Black Metropolis. By using an extensive range of sources—not just the holdings at Beinecke Library but also parole records, prison records, and legal records—and above all by closely reading the black newspapers the *New York Age* and the *Amsterdam News,* we have been able to lay bare the world of numbers, one of the most important aspects of everyday life in Harlem between the wars.

I. HISTORY

1. On lotteries, see John Samuel Ezell ("one historian"), *Fortune's Merry Wheel: The Lottery in America* (Cambridge, Mass.: Harvard University Press, 1960), 79–100; Herbert Asbury, *Sucker's Progress: An Informal History of Gambling in America* (1938; repr. New York, 2003),

72-87, *New York Evening Post* quoted on p. 77; Ann Fabian, *Card Sharps, Dream Books, and Bucket Shops: Gambling in Nineteenth-Century America* (Ithaca: Cornell University Press, 1990), 113-128.

2. On policy, see Asbury, *Sucker's Progress*, 88-106; Ezell, *Fortune's Merry Wheel*, 95-98; Fabian, *Card Sharps, Dream Books, and Bucket Shops*, 136-142.

3. *The People v. Benjamin F. Haskins*, filed April 10, 1815, District Attorney's Closed Case Files (DACCF), Municipal Archives of the City of New York.

4. On the scandal over the Medical Science Lottery in 1818, see *New York Evening Post*, October 1, 1818; October 2, 1818; October 3, 1818; October 5, 1818; and October 6, 1818. See also *New-York City-Hall Recorder* (November 1818): 161-191.

5. *New York Evening Post*, February 12, 1818.

6. Ezell, *Fortune's Merry Wheel*, 95-96. Usually the numbers were drawn from the first seventy-eight, but occasionally it was the first ninety or seventy-five or some other number.

7. Ibid., 204-229; Asbury, *Sucker's Progress*, 82-83. For details of when the results arrived in New York City, see *National Police Gazette*, December 5, 1846.

8. *National Police Gazette*, December 5, 1846; and October 10, 1846.

9. *New York Daily Times*, April 26, 1856.

10. On dream books, see Fabian, *Card Sharps, Dream Books, and Bucket Shops*, 142-150. On agents charging to look at dream books, see Asbury, *Sucker's Progress*, 94.

11. *Journal of Commerce*, September 9, 1839.

12. Quoted in *National Police Gazette*, March 20, 1847.

13. *National Police Gazette*, May 2, 1846; June 13, 1846; and May 30, 1846.

14. *National Police Gazette*, October 11, 1845; and February 19, 1848.

15. On the end of slavery and the position of blacks in New York in the 1820s and 1830s, see Shane White, *Stories of Freedom in Black New York* (Cambridge, Mass.: Harvard University Press, 2002), 7-68.

16. *New York Daily Times*, April 26, 1856.

17. *New York Herald,* September 9, 1839; *Journal of Commerce,* January 15, 1839.

18. *National Police Gazette,* June 13, 1846. The best account of the flash newspapers is the excellent book by Patricia Cline Cohen, Timothy J. Gilfoyle, and Helen Lefkowitz Horowitz, *The Flash Press: Sporting Male Weeklies in 1840s New York* (Chicago: University of Chicago Press, 2008). See also Donna Dennis, *Licentious Gotham: Erotic Publishing and Its Prosecution in Nineteenth-Century New York* (Cambridge, Mass.: Harvard University Press, 2009), 43-92.

19. *New York Sporting Whip,* February 11, 1843.

20. Ibid., February 18, 1843; *Flash,* July 31, 1842. On the flash papers and extortion, see Cohen, Gilfoyle, and Horowitz, *The Flash Press,* 51-52.

21. Cohen, Gilfoyle, and Horowitz, *The Flash Press,* 2-3.

22. Shane White, Stephen Garton, Stephen Robertson, and Graham White, "The Envelope, Please," in *The Cultural Turn,* ed. James Cook, Lawrence Glickman, and Michael O'Malley (Chicago: University of Chicago Press, 2008), 121-151. On decoy houses see, for example, *Journal of Commerce,* August 14, 1839; on Peter Funks see *Tricks and Traps of New York City,* Part 1 (Boston: Charles H. Brainard, 1857), 6.

23. On the problem of counterfeiting, see the excellent Stephen Mihm, *A Nation of Counterfeiters: Capitalists, Con Men, and the Making of the United States* (Cambridge, Mass.: Harvard University Press, 2007). "Fraudulent at its core": Steve Fraser, *Every Man a Speculator: A History of Wall Street in American Life* (New York: HarperCollins, 2005), 67. See also Steve Fraser, *Wall Street: America's Dream Palace* (New Haven: Yale University Press, 2008).

24. *Subterranean,* November 18, 1843.

25. Ibid. See also the *Weekly Herald,* November 18, 1843.

26. *New York Herald,* March 17, 1842; *Flash,* July 31, 1842.

27. *Journal of Commerce,* September 15, 1840.

28. Edward Winslow Martin [James D. McCabe], *The Secrets of the Great City* (Philadelphia, 1868), 517; Jacob A. Riis, *How the Other Half Lives:*

Studies among the Tenements of New York (New York: Dover Publications, 1971; orig. pub. 1890), 118.

29. *New York Times,* August 27, 1893; and April 3, 1892.

30. On the Lexow Committee, see Edwin G. Burrows and Mike Wallace, *Gotham: A History of the New York City to 1898* (New York: Oxford University Press, 1999), 1192-93. [Lexow Committee], *Report and Proceedings of the Senate Committee Appointed to Investigate the Police Department of the City of New York,* 5 vols. (Albany: James B. Lyon, State Printer, 1895), III, 3243, 3238; and II, 2015.

31. [Lexow Committee], *Report and Proceedings,* III, 3246; and II, 2417-20.

32. Ibid., III, 3138.

33. Asbury, *Sucker's Progress,* 101-106; Riis, *How the Other Half Lives,* 118.

34. *New York Age,* May 3, 1924, p. 4.

35. We have rummaged extensively through the surviving legal records of the 1910s and 1920s in search of material for this book. We have read all the DACCF records for Manhattan for the second half of 1916, and for 1917, 1920, 1925, 1926, 1928, and 1930, and have scanned every case dealing with blacks. In order to work out if blacks are involved in a particular case, one usually has to undo the string tying up the file, open the file, and read several pages looking for clues. We untied somewhere in excess of 39,500 files and scanned roughly 3,800 cases. We also went through the parole records for the 1920s scanning African Americans, and combed the records of Elmira Reformatory and copied every record pertaining to Harlem blacks down to 1930. Obviously, much of the material we uncovered does not concern numbers and will be used in other publications and also on the website, Digital Harlem, that accompanies this book. See www.acl.arts.usyd.edu.au/harlem.

36. [*Joseph McCormack*] *against Chu Gum* (1917) #114457, DACCF; *Dennis H. Mitchell against Knita Genaka* (1917) #117671, DACCF. On the game of Gee Far, see *New Yorker,* April 18, 1936, pp. 13-14.

37. *James C. Sterett against Frederico Valentino* (1917) #114076, DACCF.

Gustav Carlson, in his remarkable study of numbers, did not find any references to Italian policy prior to 1928, but on the basis of his "informants" he surmised that it was introduced at the beginning of the twentieth century. See Gustav G. Carlson, "Number Gambling: A Study of a Culture Complex," (Ph.D. diss., University of Michigan, 1940), 30–34.

38. See, for example, *Alfred T. Simpson against Julian Garcia* (1917) #115662, DACCF. Garcia was a fifty-nine-year-old cigar maker who was born in Cuba and arrested on East 86th Street.

2. BEGINNINGS

1. Claude McKay, *Harlem: Negro Metropolis* (New York: E. P. Dutton, 1940), 107–109. For a similar account from McKay, but this time embedded in the beginnings of a novel first published decades after his death, see Claude McKay, *Harlem Glory: A Fragment of Aframerican Life* (Chicago: Charles H. Kerr, 1990).

2. *New York Age,* January 31, 1925, pp. 1–2.

3. *New York Times,* July 25, 1937, p. 56. Henry Lee Moon is one of the featured characters in Thomas Sugrue's recent study of civil rights in the North. See Thomas J. Sugrue, *Sweet Land of Liberty: The Forgotten Struggle for Civil Rights in the North* (New York: Random House, 2008), 87–90.

4. There are innumerable spellings of Cardenas's name. For consistency, unless the name is in quotes, we are arbitrarily using "Marcelino."

5. *Pittsburgh Courier,* September 24, 1938, p. 13. In a piece in the *Amsterdam News* in 1979, James Lawson claimed that in 1913 Carlos Duran, known as Dominique, arrived in New York from Santo Domingo "and introduced the numbers game to New York City." In 1979, Duran was in the hospital—he claimed to be eighty-two or eighty-three, but Lawson reckoned him to be ninety-two or ninety-three. It seems likely that Duran was involved in the early years of

numbers, but was not responsible for first introducing the game. See *New York Amsterdam News,* February 10, 1979, p. 25.

6. *New York Age,* July 5, 1924, p. 2.

7. See J. Saunders Redding, "Playing the Numbers," *North American Review* 238 (December 1934), 533–534.

8. McKay, *Harlem,* 107.

9. Ibid., 101.

10. *New York Age,* January 31, 1925, pp. 1–2.

11. Ibid., June 28, 1924, pp. 1–2. For details of Marcelino's house, see *Pittsburgh Courier,* September 24, 1938, p. 13.

12. Redding, "Playing the Numbers," 533–534. The "farmland in Virginia" is puzzling. As we shall see in Chapter 6, Holstein bought extensive tracts of land in his native Virgin Islands, and it is tempting to believe that Redding slightly misheard the details when his informant spoke to him.

13. *Chicago Defender,* September 30, 1922, p. 9; and February 3, 1923, p. 9.

14. *Amsterdam News,* February 7, 1923, p. 1.

15. *New York Age,* May 3, 1924, pp. 1–2; May 10, 1924, pp. 1–2; and July 12, 1924, p. 1.

16. Ibid., May 17, 1924, p. 1.

17. Ibid., January 16, 1926, p. 2.

18. Ibid., December 6, 1924, p. 1.

19. Ibid., July 10, 1926, p. 2.

20. Winthrop D. Lane, "Ambushed in the City: The Grim Side of Harlem," *Survey Graphic* 6, no. 6 (March 1925), 692; Thurman, "Few Know Real Harlem," in *The Collected Writings of Wallace Thurman: A Harlem Renaissance Reader,* ed. Amritjit Singh and Daniel M. Scott III (New Brunswick, N.J.: Rutgers University Press, 2003), 69; *New York Age,* May 10, 1924, pp. 1–2; *Interstate Tattler,* August 3, 1928, p. 1.

21. *New York Age,* May 3, 1924, p. 1; March 21, 1925, p. 2; and December 27, 1924, pp. 1–2.

22. Michael Taft, *Talkin' to Myself: Blues Lyrics, 1921–1942* (1983; rev. ed. New York: Routledge, 2005), 538. On the blues and policy, see Paul Oliver, *Screening the Blues: Aspects of the Blues Tradition* (1968; repr. New York: Da Capo, 1989), 128–147; Paul Oliver, *Blues Fell This Morning: Meaning in the Blues* (1960; repr. New York: Cambridge University Press, 1990), 132–137.

23. Quoted in Oliver, *Screening the Blues*, 131.

24. Taft, *Talkin' to Myself*, 367.

25. *Amsterdam News*, March 4, 1925, p. 3.

26. *New York Age*, May 10, 1924, pp. 1–2; and December 12, 1925, p. 3.

27. "City of Refuge" comes from a Rudolph Fisher short story. See Rudolph Fisher, "The City of Refuge," in *The New Negro*, ed. Alain Locke (1925; repr. New York, 1992), 57–74. The phrase has been variously used for chapter or section titles in books about Harlem. See, for example, David Levering Lewis, *When Harlem Was in Vogue* (New York: Alfred A. Knopf, 1984), 25–49; James De Jongh, *Vicious Modernism: Black Harlem and the Literary Imagination* (New York: Cambridge University Press, 1990), 15–32.

28. Lane, "Ambushed in the City," 692.

29. *New York Age*, July 5, 1924, p. 2.

30. Thurman, "Harlem: A Vivid Word Picture of the World's Greatest Negro City," 34.

31. *Interstate Tattler*, April 5, 1929, p. 1.

32. *New York Age*, November 20, 1926, p. 2; and March 8, 1930, pp. 4–6.

33. Ibid., May 10, 1924, pp. 1–2; and June 28, 1924, pp. 1–2.

34. Thurman, "Odd Jobs in Harlem," in *The Collected Writings of Wallace Thurman*, ed. Singh and Scott, 75; *New York Age*, June 12, 1926, p. 2.

35. *New York Age*, March 9, 1935, p. 6.

36. Ibid., December 6, 1924, p. 1.

37. *Amsterdam News*, February 8, 1928, p. 4; *New York Age*, February 11, 1928, p. 1.

38. *New York Age*, December 31, 1931, p. 1.

39. *Amsterdam News*, March 2, 1935, p. 2.

40. Gilbert Osofsky, *Harlem: The Making of a Ghetto* (New York: Harper Torchbooks, 1971), 113-117; Marcy S. Sacks, *Before Harlem: The Black Experience in New York City before World War I* (Philadelphia: University of Pennsylvania Press, 2006), 179-186; Cynthia Hickman, *Harlem Churches at the End of the Twentieth Century* (New York: Dunbar Press, 2001).

41. *New York Age,* May 10, 1924, p. 2.

3. DREAMS

1. See the New York Clearing House's website at www.theclearinghouse.org/home.php. There is a brief official history of the Clearing House under "History." No mention is made of the Clearing House numbers.

2. "Statistical Thrills," *Time* magazine, March 17, 1924; *New York Times,* December 23, 1930, p. 28.

3. *New York Age,* August 2, 1924, p. 1; June 15, 1925, p. 1; and March 14, 1925, p. 1.

4. *Jim Nairne against Harold Bancroft* (1925) #159768, District Attorney's Closed Case Files (DACCF), Municipal Archives of the City of New York. On the importance of the con, see Shane White, Stephen Garton, Stephen Robertson, and Graham White, "The Envelope, Please," in *The Cultural Turn,* ed. James Cook, Lawrence Glickman, and Michael O'Malley (Chicago: University of Chicago Press, 2008), 121-151.

5. *New York Times,* August 9, 1929, p. 10; August 9, 1929, p. 13; and August, 28, 1929, p. 13.

6. Ibid., December 6, 1928, p. 1.

7. *James Carberry against Silas Holt* (1925) #160110, DACCF; *New York Age,* October 9, 1926, p. 3.

8. *New York Age,* November 22, 1930, p. 1.

9. Langston Hughes to Carl Van Vechten, January 28, 1931, Box 1, Folder 5, Zora Neale Hurston Collection, Beinecke Library, Yale University, New Haven, Conn.

10. *New York Age,* June 2, 1923, p. 1.

11. *Uriah McCoy against Douglas Jefferson and Malcolm Wright* (1926) #165707, DACCF.

12. Parole Case Files #11179 (1928), Municipal Archives of the City of New York. Researchers are granted access to these records on the condition that they not reveal probationers' names.

13. *Chicago Defender,* August 18, 1934, p. 3.

14. *Amsterdam News,* August 18, 1926, p. 7.

15. *Gurnie Roberts against Fred Woods* (1930) #181888, DACCF.

16. On dream books, see the pamphlet Harry B. Weiss, "Oneirocritica Americana; The Story of American Dream Books," (New York: New York Public Library, 1944), reprinted from the *Bulletin of the New York Public Library* (June–July 1944).

17. *Amsterdam News,* April 20, 1932, p. 6.

18. *New York Times,* August 18, 1938, p. 12.

19. *Amsterdam News,* August 28, 1937, p. 11.

20. *Pittsburgh Courier,* May 7, 1938, p. 6.

21. See, for example, the report of the christening of Konje's only son, Reginald Gilbert: *Amsterdam News,* February 24, 1932, p. 4.

22. Robert Hill, ed., *The Marcus Garvey and Universal Negro Improvement Association Papers,* vol. 2 (Berkeley: University of California Press, 1983), 541, note 3; Theodore Kornweibel Jr., *"Seeing Red:" Federal Campaigns against Black Militancy, 1919–1925* (Bloomington: Indiana University Press, 1998), 110–115; *Amsterdam News,* magazine section, January 19, 1927, p. 1. On the brawl with Julian, see *Amsterdam News,* May 13, 1925, p. 1; for an example of a divorce raid, see *Amsterdam News,* August 3, 1927, p. 1. *Interstate Tattler,* November, 7, 1930, p. 13; *Amsterdam News,* November 5, 1930, p. 1; *New York Age,* December 20, 1930, p. 10.

23. *Amsterdam News,* August 28, 1937, p. 11. Such comments were fairly common. See, for example, Claude McKay, *Harlem: Negro Metropolis* (New York: E. P. Dutton, 1940), 106.

24. *New York Age,* March 7, 1925, p. 2.

25. *Amsterdam News,* May 25, 1940, p. 13.

26. Gustav G. Carlson, "Number Gambling: A Study of a Culture Complex" (Ph.D. diss., University of Michigan, 1940), 95–96.

27. *Herbert Reid against Orville Milwood* (1930) #182456, DACCF (he is "Milwood" in the DA's files and "Millwood" in the newspapers); *Artemus Green against Vernon Mullett* (1930) #183114, DACCF (the papers dealing with Millwood are misfiled in this case file); *Amsterdam News,* June 16, 1930; *New York Age,* July 19, 1930. For a fuller explication of black cons in Harlem in the 1920s, see White, Garton, Robertson, and White, "The Envelope, Please."

28. See, for example, *New York Age,* April 12, 1930.

29. Amritjit Singh and Daniel M. Scott III, eds., *The Collected Writings of Wallace Thurman: A Harlem Renaissance Reader* (New Brunswick, N.J.: Rutgers University Press, 2003), 306–309, 324.

4. TURF WARS

1. *New York Age,* June 28, 1924, p. 1; July 5, 1924, pp. 1–2; and July 12, 1924, pp. 1, 7.

2. *New York Age,* September 27, 1924, pp. 1, 7; July 18, 1925, pp. 1, 3; June 12, 1926, pp. 1–2; and August 7, 1926, p. 2. See also Rufus Schatzberg and Robert J. Kelly, *African American Organized Crime: A Social History* (New Brunswick, N.J.: Rutgers University Press, 1997), 90.

3. *New York Age,* November 20, 1926, p. 1; and March 6, 1926, p. 3.

4. Ibid., June 26, 1926, pp. 1–2; and July 18, 1925, pp. 1, 3.

5. Ibid., June 12, 1926, pp. 1–2.

6. Ibid., June 12, 1926, pp. 1–2; and August 7, 1926, p. 2.

7. Ibid., August 7, 1926, p. 2; Claude McKay, *Harlem: Negro Metropolis* (New York: E. P. Dutton, 1940), 113; *New York Age,* December 27, 1924, pp. 1–2.

8. James Weldon Johnson, *Black Manhattan* (New York: Atheneum, 1968; orig. pub. 1930), 160–161; Rudolph Fisher, "The Caucasian

Storms Harlem," *American Mercury* (August 1927): 393–398; Langston Hughes, *The Big Sea: An Autobiography* (New York: Thunder's Mouth Press, 1986), 228.

9. Stephen Robertson, "Harlem Undercover: Vice Investigators, Race, and Prostitution, 1910–1930," *Journal of Urban History* 35 (2009): 486–504.

10. *Peter King against William Smith* (1920) #129713, District Attorney's Closed Case Files (DACCF), Municipal Archives of the City of New York, New York, New York. For other examples, see *New York Age,* August 20, 1921, p. 1; ibid., June 12, 1926, p. 1; *Amsterdam News,* August 25, 1926, p. 3; *New York Age,* July 28, 1928, p. 1; *Amsterdam News,* August 22, 1928, p. 1.

11. *Amsterdam News,* July 23, 1930, p. 2; also January 15, 1930, p. 8.

12. *New York Age,* November 27, 1926, p. 1.

13. Ibid.

14. Ibid.

15. Ibid., December 4, 1926, p. 1.

16. Ibid., December 11, 1926, p. 1.

17. Ibid., December 18, 1926, p. 1.

18. McKay, *Harlem,* 101; *Amsterdam News,* March 2, 1935, pp. 1–2.

19. *Casper Holstein against Michael Bernstein* (1928) #175778, DACCF.

20. According to the *New York Times*'s account, the kidnapping occurred shortly after 1:00 A.M.; Holstein was seized on the sidewalk by four white men as he was leaving the apartment; Holstein's chauffeur was still there and, indeed, pursued the kidnappers for a while but lost them. *New York Times,* September 23, 1928, p. 1.

21. *Amsterdam News,* September 26, 1928, pp. 1, 2.

22. Ibid.; also October 3, 1928, p. 1.

23. Ibid., October 3, 1928, p. 1.

24. *Casper Holstein against Michael Bernstein* (1928), DACCF.

25. *New York Times,* September 25, 1928, p. 30; *Amsterdam News,* October 3, 1928, pp. 1, 2; Mayme Hatcher Johnson and Karen E. Quinones

Miller, *Harlem Godfather: The Rap on my Husband, Ellsworth "Bumpy" Johnson* (Philadelphia: Oshun Publishing Company, 2008), 74–75.

26. *New York Times,* September 23, 1928, p. 1.
27. Helen Lawrenson, *Stranger at the Party: A Memoir* (New York: Random House, 1975), 175; Johnson and Miller, *Harlem Godfather,* 70–71; *Pittsburgh Courier,* December 27, 1930, p. 2.
28. *Pittsburgh Courier,* December 27, 1930, p. 2; *Amsterdam News,* January 1, 1930, p. 2; ibid., March 19, 1930, p. 1; ibid., December 10, 1930, p. 1; *New York Times,* December 9, 1930, p. 1.
29. *New York Times,* May 24, 1931, p. XX5. Thomas Dewey dated this change to 1930. See *New York Times,* August 18, 1938, p. 12.
30. *New York Age,* December 27, 1930, p. 1; *New York Times,* December 23, 1930, p. 28; *Negro World,* January 3, 1931, p. 1; *Chicago Defender,* January 3, 1931, p. 11. Saunders Redding suggested that several "well-known insurance companies" got together to pressure the Clearing House. See J. Saunders Redding, "Playing the Numbers," *North American Review* 238 (December 1934), 537. A search of the archives of the Clearing House turned up very little material. The minutes for the meeting of December 22, 1930, merely stated that "the Manager was instructed to record that the publication of the daily figures of Clearing House exchanges and balances and the Federal Reserve Bank credit balance will cease beginning January 1st, 1931." If there was any supporting material for this meeting, it was probably destroyed when the Clearing House moved to a new location in the early 1960s. Minutes of the Clearing House Committee, December 22, 1930, Archives of the Clearing House, New York.
31. *Amsterdam News,* December 24, 1930, pp. 1–2; *Negro World,* January 3, 1931, p. 4.
32. *Amsterdam News,* December 24, 1930; *New York Times,* January 28, 1931, p. 37; Ibid., August 21, 1938, p. 99.
33. This example is taken from an article in *New York Times Magazine,* August 21, 1938, pp. 15–16.

34. J. Saunders Redding, "Playing the Numbers," 537–538.

35. Emily Bernard, ed., *Remember Me to Harlem: The Letters of Langston Hughes and Carl Van Vechten, 1925–1964* (New York: Alfred A. Knopf, 2001), 83.

36. If any of this ephemeral material survives for Harlem, we have not managed to find it. Gustav Carlson, who was there and collected Detroit material in the 1930s, reproduces in his thesis a "notice" detailing that the "Mutuel Number" will be taken from Laurel Park in Maryland on the dates October 8 to October 30; from Pimlico in Maryland on the dates October 31 to November 14; and from Jefferson Park in New Orleans on November 30 and subsequent dates "until further notice." It seems likely that similar notices were used in Harlem. See Gustav G. Carlson, "Number Gambling: A Study of a Culture Complex" (Ph.D. diss., University of Michigan, 1940), 15ff.

5. NUMBERS' LORE

1. *Amsterdam News,* October 17, 1923, p. 1; *New York Age,* June 21, 1924, p. 1; ibid., July 26, 1924, p. 3.

2. *New York Age,* July 18, 1925, p. 1. For a detailed legal opinion by a "prominent lawyer" on why the old laws did not cover numbers, see *New York Age,* July 24, 1926, p. 3.

3. *Amsterdam News,* November 23, 1927, p. 000.

4. *Edward Robinson against Bolivar Garcia* (1925) #160076, District Attorney's Closed Case Files (DACCF), Municipal Archives of the City of New York; *Albert Wolcott against Peter McKay* (1925) #160905, DACCF; *Benjamin Garrick against Alex Cornelius* (1928) #172798, DACCF.

5. *New York Age,* July 10, 1926, p. 2; and January 30, 1926, p. 2.

6. *Against Samuel Johnson, Otherwise Known as Edward Turner* (1926) #165912, DACCF. For another case of impersonation, this time clearly to get the bail forfeiture vacated and rescinded, see *James Quinlivan against John Carter* (1930) #183311, DACCF.

7. On the Seabury Investigation, see William B. Northrop and John B. Northrop, *The Insolence of Office: The Story of the Seabury Investigations* (New York: G. P. Putnam's Sons, 1932).

8. *Collier's,* July 29, 1939, pp. 21, 37.

9. Accompanying this book, there is a map-based website called Digital Harlem (www.acl.arts.usyd.edu.au/harlem), which can be used to chart and examine our data on numbers arrests. For an introduction using the example of numbers, see the blog at digitalharlemblog.wordpress.com/2009/04/17/numbers/ (part of the Digital Harlem site).

10. *George Treubert against Charles Dyce* (1926) #163969, DACCF; *Ernest Walsh against George Lewis* (1926) #165420, DACCF.

11. *Charles Williams against Jacob Goldman and Doris Altman* (1926) #164009, DACCF; *James Quinlivan against Adolph Isles* (1926) #163885, DACCF; *Harry Ervin against John Diamond* (1925) #160317, DACCF.

12. *George Treubert against Charles Dyce* (1926) #163969, DACCF.

13. Mayme Hatcher Johnson and Karen E. Quinones Miller, *Harlem Godfather: The Rap on My Husband, Ellsworth "Bumpy" Johnson* (Philadelphia: Oshun Publishing Company, 2008), 155-156.

14. *Harold Peace against John Jackson, Charlie Taylor and William Whitson* (1926) #163786, DACCF; *John Mehrtens against Charles Dyce* (1926) #164319, DACCF.

15. *New York Age,* May 17, 1924, p. 1; and July 19, 1924, pp. 1, 3.

16. *New York Age,* July 26, 1924, p. 1; and February 19, 1927, p. 3.

17. See, for example, *Joseph Miller against Eli McClain* (1925) #162342, DACCF.

18. *New York Age,* August 10, 1929, p. 1; *Amsterdam News,* February 12, 1930, p. 1; *New York Age,* November 8, 1930, p. 1.

19. *New York Age,* August 15, 1925, p. 1; and November 14, 1925, p. 1.

20. *Hazel Dickson against Alice Hooker* (1917) #116922, DACCF.

21. *Edward Atkins against Frank Joyner* (1926) #165144, DACCF.

22. Thurman, "Odd Jobs in Harlem," in *The Collected Writings of Wallace*

Thurman: A Harlem Renaissance Reader, ed. Amritjit Singh and Daniel M. Scott III (New Brunswick, N.J.: Rutgers University Press, 2003), 74. On the importance of dress and style, see Shane White and Graham White, *Stylin': African American Expressive Culture from Its Beginnings to the Zoot Suit* (Ithaca: Cornell University Press, 1998), 220–247.

23. *New York Age,* May 3, 1924, pp. 1–2; and June 4, 1927, p. 2.
24. Ibid., May 3, 1924, p. 1.
25. Ibid., January 10, 1925, pp. 1–2; and July 31, 1926, p. 1.
26. *Amsterdam News,* August 3, 1927, p. 1; and December 25, 1929, p. 2.
27. *New York Age,* March 12, 1927, p. 2; and October 26, 1926, p. 2.

6. OF KINGS AND QUEENS

1. *Amsterdam News,* magazine section, February 23, 1927, p. 1.
2. *New York Age,* July 10, 1926, p. 2; *Pittsburgh Courier,* September 24, 1938, p. 13; *New York Age,* September 20, 1930, p. 1; ibid., July 15, 1933, p. 1.
3. *New York Times,* July 18, 1905, p. 2.
4. Baxter Leach, "Short Outline of Fraternal and Social Organizations," "Negro Organizations," Roll 3, WPA Writers Program Collection, Schomburg Center for Research in Black Culture, New York Public Library; Irma Watkins-Owens, *Blood Relations: Caribbean Immigrants and the Harlem Community, 1900–1930* (Bloomington: Indiana University Press, 1996), 72–73, 169.
5. *Amsterdam News,* February 15, 1936, p. 1; *Chicago Defender,* January 15, 1916, p. 3; ibid., January 13, 1917, p. 2.
6. *Chicago Defender,* September 29, 1928, p. 3; *Amsterdam News,* February 22, 1936, pp. 1, 17; *Chicago Defender,* February 8, 1936, pp. 1, 2; *Amsterdam News,* April 15, 1944, p. A1.
7. *Chicago Defender,* March 5, 1927, p. A1; ibid., September 29, 1928, p. 3; *Amsterdam News,* February 29, 1936, p. 2; Watkins-Owens, *Blood Relations,* 144.

8. *Chicago Defender*, September 29, 1928, p. 3; *Amsterdam News*, February 22, 1936, pp. 1, 7.

9. *Amsterdam News*, August 3, 1927, p. 1; *New York Age*, August 20, 1927, p. 1; *Amsterdam News*, August 22, 1927, p. 1.

10. *Charles Williams against Howard Brown* (1925) #158694, District Attorney's Closed Case Files (DACCF), Municipal Archives of the City of New York; *Harold Moore against Alexander Hansen* (1925) #159412, DACCF.

11. Claude McKay, *Harlem: Negro Metropolis* (New York: E. P. Dutton, 1940), 104-105; Langston Hughes, *The Big Sea: An Autobiography* (New York: Thunder's Mouth Press, 1986), 214-215. On his distance from elite society, see also Jervis Anderson, *This Was Harlem: 1900–1950* (New York: Farrar Straus Giroux, 1982), 336.

12. *New York Times*, December 24, 1935, p. 3; *Amsterdam News*, February 15, 1936, p. 1; *Chicago Defender*, February 15, 1936, p. 1; *Amsterdam News*, February 29, 1936, p. 2.

13. *New York Times*, April 9, 1944, p. 35; *Amsterdam News*, April 15, 1944, p. A1.

14. Colin Grant, *Negro with a Hat: The Rise and Fall of Marcus Garvey and His Dream of Mother Africa* (London: Jonathan Cape, 2008), 349-455; Ethel Collins to Amy Jacques Garvey, July 30, 1940, in Robert Hill, ed., *The Marcus Garvey and Universal Negro Improvement Association Papers*, vol. 7 (Berkeley: University of California Press, 1990), 945-948.

15. On Walker, see A'Lelia Bundles, *On Her Own Ground: The Life and Times of Madam C. J. Walker* (New York: Scribners, 2001); and Beverly Lowry, *Her Dream of Dreams: The Rise and Triumph of Madam C. J. Walker* (New York: Alfred A. Knopf, 2003).

16. *New York Times*, April 9, 1944, p. 34; Hughes, *The Big Sea*, 214-215.

17. *Amsterdam News*, November 20, 1929, p. 13.

18. St. Clair was by far the most prominent Numbers Queen, but there were other Queens and other female bankers, although very

little is known about any of them. In June 1935, a Mrs. Anita Soas-Howell, a "Reputed Numbers Queen of New York City," drowned while on a two-month vacation in the Bermuda Islands, and the news was reported in the black press. See *New York Age,* June 15, 1935.

19. *Amsterdam News,* March 19, 1930, p. 1; *New York Age,* September 24, 1932, p. 1.

20. *New York Age,* September 24, 1932, p. 1; ibid., December 12, 1931, p. 1; *Interstate Tattler,* December 10, 1931, p. 2.

21. *Amsterdam News,* November 20, 1937, p. 1; ibid., March 26, 1938, p. 1; ibid., October 28, 1939, p. 15; Mayme Hatcher Johnson and Karen E. Quinones Miller, *Harlem Godfather: The Rap on My Husband, Ellsworth "Bumpy" Johnson* (Philadelphia: Oshun Publishing Company, 2008), 115.

22. *People of the State of New York against Herbert Russell* (1936), 132, 143, 319, 493, 251, 356-357, 486, 757, and 869, Court of Appeals of the State of New York; *Amsterdam News,* March 15, 1933, pp. 1, 7; *New York Age,* March 18, 1933, p. 1.

23. John H. Johnson, *Fact Not Fiction in Harlem* (Glen Cove, N.Y.: Northern Type Printing, 1980), 100.

24. Johnson and Miller, *Harlem Godfather,* 39; Johnson (Colored) #32662, New York State Reformatory Files, New York State Archives, Albany, N.Y. Helen Lawrenson stated that he was born on October 16, 1906. See Helen Lawrenson, *Stranger at the Party: A Memoir* (New York: Random House, 1975), 180.

25. Johnson #32662; Johnson and Miller, *Harlem Godfather,* 47, 65-66.

26. Stewart #32661, New York State Reformatory Files; Johnson #32662.

27. Lawrenson, *Stranger at the Party,* 181; Johnson and Miller, *Harlem Godfather,* 69.

28. *New York Times,* July 10, 1968, p. 46; Johnson and Miller, *Harlem Godfather,* 220-225.

29. Lawrenson, *Stranger at the Party,* 163-164.

30. Ibid., 168-169.

31. Johnson and Miller, *Harlem Godfather*, 68; Lawrenson, *Stranger at the Party*, 181; Johnson, *Fact Not Fiction in Harlem*, 111–112.
32. *New York Times*, July 10, 1968, p. 46; Lawrenson, *Stranger at the Party*, 170; *New York Times*, July 12, 1968, p. 13; Johnson, *Fact Not Fiction in Harlem*, 106.
33. Johnson, *Fact Not Fiction in Harlem*, 103.
34. Ibid., 115; Lawrenson, *Stranger at the Party*, 164–167.
35. *New York Times*, July 12, p. 13.
36. Lawrenson, *Stranger at the Party*, 181–182, 184, 166.

7. THE DUTCHMAN COMETH

1. *New York Times*, August 20, 1938, p. 7.
2. Mayme Hatcher Johnson and Karen E. Quinones Miller, *Harlem Godfather: The Rap on My Husband, Ellsworth "Bumpy" Johnson* (Philadelphia: Oshun Publishing Company, 2008), 74.
3. Quoted in Ron Chepesiuk, *Gangsters of Harlem: The Gritty Underworld of New York's Most Famous Neighborhood* (Fort Lee, N.J.: Barricade Books, 2007), 80. See also Kenneth T. Jackson, ed., *The Encyclopedia of New York City* (New Haven: Yale University Press, 1995), 1048.
4. *Collier's*, July 29, 1939, p. 38; August 5, 1939, p. 43; and July 29, 1939, p. 21.
5. *New York Times*, August 20, 1938, p. 7; *Amsterdam News*, August 27, 1938, p. 10.
6. *Collier's*, July 29, 1939, p. 38.
7. Ibid., pp. 38, 40.
8. *New York Times*, August 18, 1938, p. 12.
9. Ibid., August 20, 1938, p. 7; *Collier's*, July 29, 1939, p. 40. According to Mayme Johnson, after liquidating his bank, Ison was $18,000 short and not $12,000; see Johnson and Miller, *Harlem Godfather*, 77.
10. *Amsterdam News*, August 27, 1938, p. 10.
11. *New York Times*, August 19, 1938, p. 11.

12. *New York Age,* August 13, 1932, pp. 1, 3.
13. *Collier's,* July 29, 1939, p. 40.
14. *Pittsburgh Courier,* August 27, 1938, p. 4.
15. Ibid., October 16, 1937, p. 1.
16. Thomas E. Dewey, *Twenty against the Underworld* (New York: Doubleday, 1974), 215. On prostitution, see pp. 187-226.
17. *New York Age,* August 13, 1932, pp. 1, 3.
18. Dewey, *Twenty against the Underworld,* 379.
19. *New York Times,* August 18, 1938, p. 15.
20. *Collier's,* July 29, 1939, p. 40.
21. *New York Times,* August 18, 1938, p. 1.
22. *Collier's,* July 29, 1939, p. 40.
23. Dewey, *Twenty against the Underworld,* 383.
24. *Pittsburgh Courier,* August 27, 1938, p. 4. The link with the Democratic Party continued throughout the life of numbers. In 1964, the voter turnout in Harlem was huge. This was due partly to the fact that Harlem blacks were anti-Goldwater, and partly to the fact that many supported Robert Kennedy's run for the Senate, but mostly to the fact that almost all of the numbers bankers "agreed to give a $1 free play on the numbers to those who would register and vote." See *New York Times,* April 4, 1971, p. SM108.
25. *New York Age,* August 13, 1932, pp. 1, 3; and August 20, 1932, pp. 1, 5. The use of "artichoke" in our text was not random. Supposedly, one of Schultz's backers was Ciro Terranova, also known as the "millionaire 'artichoke king.'"
26. Cheryl Greenberg, *"Or Does It Explode?" Black Harlem in the Great Depression* (New York: Oxford University Press, 1991), 3-6, 93-139; Mark Naison, *Communists in Harlem during the Great Depression* (Urbana: University of Illinois Press, 1983).
27. *New York Age,* September 24, 1932, p. 1; *Amsterdam News,* March 15, 1933, pp. 1, 7; Johnson and Miller, *Harlem Godfather,* 82-83; *New York Times,* April 4, 1971, p. SM108.

28. William E. Leuchtenburg, *Franklin D. Roosevelt and the New Deal: 1932–1940* (New York: Harper and Row, 1963), 39; *New York Age,* March 4, 1933, p. 1. On the economic collapse and the early weeks of FDR's administration, see Anthony J. Badger, *FDR: The First Hundred Days* (New York: Hill and Wang, 2008); Adam Cohen, *Nothing to Fear: FDR's Inner Circle and the Hundred Days that Created Modern America* (New York: Penguin, 2009).

29. Leuchtenburg, *Franklin D. Roosevelt and the New Deal,* 18; *Amsterdam News,* March 8, 1933, p. 1; *New York Age,* March 11, 1933, p. 1.

30. *Amsterdam News,* March 15, 1933, p. 1; ibid., March 22, 1933, pp. 1–2; Helen Lawrenson, *Stranger at the Party: A Memoir* (New York: Random House, 1975), 176; Johnson and Miller, *Harlem Godfather,* 83–105. The *New York Age* may well have made such a comment, but we did not notice it in our many readings of the newspaper.

31. *Amsterdam News,* March 22, 1933, pp. 1–2; *New York Age,* March 25, 1933, p. 1. For St. Clair's later claim that she furnished the tip to police, see *Amsterdam News,* August 27, 1938, pp. 1–2.

32. *Amsterdam News,* April 5, 1933, pp. 1, 10.

33. Ibid., August 27, 1938, pp. 1–2.

34. See, for example, *New York Age,* August 13, 1932, pp. 1, 3.

35. *Amsterdam News,* June 21, 1933, pp. 1–2.

36. *New York Age,* August 20, 1932, pp. 1, 5.

37. *Amsterdam News,* July 5, 1933, p. 2.

38. *New York Age,* June 17, 1933, p. 1.

39. Ibid.

40. *Amsterdam News,* July 19, 1933, p. 1; *New York Age,* August 5, 1933, p. 1.

41. *New York Times,* February 27, 1935, p. 1, 9; *Collier's,* July 29, 1939, p. 40.

42. *New York Times,* August 18, 1938, p. 12; Dewey, *Twenty against the Underworld,* 321–322.

43. *New York Age,* January 12, 1935, p. 1; and January 19, 1935, p. 1.

44. *New York Age,* January 12, 1935, p. 1.
45. *Amsterdam News,* March 2, 1935, pp. 1–2.

8. OF BANKS AND BANKERS

1. *Pittsburgh Courier,* April 2, 1927, p. 5; Harry H. Pace, "The Business of Banking among Negroes," *Crisis* (February 1927), 184–188. More generally, see Abram L. Harris, *The Negro as Capitalist: A Study of Banking and Business among American Negroes* (Philadelphia: American Academy of Political and Social Science, 1936), a book that remains the best study of blacks and business.

2. We have read every case for Manhattan in the District Attorney's Closed Case Files for the second half of 1916, as well as for 1917, 1920, 1925, 1926, 1928, and 1930, and have scanned all cases that involved African Americans. See District Attorney's Closed Case Files (DACCF), Municipal Archives of the City of New York. Some cases involving blacks with bank accounts are discussed in Shane White, Stephen Garton, Stephen Robertson, and Graham White, "The Envelope, Please," in *The Cultural Turn in U.S. History: Pasts, Presents, Futures,* ed. James Cook, Lawrence Glickman, and Michael O'Malley (Chicago: University of Chicago Press, 2008), 121–151.

3. *Amsterdam News,* November 11, 1931, p. 10.

4. *Pittsburgh Courier,* April 2, 1927, p. 5; *Atlanta Daily World,* November 16, 1941, p. 4.

5. *Chicago Defender,* September 22, 1928, p. 2.

6. *Richardson against Geter and Webb* (1930) #183993, DACCF.

7. Ibid.

8. Ibid.

9. *Franklin Mathews against Roland Wilson* (1930) #180181, DACCF; *David Diaz against James Hurtt* (1930) #180134, DACCF.

10. Parole Case Files #11076 (1928), Municipal Archives of the City of New York. Researchers are granted access to these records on the condition that they not reveal probationers' names.

11. *New York Age,* September 6, 1924, p. 3; *Herbert Reid against Orville*

Milwood (1930) #182456, DACCF. These and other cases are discussed in White, Garton, Robertson, and White, "The Envelope, Please."

12. *Atlanta Daily World,* November 16, 1941, p. 4.
13. See Ivan Light, "Numbers Gambling among Blacks: A Financial Institution," *American Sociological Review* 42 (December 1977): 892–904; Jackson Lears, *Something for Nothing: Luck in America* (New York: Viking, 2003), 260-261.
14. *New York Times,* April 4, 1971, pp. SM26, 108.
15. *Amsterdam News,* February 22, 1936, p. 17; *New York Age,* August 13, 1932, pp. 1, 3.
16. *Atlanta Daily World,* November 16, 1941, p. 4.
17. *Chicago Defender,* April 39, 1932, p. 13; *Pittsburgh Courier,* September 24, 1938, p. 13.
18. *Chicago Defender,* April 30, 1932, p. 13; *Pittsburgh Courier,* September 24, 1938, p. 13. For a very good discussion of the role of policy in Chicago's business world, see Davarian L. Baldwin, *Chicago's New Negroes: Modernity, the Great Migration, and Black Urban Life* (Chapel Hill: University of North Carolina Press, 2007), 46-51.
19. Juliet E. K. Walker, *The History of Black Business in America* (New York: Macmillan Library Reference USA, 1998), 238.
20. We have relied heavily on the excellent study Lewis A. Erenberg, *The Greatest Fight of Our Generation: Louis vs. Schmeling* (New York: Oxford University Press, 2006), 29-30. See also David Margolick, *Beyond Glory: Joe Louis vs. Max Schmeling, and a World on the Brink* (New York: Alfred A. Knopf, 2005), 60-61.
21. Neil Lanctot, *Negro League Baseball: The Rise and Ruin of a Black Institution* (Philadelphia: University of Pennsylvania Press, 2004), 60; Adrian Burgos Jr., *Playing America's Game: Baseball, Latinos, and the Color Line* (Berkeley: University of California Press, 2007), 130.
22. Lanctot, *Negro League Baseball,* 42-43; Burgos, *Playing America's Game,* 121-134; *Amsterdam News,* April 3, 1937, p. 23.

23. *Amsterdam News*, January 16, 1937, p. 1; ibid., April 3, 1937, p. 1; quoted in Lanctot, *Negro League Baseball*, 60.
24. *New York Times*, April 4, 1971, pp. SM109-110.
25. James Weldon Johnson, *The Autobiography of an Ex-Colored Man* (New York: Hill and Wang, 1960; orig. pub. 1912), 103-125, 192-196. We have been strongly influenced by Ann Fabian's reading of this novel. See Fabian, *Card Sharps, Dream Books, and Bucket Shops: Gambling in Nineteenth-Century America* (Ithaca, N.Y.: Cornell University Press, 1990), 108-113.
26. *New York Age*, February 12, 1927, p. 9.
27. Claude McKay, *Harlem: Negro Metropolis* (New York: E. P. Dutton, 1940), 114.
28. The letter is contained in the file for *Morris Popkin against Harold Jones and James Cooper* (1930) #184319, DACCF.
29. *New York Age*, January 10, 1925, pp. 1-2; and December 17, 1932, p. 1.
30. Ibid., March 26, 1927, p. 2.
31. On these points, see the excellent article Ross McKibbin, "Working-Class Gambling in Britain, 1880-1939," *Past and Present* 82 (1979), 160-162.
32. Gustav G. Carlson, "Number Gambling: A Study of a Culture Complex," (Ph.D. diss., University of Michigan, 1940), 81, Appendix B (unpaginated).
33. *Amsterdam News*, February 22, 1936, p. 17.
34. Carlson, "Number Gambling," 139, 145; Reuven Brenner, Gabrielle A. Brenner, and Aaron Brown, *A World of Chance: Betting on Religion, Games, Wall Street* (New York: Cambridge University Press, 2008).
35. *Chicago Defender*, May 30, 1931, p. 3; *Amsterdam News*, July 20, 1932, p. 1.

9. ALL OVER TOWN

1. *Collier's*, August 5, 1939, p. 44.
2. Thomas E. Dewey, *Twenty against the Underworld* (New York: Doubleday, 1974), 272-278.

3. *New York Times,* October 25, 1935, pp. 1, 16; *Time,* November 4, 1935; *Collier's,* July 22, 1939, p. 41; *New York Times,* October 8, 1989, p. NJ23.

4. *New York Times,* October 25, 1935, p. 16. In this story the *Times* reporter misspelled St. Clair's name as "Sinclair."

5. *Time,* November 4, 1935.

6. *New York Age,* March 9, 1935, p. 6.

7. Dewey, *Twenty against the Underworld,* 150.

8. *New York Age,* March 9, 1935, p. 6.

9. *Time,* January 4, 1937.

10. *Time,* November 13, 1933; and January 4, 1937. See, for example, *New York Daily Mirror,* March 11, 1937, p. 32; *New York Sunday Mirror,* July 9, 1938, p. 25.

11. *New York Times,* October 25, 1935, pp. 1, 16; *Time,* November 4, 1935.

12. *Collier's,* August 5, 1939, p. 44.

13. Ibid. For a different view of what was going on in the Mafia, in a book that includes strikingly little mention of numbers, see David Critchley, *The Origin of Organized Crime in America: The New York City Mafia, 1891–1931* (New York: Routledge, 2009).

14. Supposedly it was either Lansky or Luciano, or both, who authorized the hit on Siegel (shot in 1947). But in this sort of milieu, that was what friends were for. See T. J. English, *Havana Nocturne: How the Mob Owned Cuba . . . and then Lost It to the Revolution* (New York: William Morrow, 2008), 35–38.

15. Mayme Hatcher Johnson and Karen E. Quinones Miller, *Harlem Godfather: The Rap on My Husband, Ellsworth "Bumpy" Johnson* (Philadelphia: Oshun Publishing Company, 2008), 108–109. Details of the incident in which Johnson saved Luciano from a knifing in prison are on 143.

16. *New York Times,* July 25, 1937, p. 56; and August 21, 1938, p. 99.

17. Quoted in Cheryl Lynn Greenberg, *"Or Does It Explode?" Black Harlem in the Great Depression* (New York: Oxford University Press, 1991), 102.

18. *Chicago Defender,* April 1, 8, 15, and 22, 1939.

19. *Pittsburgh Courier,* January 5, 1935, p. 6; *Amsterdam News,* November 20, 1937, pp. 1, 2.

20. Jacqueline Najuma Stewart, *Migrating to the Movies: Cinema and Black Urban Modernity* (Berkeley: University of California Press, 2005), 247-248; Donald Bogle, *Toms, Coons, Mulattoes, Mammies and Bucks: An Interpretive History of Blacks in American Films* (New York: Continuum, 1991), 108-109.

21. Quoted in Thomas Cripps, *Slow Fade to Black: The Negro in American Film, 1900-1942* (New York: Oxford University Press, 1977), 328; Paula J. Massood, *Black City Cinema: African American Urban Experiences in Film* (Philadelphia: Temple University Press, 2003), 61.

22. Ralph Cooper with Steve Dougherty, *Amateur Night at the Apollo: Ralph Cooper Presents Five Decades of Great Entertainment* (New York: HarperCollins, 1990), 128.

23. See, for example, *Chicago Defender,* January 23, 1937, p. 11.

24. Film Script, *Dark Manhattan* (1937), File 3250, Box 510, New York State Archives, Albany, N.Y.

25. Our discussion of the film is based on the shooting script, filed away in the State Archives in Albany, N.Y., and on the film itself, readily available on DVD.

26. Quoted in John Kisch and Edward Mapp, *A Separate Cinema: Fifty Years of Black-Cast Posters* (New York: Noonday Press, 1992), xxvii; Cripps, *Slow Fade to Black,* 322-323.

EPILOGUE

1. See Claude McKay, *Harlem: Negro Metropolis* (New York: E. P. Dutton, 1940), 114.

2. *New York Age,* January 19, 1935, p. 1.

3. McKay, *Harlem,* 114.

4. *Amsterdam News,* February 6, 1937, p. 1 (second section).

5. On *Gone with the Wind,* see Lawrence W. Levine, *The Unpredictable*

Past: Explorations in American Cultural History (New York: Oxford University Press, 1993), 218. The reference in this sentence is, of course, to the last page of another blockbuster novel of the twentieth century. See Ralph Ellison, *Invisible Man* (Harmondsworth: Penguin, 1965; orig. pub. 1952), 469.

ACKNOWLEDGMENTS

Genuinely collaborative work, not that common among historians, has its pleasures, some guilty, some not. Many things are much simpler. For this project, we read somewhere in excess of 50,000 case files, probation files, and prison files, as well as decades' worth of newspapers. Often working in the archives in pairs, occasionally as a trio, we developed brutally efficient ways of doing things that enabled us to proceed much faster than if we had been lone researchers. As well, having someone to talk to helps keep at bay jetlag, tedium, and torpor. Indeed, more generally, conversation about work—having other people around who are just as familiar with the details of everyday life in Harlem—has been one of the great benefits of this collaboration. Writing becomes less lonely, less monastic; we would also like to think that the history is better. On the other hand, collaboration makes some things unbelievably complicated. There is a group photograph of the four authors. For understandable reasons Harvard University Press did not use it on the jacket—after all, their business is selling books, and there are limits to the skill of even the best photographer—but it is on the press's website and on our Harlem website. Arranging a day when one professional photographer and four academics were all in Sydney and available took in excess of three months. By comparison, herding cats is simple.

The title page of *Playing the Numbers* may suggest to some that this is a report written by a committee (perhaps the most devastating comment it is possible to make about a piece of prose), or even "workshopped." It wasn't written that way at all. Not only are there no dot points or executive summaries, but we'd reckon that there are almost as many verbs as sentences in this book. Indeed, perhaps strangely, the occasion of our photograph was one of the two, maybe three, times on which we all ended up in the same room in the past six or seven years. Rather, innumerable drafts of sentences, paragraphs, and chapters were passed around among ourselves, large slabs of text were tried out over the phone, and the whole slightly ungainly process was greased by discussion and truly prodigious quantities of coffee.

Writing the history of Harlem from the other side of the globe is expensive and we would like to use this occasion to acknowledge our considerable debts to the University of Sydney (our employer) and the Australian Research Council. The support of the ARC was essential to the writing of *Playing the Numbers*. A Discovery Grant, "Black Metropolis: Harlem 1915-1930," funded our larger Harlem project, including this book and the website; and Shane White's Australian Professorial Fellowship, "The Making of Black Manhattan," underwrote the research for Chapter 1. We are extraordinarily grateful for the ARC's generosity. At the University of Sydney, the Research Office, particularly Warwick Dawson, its director, has been an exemplary intermediary between us and the ARC.

Playing the Numbers may have been conceived, funded, and written in Sydney, but most of the research was conducted 10,000 miles away on the East Coast of the United States. We owe a very large debt to various libraries and repositories, and their invariably helpful staff, who house the material that we have used in this book. These include the American Antiquarian Society, the Beinecke Rare Book and Manuscript Library at Yale University, the Library of Congress, the New York Clearing House Archives, the New York Historical Society, the New York Public Library, the New York State Archives in Albany, and the Schomburg Center for Research in Black Culture. Most of all, though, we are indebted to the Municipal Archives of the City of New York, an institution with the most extraordinary holdings. Year after year, we camped out there for weeks at a time and the staff went out of their way to facilitate our research. In particular, we would like to thank Ken Cobb and Leonora Gidlund, who could not have been more knowledgeable and helpful.

When in New York, the authors of this book choose to stay at the Milburn Hotel, near 76th and Broadway. For almost a decade, several times a year and usually for weeks at a time, the Milburn has been a home away from home and we would like to thank very much all the staff, particularly Adam, who is usually manning the front desk late at night as, shattered by the twenty-four-hour trek from Sydney, individual Australian historians stagger into the lobby.

This book first saw the light of the day as a much shorter piece, "When Black Kings and Queens Ruled in Harlem." Stephen Garton gave a brief version of this as a paper at the Organization of American Historians annual meeting in New York in 2008. Shane White delivered versions of it as the Annenberg Lecture at the University of Pennsylvania and, thanks to the efforts of Emily West, as a seminar paper at the American History Seminar Series of the Institute for Historical Research at University College London, and at La

Trobe University. We would all like to thank the audiences on these occasions for their helpful comments. In particular, we are indebted to Rhys Isaac, John Salmond, and Bill Breen, who on hearing of the manifest lack of interest shown by some journals in even reading, let alone publishing, our article, urged us to write a short book.

Many years ago now, Alex Bontemps ferreted out some material, unavailable to us in Australia, that turned out to be crucial to this book. George Thompson, indefatigable chronicler of nineteenth-century New York, graciously gave us a number of items that made their way into Chapter 1. Helen Horowitz and Tim Gilfoyle, in a hurried conversation at an OAH meeting, helped our understanding of the flash press. Before he decamped for Los Angeles, Robin Kelley, on most of our trips to New York, made all sorts of suggestions about numbers, leavened with many observations about Thelonious Monk. A decade and a half ago, Peter Agree set himself the task of explaining American publishing to Shane White; he's still trying, but his efforts have been much appreciated. We are grateful to all of these people.

Whether the institution likes it or not, this book is very much a product of the University of Sydney. As students, academics, and of late, God forbid, administrators, between the four of us, we have racked up over a century spent within a well-struck pitching wedge of the splendid jacaranda tree that graces the corner of the quadrangle. It is a great place to write American history. The American Area Reading Group, particularly the regulars Frances Clarke, Clare Corbould, and Mike McDonnell, have, with helpful critical comments, heard a lot about Harlem. For almost two decades now, Glenda Sluga has been a wonderful friend and colleague. In combination with others such as those mentioned above and Andrew

Fitzmaurice, Chris Hilliard, Iain McCalman, and Richard Water-house, she has helped transform the History Department over the past few years. Richard and, more recently, Duncan Ivison, as successive Heads of School, always "got" what we were trying to do and supported wholeheartedly our endeavors. And elsewhere in Australia, Richard Bosworth, David Goodman, Rhys Isaac, Donna Merwick, John Salmond, and Ian Tyrrell have all contributed to the intellectual environment in which we work.

There is a website that accompanies this book. It was created in collaboration with the University of Sydney's Archaeological Computing Laboratory, directed by Ian Johnson. Damian Evans designed the site and the database behind it, and tweaked them innumerable times as problems arose and our sources led us in unexpected directions—until he fled to Cambodia, to take up a post-doctoral fellowship. Since then, Steve White has taken on the task of making fixes, often from locations far removed from Sydney. Andrew Wilson and his team worked to transform the modern map of Harlem into what it looked like in the 1920s, initially hand-drawing buildings, and more recently overlaying and correcting a 1932 real estate map that we were able to buy. That last project was funded by the American Historical Association's 2010 Roy Rosenzweig Fellowship for Innovation in Digital History; we are grateful to the prize committee and to Roy's many friends and colleagues for this award. One of the strengths of the site is the quantity of material it makes available, on numbers and many other facets of everyday life in Harlem. Entering the data is a tedious, complicated, and immensely time-consuming task—which is why the site currently contains only a fraction of what we have gathered. That even that much is available is due to the work of a series of research assistants. Delwyn Elizabeth battled through the database's many teething problems and spent by far the most time with the data, including entering the hundreds of arrests for numbers. When Delwyn declared she'd had enough, Nick Irving (who also spent countless hours scanning microfilm) and Michael Thompson took on the job. We thank them all.

We would also like to thank Mary Cunnane, our agent, for her advice and sterling efforts on our behalf. At Harvard University Press, Joyce Seltzer has been simply terrific—she knows what she wants, and more often than not gets it. Working with Joyce is always a pleasure. Maria Ascher copyedited the manuscript with sensitivity, contributing a number of very nice changes that improved the text, and looked after the production of the book. Ira Berlin gave the manuscript the perceptive and helpful reading that everyone expects from him as a matter of course. We thank them all as well.

Larry Levine, Roy Rosenzweig, and Greg Dening died, in quick succession, while we were working on this book. All three were truly creative historians—and they were also our friends. Roy, of course, was the original inspiration for the Harlem website. But all three of them, in the way they thought about and, above all, wrote history, have influenced every page of this book. *Playing the Numbers* is for them.

And last, we come to our long-suffering families. Graham White would like to thank Sue for decades of support and encouragement. We would all like to thank Sue for the sharp-eyed reading she gave the entire manuscript just before it was sent off. Stephen Robertson would like to thank Delwyn and Cleo for keeping him happy, putting up with his disappearing to the U.S. for several weeks a year, and not laughing (too hard) as he spent days moving pins in Google Earth so the website didn't put Harlem addresses in the Hudson River. Craig Robertson, during hours of conversation on our side trips to Boston, helped in so many ways, as did time spent with Erin and the adorable Edie. And to Doug Robertson, a proud supporter of this book until his unexpected death in 2009: Go well, Dad. Stephen Garton would like to thank Julia and Anna for allowing themselves to be dragged off (although they certainly weren't kicking and screaming) to a city that has a very special place in our family lore. For nigh on three decades Lexie Macdonald has reminded Shane White that there is more to life than history. He would like to thank her for being a constant source of encouragement and advice. Mac is the apple of his parents' eyes. Watching a son grow up into an "awesome" young boy is even more fun than writing history. And finally, all Monty Macdonald wanted was to see his name in print for the first time.

University of Sydney
February 2010

INDEX